Law, Alcohol, and Order

From *A Prohibition Primer* (New York: John Day, 1931), p. 53. Used with permission.

Law, Alcohol, and Order

PERSPECTIVES ON NATIONAL PROHIBITION

EDITED BY David E. Kyvig

SPONSORED BY ELEUTHERIAN MILLS–HAGLEY
FOUNDATION INCORPORATED

CONTRIBUTIONS IN AMERICAN HISTORY, NUMBER 110
Greenwood Press
WESTPORT, CONNECTICUT · LONDON, ENGLAND

Library of Congress Cataloging in Publication Data
Main entry under title:

Law, alcohol, and order.

(Contributions in American history, ISSN 0084-9219 ; no. 110)
Based on papers originally presented at a conference held in April 1983 in Wilmington, Delaware at the invitation of the Delaware Humanities Forum and the Eleutherian Mills Historical Library.
Bibliography: p.
Includes index.
1. Prohibition—United States—History—Congresses. I. Kyvig, David E. II. Eleutherian Mills–Hagley Foundation. III. Series.

HV5089.L33   1985   363.4'1'0973   84-25225
ISBN 0-313-24755-2 (lib. bdg.)

Library of Congress Catalog Card Number: 84-25225
ISBN: 0-313-24755-2
ISSN: 0084-9219

First published in 1985

Greenwood Press
A division of Congressional Information Service, Inc.
88 Post Road West
Westport, Connecticut 06881
Printed in the United States of America

10 9 8 7 6 5 4 3 2 1

Copyright Acknowledgments

The frontispiece is reprinted from *A Prohibition Primer* (New York: John Day, 1931), p. 53.

Every reasonable effort has been made to trace the owners of copyright materials used in this book, but in some instances this has proven impossible. The publishers will be glad to receive information leading to more complete acknowledgments in subsequent printings of this book, and in the meantime extend their apologies for any omissions.

Contents

Introduction

On December 5, 1983, American press attention turned briefly to the fiftieth anniversary of the adoption of the Twenty-first Amendment to the United States Constitution. An Associated Press feature story proclaimed, "Drinkers can raise a glass tonight to toast 50 uninterrupted years of legal imbibing." On December 5, 1933, the Twenty-first Amendment repealed the fourteen-year-old Eighteenth Amendment, which had banned the manufacture, sale, and transportation of alcoholic beverages. The end of national prohibition was greeted with enthusiasm at the time and, if press accounts are any indication, with bemusement a half century later. From the perspective of fifty years, prohibition appeared an historical quirk, a curious aberration totally without consequence, a matter solely of nostalgic interest.

National prohibition was, however, a far from trivial phenomenon. It represented the culmination of a century-long, broad-based social reform movement. It produced two constitutional alterations within a decade and a half, including the only repeal of a constitutional amendment in American history. And, most importantly, it spawned major and long-lasting consequences for American law, politics, government, labor, criminal enterprise, and social order. Prohibition repeal ended an important phase of the continuing effort to develop a satisfactory public policy toward America's most widely used and accepted drug. And like the law which provoked it, repeal had subtle but significant effects upon many aspects of American life.

In April 1983 a group of scholars gathered to discuss and consider the consequences of the liquor ban and its repeal at a conference entitled "Prohibition Fifty Years Later: Implications for Law, Alcohol, and Order." They met in Wilmington, Delaware, at the invitation of the Delaware Humanities Forum and the Eleutherian Mills Historical Library, a major private historical research institution with a notable collection of prohibition-related materials. The conference hosts received assistance from Scholarly Resources, Inc. of Wilmington and the Joseph E. Seagram and Sons, Inc. Fund. During two days of formal presentations and lively informal discussion, the exchange of ideas and information underscored the multifaceted significance of the national prohibition episode and its enduring importance in a variety of fields.

The participants in the Eleutherian Mills conference represented a range of disciplines: alcohol studies, anthropology, criminology, law, political science, public health, sociology, and a variety of historical specialities—constitutional, criminal, legal, medical, political, and social history. The principal speakers were all active scholars, and in some cases also participants in alcohol reform, constitutional amending efforts, or labor politics. For instance, one of the senior members of the group, Mark Keller, had been involved with the Center for Alcohol Studies, first at Yale and then at Rutgers University, since the year of repeal. He brought a unique and useful personal perspective to the discussion. Also attending were congressional staff members, law enforcement officials, and representatives of such disparate groups as the National Task Force on Cannabis Regulation and Mothers Against Drunk Driving. The mix of viewpoints generated a richness and freshness of discussion which many conference participants, accustomed to a single discipline's approach to the subject, found stimulating.

This volume brings together most of the formal presentations from the Eleutherian Mills conference along with three essays prepared thereafter by conference participants who were stimulated to set forth their thoughts. The authors have revised their papers, in some cases very substantially, to respond to questions raised at the conference, expand on ideas addressed in the discussion, and indicate sources of evidence for their conclusions. The editor's intent has been to preserve the tone and clarity of the original conference papers while at the same time enabling each author to support his or her arguments in greater detail. The resulting collection reflects a variety of styles and conclusions but is integrated by a shared concern with defining the impact of national prohibition upon a half century of American development.

The first essay in this collection is David E. Kyvig's conference keynote speech. It sets the stage for what follows by contrasting national prohibition's popular image with the historical reality. Briefly reviewing the history of the long temperance crusade which led to the adoption of the Eighteenth Amendment, the essay calls attention both to the importance of alcohol as a social issue and to the necessary magnitude of a political movement powerful enough to produce constitutional change. The paradox of national prohibition is shown in the law's simultaneous substantial reduction of alcohol consumption and its loss of popular support because of perceived ineffectiveness. Declining public enthusiasm for the liquor ban did not lead inevitably to repeal, the essay argues, because the actual and assumed difficulties of further constitutional amendment were so formidable. A well-organized pressure group and the unique method of amendment ratification by popularly elected state conventions contributed to the success of the repeal effort. Among the consequences of national prohibition's perceived failure and rapid fall, the essay concludes, are as yet unresolved questions about the proper role of law in dealing with alcohol abuse as well as continuing political caution regarding any proposed constitutional amendment. Many of the essays which follow deal in one way or another with issues of alcohol control and the impact of constitutional change.

Prior to 1919 the scientific and medical community, the American Medical Association in particular, contributed influential arguments in support of a national ban on alcoholic beverages despite its own internal divisions of opinion on the issue, Steven Goldberg shows. The implementation of the Eighteenth Amendment led to restrictions on medical practice and caused physicians to acknowledge their own scientific uncertainty. Until recently, the unhappy experience with national prohibition led the scientific community to be more cautious about taking sides in public policy debates, Goldberg observes. In a reversal of this pattern, scientists have become involved in the fierce debate over abortion. Justice Harry Blackmun in the 1973 Supreme Court decision in *Roe v. Wade* and both sides in the subsequent debate over a constitutional ban on abortion have relied heavily on scientific arguments. Goldberg concludes that the instability of scientific opinion as a foundation for constitutional policy is one lesson of prohibition repeal which appears to have been forgotten.

The battle over adoption of national prohibition and the implementation of the law disrupted organized labor, Nuala McGann Drescher points out. The alcohol ban not only divided the ranks of labor on a policy issue but also destroyed a significant component of the American labor movement. Drescher, a state faculty union president herself, regards brewery workers as a distinctive and influential force within the American Federation of Labor before World War I. An industrial union in the Samuel Gompers era of craft unionism, a union with strong commitments to racial and sexual equality and to socialism, and a prosperous, stable union which had organized 90 percent of its industry, the United Brewery Workers would have been a force which, she argues, might have altered the course of American unionism had it not been undermined by prohibition.

Looking at constitutional evolution once national prohibition was adopted, William F. Swindler attributes a variety of significant developments to the effort to enforce the law. He calls particular attention to the Supreme Court's authorization of wiretapping and its broadened interpretation of legitimate search and seizure. Even repeal, he concludes, left the federal government with wider constitutional authority. At the conference, commentator Maeva Marcus of the Supreme Court Documentary Project confirmed this, pointing out that the Court in its 1972 decision *California v. La Rue* held that the Twenty-first Amendment expanded state police power over places where liquor is sold in order to protect public health, welfare, and morals. In the case in question, the Court let stand a state ban on nude dancers in bars.

Like Goldberg and Swindler, Paul L. Murphy views the Eighteenth Amendment as a manifestation of Progressive attitudes toward reform. Early twentieth-century Progressives believed, he points out, that proper moral conduct was a social need which should be placed above the liberty of the individual. The encounter with national prohibition contributed in important ways during the 1920s to rising concern for the rights of the individual against the state. In particular, Murphy shows that a series of Supreme Court decisions in prohibition enforcement cases contained the seeds of modern concepts of the right to privacy and individuality which would ripen in the 1960s but which are again under challenge in the 1980s.

Legal enforcement of national prohibition had other significant judicial consequences, as Rayman L. Solomon points out. Having examined the entire body of cases heard by the U.S. Court of Appeals for the Seventh Circuit (Indiana, Illinois, and Wisconsin) from the 1890s through the 1930s, he observes a pronounced shift from private disputes to litigation involving the government during the 1920s, the decade in which prohibition enforcement cases became the largest single source of appeals. Solomon notes an unusually high rate of judicial intervention in cases involving questions of the proper conduct of government prohibition agents. National prohibition, he concludes, initiated an important tradition of judicial supervision of federal bureaucratic regulation on the eve of the great New Deal expansion of such activity.

The manner in which the Eighteenth Amendment was adopted provoked a reaction which in turn produced one of national prohibition's notable consequences, in the estimate of Clement E. Vose. Antiprohibitionist resentment toward the political process used to obtain the constitutional liquor ban led to a unique use of popularly elected state conventions for ratification of the repeal amendment in 1933, a process which Vose describes in detail. The implications of this referendum-like procedure for democratic constitutional change are profound, he suggests, even though this alternative ratification method has received little attention since prohibition repeal.

Humbert S. Nelli and Mark H. Haller agree that national prohibition had great consequences for the evolution of criminal activity in the United States. They diverge, however, in their assessments of that impact. They differ initially on whether bootlegging principally attracted already established criminals or drew upon novices. Nelli traces the evolution of criminal syndicates created as bootlegging operations into post-repeal involvement in labor racketeering, loan sharking, gambling, and narcotics. He characterizes syndicate crime as highly organized and interconnected. Haller, in contrast, pictures bootleggers as independent entrepreneurs who specialized in one aspect of the trade rather than developing a vertically integrated business. Their joint ventures involved temporary, limited partnerships. He describes how, after repeal, former bootleggers used their accumulated capital, skills, and network of contacts to enter the legitimate liquor distribution business and, following World War II, pooled their resources to develop the national gambling mecca, Las Vegas.

Mark Keller offers a reminder that the problem of alcohol control has perplexed many societies over many centuries. The drink dilemma exists because of alcohol's capacity to produce genuine pleasure as well as distress. Keller, who worked with the renowned E. M. Jellinek at the Center of Alcohol Studies, describes from personal observations the post-repeal evolution of American scientific approaches to alcohol. He perceives a significant divergence between the alcohol study and alcoholism treatment movements. The latter, far more successful, rejected the notion that alcohol problems could be prevented and instead propounded that "alcoholism is a treatable disease" as a deliberate tactic to gain public support and funding. In his subtle and provocative essay, Keller suggests that one consequence of the scientific community's reaction to prohibition repeal has been ongoing uncertainty regarding appropriate social policy toward alcohol.

These ten essays call attention to some of the variety and significance of national prohibition's consequences. Building on this theme, Mark Edward Lender's essay, which concludes this volume, surveys the current state of prohibition history research and identifies a number of unmet needs. Lender points particularly to the value of further examination of the politics of repeal and the nature of post–1933 federal and state alcohol policy. The elaborate agenda which he sets forth suggests, as do all the essays in the collection, what a stimulating and worthwhile topic the history of public policy toward alcohol remains.

An awareness of the importance of historical understanding for dealing successfully with contemporary public policy issues permeated the Eleutherian Mills conference, just as it does this volume. Several conference participants called attention to the serious ongoing social problem of alcohol abuse. Public health specialist Dan E. Beauchamp, describing alcohol as "America's second most lethal drug" (second only to tobacco), suggested that flawed historical understanding of the prohibition episode helps account for the modern-day difficulty in developing a social policy toward alcohol responsive to public health and safety needs. Medical historian David Musto attributed the rise of a new wave of alcohol reformers (such groups as Mothers Against Drunk Driving) to a fading historical memory of prohibition together with a heightened concern with the social damage done by alcohol excess. Neither Beauchamp nor Musto showed any enthusiasm for a return to national prohibition, but both held out hope for the development of socially responsible, historically well-informed public policies regarding alcohol.

Those scholars at the conference who were more concerned with general questions of law and constitutionalism than with alcohol *per se* shared the sense of the value of historical awareness in public policy considerations. Careful analysis of the history of prohibition illuminates not only specific subjects such as effective methods of constitutional alteration but also broad issues such as the appropriate limits of law and the consequences of using law as a tool of social reform. As citizens and public officials are moved to call for various statutory innovations and constitutional changes, they will benefit from the availability of careful historical assessments of national prohibition and its results.

In the final analysis, it was this sense that national prohibition was an important historical phenomenon and that its continuing study could have broad public policy benefits which led to the convening of the Eleutherian Mills conference. It is in the same spirit that this volume of essays is offered. Far from being an occasion of merely antiquarian interest, the fiftieth anniversary of national prohibition repeal can contribute to a worthwhile reevaluation of an historical episode which had a noteworthy impact upon the United States.

Law, Alcohol, and Order

1

Sober Thoughts: Myths and Realities of National Prohibition after Fifty Years

Nineteen eighty-three marked the five hundredth anniversary of the birth of Martin Luther. It represented as well the two hundredth anniversary of the Treaty of Paris which ended America's war for independence from Great Britain. Also, 1983 was the one hundredth anniversary of the death of Karl Marx. And the same year marked the fiftieth anniversary of the practically simultaneous coming to power of Adolf Hitler with his Third Reich in Germany and Franklin Roosevelt with his New Deal in the United States. Each of these anniversaries symbolized a milestone in the course of Western civilization worthy of contemplation.

In the face of these monumental anniversaries, why should scholars and sensible citizens gather to observe the fiftieth anniversary of the repeal of the Eighteenth Amendment to the United States Constitution, the measure which sought to prohibit the manufacture, sale, transportation, importation, and exportation of alcoholic beverages, a law widely scorned ever since as one of the most ineffectual, misguided, and foolish undertakings in the history of social reform? Many academics do, of course, possess considerable personal enthusiasm for celebrating the demise of national prohibition. It is perhaps not entirely inappropriate for Martha's hard-drinking husband, George, in Edward Albee's masterpiece *Who's Afraid of Virginia Woolf* to be a professor of history. But personal predilections aside, can there be any point in devoting attention to the end of a failed and frequently mocked attempt at reforming society?

The popular image of national prohibition certainly suggests little reason. That image rests on a foundation of contemporary opinions, such as that of the acerbic Baltimore writer H.L. Mencken, who called it an effort "to punish the other fellow for having a better time in the world."[1] Perhaps more devastating and certainly better remembered was the innocent declaration of 1928 Republican presidential candidate Herbert Hoover, an admirer of prohibition, in his campaign against the first serious political challenger of the national liquor ban, Democratic nominee Alfred E. Smith. Hoover called prohibition "a great social and economic experiment, noble in motive and far-reaching in purpose."[2] The "noble experiment" label soon became national prohibition's nickname, inadvertently but effectively undermining the law's image by implying that it was less than a genuine and serious reform.

Historians have strengthened prohibition's popular image. Frederick Lewis Allen, the journalist-historian whose influential, if unbalanced, 1931 book, *Only Yesterday*, created a vivid picture of the 1920s as a frivolous "lost weekend" between the traumas of World War I and the Great Depression, portrayed prohibition as completely ineffective. Its results, he wrote, were

rum-ships rolling in the sea outside the twelve-mile limit and transferring their cargoes of whiskey by night to fast cabin cruisers, beer-running trucks being hijacked on the interurban boulevards by bandits with Thompson sub-machine guns, illicit stills turning out alcohol by the carload, the fashionable dinner party beginning with contraband cocktails as a matter of course, ladies and gentlemen undergoing scrutiny from behind the curtained grill of the speakeasy, and Alphonse Capone, multi-millionaire master of the Chicago bootleggers, driving through the streets in an armour-plated car with bullet-proof windows.[3]

Subsequent historians, unable to reconcile prohibition with their admiring views of American social reform, reinforced the negative image. The distinguished scholar Richard Hofstadter in his much-acclaimed book *The Age of Reform* scorned prohibition as "a psuedo-reform, a pinched, parochial substitute for reform . . . not merely an aversion to drunkenness and to the evils that accompanied it, but to the immigrant drinking masses, to the pleasures and amenities of city life, and to the well-to-do classes and cultivated men." National prohibition, Hofstadter concluded, "was a means by which the reforming energies of the country were transformed into mere peevishness."[4]

These influential voices and others, shaped a powerful myth of national prohibition. An historical myth can be defined as any popularly held and acted-upon historical account, however true or false. The prohibition myth holds that national prohibition was a foolish idea put over by well-organized special interests—a few fanatical, conservative, small-town and rural, white, Anglo-Saxon, Protestant Americans seeking to hold back the rising tide of urban immigrant America. This impractical dry law, so the myth continues, lacked public support, could not be policed, and turned the 1920s into a riot of uncontrolled, illicit drinking. Speakeasies, bathtub gin, and hip flasks appeared everywhere. As the lost weekend of the 1920s turned into the Great Depression of the 1930s, replacing frivolity with serious economic and social problems, the "noble experiment" was quickly, sensibly, and effortlessly laid aside. The myth concludes that the law which Hofstadter termed "a ludicrous caricature of the reforming impulse"[5] lacks any relevance whatsoever to post–1933 America.

Historical myths can have a powerful hold on public thinking and policy-making. For example, American foreign relations provides the "appeasement" myth that Western concessions encouraged Hitler's expansionist appetite and that strict and absolute containment of adversaries is therefore essential to prevent a "domino effect" leading to total collapse. This perception, however inadequate, shaped post–World War II U.S.-Soviet relations and the U.S. encounter, in far different circumstances, with third-world nationalism in Southeast Asia in the 1960s and Central America in the 1980s.[6] The national prohibition myth has encouraged the belief that restriction of private, consensual behavior through law is both intolerant and ineffective, that the negative consequences of the attempt dwarf the benefits, and that constitutional stability is threatened by use of the amending process to reform social policy. The wisdom of conclusions based upon this, or any, myth, can only be determined after a careful consideration of the historical reality upon which the myth is founded.

The very requirements for constitutional amendment ought to remind us at the outset that the national prohibition myth may be flawed. For an amendment to be adopted, it must first be approved by a two-thirds vote in each house of Congress and then ratified by three-fourths of the states, through either their legislatures or specially convened state conventions, whichever Congress directs. The founding fathers, though they recognized that it might be necessary to alter their creation, did not intend for it to be easy. Constitutional amendment requires the largest super-majorities, the greatest degree of democratic consensus, of any political decision in the American governmental system. In our own time, the difficulty of constitutional amendment is attested to by the equal rights amendment (ERA), which obtained the approval of over two-thirds of Congress and the legislatures of thirty-five states between 1972 and 1977 yet fell short of ratification. ERA supporters certainly now appreciate how enormously difficult it is to amend the Constitution. The adoption of the Eighteenth Amendment, at that time only the sixth amendment in over a century, reflected the strength of prohibitionist sentiment. The repeal of the amendment fourteen years later required the same degree of support and thus represented a tremendous political reversal. These were not narrowly backed, casually accomplished changes in either case. They were far more important events than the popular myth of prohibition acknowledges. It is essential to blow the foam off the prohibition myth and look beneath that appealing but insubstantial effervescence.

The myth has obscured the reality that the national prohibition amendment was arguably the most radical and significant constitutional reform ever adopted. Only the Thirteenth Amendment abolishing slavery rivals it . Other amendments to the 1787 Constitution adjusted governmental powers or procedures, clarified or verified assumed individual rights, or extended their coverage to additional classes of people. Only the Thirteenth and Eighteenth Amendments represented fundamental departures from previous American governmental principles. They destroyed large-scale private property holdings and economic arrangements—slave holdings in one case, an entire industry in the other—for the object of social restructuring. The Eighteenth Amendment furthermore asserted the federal government's power to determine whether personal conduct had social consequences and then to regulate or restrain individual behavior. Direct intervention of the federal government into citizens' lives increased dramatically, at least in principle. The balance of power in the federal relationship shifted sharply away from the states and toward the national arena.

The prohibition amendment sought to redraw for all time the boundary between the public and private spheres of American life. From the founding of the republic, the right of the individual to be free from government intervention in purely private affairs received endorsement after endorsement. Only actions which had a negative impact on others were regarded as the proper concern of government. Prohibition redefined behavior once considered private and therefore beyond the proper reach of government as social and appropriate for government regulation. Adoption of the Eighteenth Amendment set a new standard for governmental intervention into personal lives, a step long discussed but not taken until 1919.[7]

National prohibition had its origins in a century-old debate over the proper role of alcohol in American society. Colonial Americans, most of them farmers, needed an economical way to transport their crops or to market imported West Indies molasses. They wanted a dependable, pure beverage when water and milk were not, and they sought a less expensive alternative to tea and coffee. So they made beer, rum, gin, and whiskey a routine feature of their daily lives. Beer and hard cider were the usual mealtime beverages; farmers in their fields sipped throughout the day; and group projects, whether church raisings or harvests, normally featured a cask of spirits. The pattern appears to have been steady low-volume consumption rather than binge drinking. Work was strenuous and physically punishing, but seldom fast-paced or precise. So regular drinking might soften the burden without endangering the job. No wonder alcohol was considered beneficial and drinking normal and necessary.

And drink they did. With few exceptions, men and women drank, and many children did also. Fairly reliable estimates of consumption are available beginning in 1790, measured in the absolute alcohol consumed per capita by the population aged fifteen and older.[8] (Beer and cider were assumed to be 10 percent alcohol until 1840, 5 percent thereafter, wine a constant 18 percent, and distilled spirits 45 percent.) In 1790—which probably typified the eighteenth century—per capita absolute alcohol consumption averaged just under six gallons a year. By comparison, it was about two and two-thirds gallons during the 1970s. Between 1800 and 1830 consumption rose to about seven gallons of alcohol a year. (That represented seventy gallons of beer and cider, thirty-nine gallons of wine, or fifteen and one-half gallons of distilled liquor.) No wonder that W. J. Rorabaugh calls this the heaviest-drinking era in American history in his aptly titled book *The Alcoholic Republic*. However, while most Americans were sipping literally morning, noon and night, with whiskey (instead of coffee) breaks at 11 A.M. and 4 P.M. customary, and a nightcap before bedtime common, their country was changing.

The early nineteenth century saw the beginnings of the rapid modernization of the country. Increasing industrialization, expanding commercial agriculture, and growing urban centers encouraged each other. Transportation improved, first with better roads and canals, then with railroads. Even family life and relations between the genders changed as workplace and homesite were separated and a wage economy emerged. All of this produced a new attitude about time: schedules had to be kept for a modern society to function, and the notion of time as a valuable commodity, one to be used efficiently or lost irretrievably, replaced the traditional notion of a cycle of seasons with alternating periods of working and waiting and annually recurring opportunity. Alcohol use caused difficulties in a modern society which had mattered little in traditional society.

Early criticism of hard liquor came from Dr. Benjamin Rush of Philadelphia, a signer of the Declaration of Independence and respected late eighteenth-century physician. He doubted the effectiveness of soldiers who consumed a daily liquor ration. Liquor still posed danger to the republic after the revolution, Rush argued, because chronic drunkenness undermined the health of its citizens. Protestant churches took up the battle, considering liquor religion's rival for popular attention and intemperance an obstacle to moral behavior. By the 1830s and 1840s liquor came to be blamed in large measure for poverty. It reduced worker's productively and drained off wages which could otherwise be used to raise their living standards. Crime, child neglect, and other social ills were likewise attributed to alcohol.

The crusade against alcohol began with appeals for moderation in the use of liquor. But by 1825 respected voices, in particular that of Connecticut Presbyterian minister Lyman Beecher, began to argue that drinking was addictive, that alcohol in any form was still alcohol, that moderate drinking led progressively and inevitably to immoderate drinking, and therefore that the only true temperance was total abstinence. The American Temperance Society, which began urging Americans to voluntarily pledge themselves to avoid distilled spirits, gradually by 1840 came to support total abstinence, or, to use the popular term, went all the way ''dry.''

The temperance agitation of the 1830s helped produce a sharp decline in drinking. Many people stopped altogether, and others reduced their intake. Annual per capita alcohol consumption fell to about three gallons by 1840. But temperance advocates were not satisfied. The continued presence of liquor, they maintained, perpetuated social problems and personal temptations. They posed the question: If abolishing "the liquor traffic" altogether would be in the common good, why not legislate a ban on alcohol instead of relying on voluntary individual action, at best a partial solution? Legal action applying to all of society quickly attracted those persuaded that liquor was harmful. Before the Civil War a dozen states, led by Maine in 1851, adopted some sort of legal prohibition. The next half century saw new anti-alcohol organizations formed (the Prohibition party in 1869, the Women's Christian Temperance Union in 1873, the Anti-Saloon League in 1893), political support ebb and flow, but no real change in the basic temperance notions that abstinence from alcohol was in society's best interest and most effective if legally imposed.

By 1913, when the Anti-Saloon League first proposed a federal constitutional amendment to impose prohibition nationally, nine states had decided to legally abolish the liquor traffic, as had many communities by local option. Within the next six years, the Congress and forty-six states endorsed the constitutional solution. Why, one may ask, did national prohibition become so popular? Most explanations emphasize the effective political organization and pressure tactics of the Anti-Saloon League and its temperance group allies. Mention is also made of old-stock, by now nondrinking, Americans' hostility to the new wave of immigrants with unfamiliar cultures and drinking habits. No doubt these were important, even vital. But it is necessary to look at the beliefs which appealed to many outside the temperance societies.

Overall American drinking had continued the decline begun in the 1830s. During the early years of the twentieth century, per capita consumption of alcohol hovered around two and one-half gallons (keeping in mind that 30 to 40 percent of the population now abstained altogether, a much higher percentage than had been the case a century before. Those who still drank were keeping up their rate of consumption nicely, one suspects). By the eve of World War I, however, the United States had become a highly industrialized, increasingly urban nation. Employers had become sensitive to the negative effects of drinking on workers' schedules, productivity, and safety habits. Railroads, the DuPont powder mills, and many other companies realized the damage a drunken worker could do and strictly forbade drinking. Observers of the urban poor saw drink taking their money, damaging their health, and causing them to neglect their families. Jane Addams and other social workers concluded the poor would be far better off without alcohol. A general obstacle to urban reform was the graft-ridden local political machine which found the neighborhood saloon the ideal site to contact constituents, dispense favors, and on election day rally support and buy votes. Without saloons, urban politics would be much more clean and honest, reformers thought. These concerns with efficiency, safety, health, poverty, child and wife abuse, and political corruption ignored, of course, the role of alcohol in various cultures and the possibility that alcohol was the means of relief from the problems of modern life, not their cause.

A great variety of early twentieth-century reform interests shared underlying assumptions which came to be called Progressive. Mankind had the capacity, through the use of intellect, to rationally analyze and solve social problems. By creating the proper laws and institutions, Progressives believed, they would mold a far more satisfactory world. Inspired by technological modernization, Progressives were exceedingly confident that human free will and intelligence could uplift society. Cultural variations—which they viewed as defects instead of alternatives—could be eliminated. They placed great confidence in law as the instrument of "social engineering." Alcohol prohibition made perfect sense to many Progressives.[9] Since liquor so obviously spawned a multitude of social, political, and economic evils, why not eliminate them by outlawing it? "The first consideration," a leading prohibitionist argued, "is not the individual, but society. . . . You may exercise your personal liberty only in so far as you do not place additional burdens upon your neighbor, or upon the state."[10]

U.S. entry into World War I accelerated growing sentiment for national prohibition. Hostility to all things German—including beer—and a widespread sense of the need for patriotic self-sacrifice for the nation's defense gave the prohibition amendment a final boost toward bipartisan congressional approval late in 1917 and rapid state ratification within thirteen months. The liquor industry was given one year to wind up its business. During that time Congress adopted the Volstead Enforcement Act, which declared all beverages with .5 percent alcohol content illegal—thus assuring that beer and wine as well as hard liquor would be prohibited (implementing Beecher's abstinence theory). The act created only a modest enforcement budget, on the clear assumption that the American people would abide by the law. On January 16, 1920, national prohibition took effect.

How many Americans favored national prohibition when it was

adopted? That cannot be determined for certain because no general popular vote was taken and reliable public opinion polling lay two decades in the future. However, in nineteen of twenty-three states where referendums on statewide prohibition measures were held in the five years prior to adoption of the Eighteenth Amendment, voters approved antiliquor laws (not all of them as strict as national prohibition) by majorities of from 52 to 76 percent. Ohio had a state constitutional provision allowing voters to petition for a referendum on legislative ratification of a federal amendment. Such a referendum was held on the Eighteenth Amendment in November 1919, and by 479 votes out of a million cast, voters rejected the amendment. Although the U.S. Supreme Court disallowed this referendum and no other state held one, the Ohio vote fertilized the image of popular disapproval of prohibition. Yet considering all the state referendum results and the federal and state legislative actions, it seems likely that a nationwide majority, though not necessarily a large one, endorsed the temperance and Progressive arguments.[11]

National prohibition clearly passed the Constitution's demanding standards for establishing its legitimacy. Between 1917 and 1919 it gained legislative approval as broad as any other twentieth-century amendment. We do not doubt the legitimacy of the contemporary women's suffrage or federal income tax amendments (well, at least most of us don't most of the time). Yet a unique cloud hangs over prohibition, leading one to ask: Do different sorts of law require different levels of public approval? What degree and manner of dissent from its law can a society tolerate and yet remain cohesive? In the face of various levels of objections, to what lengths should government go to enforce its statutes?

Questions about the extent of support for national prohibition naturally arise in light of apparent widespread violation of the law. The image was abysmal. Franklin P. Adams made fun of it and its supporters in 1931.

Prohibition is an awful flop.
  We like it.
It can't stop what it's meant to stop.
  We like it.
It's left a trail of graft and slime
It don't prohibit worth a dime
It's filled our land with vice and crime,
  Nevertheless, we're for it.[12]

Newspapers were constantly carrying stories of police raids on stills and speakeasies, not to mention wars between rival gangs of bootleggers in Chicago and elsewhere. Motion pictures, which were attracting huge audiences in the 1920s and shaping perceptions of what was going on in society, showed a great deal of drinking. A 1930 survey found drinking depicted in two-thirds of the 115 films studied. Cinema heroes and heroines were imbibing three times as often as villains.[13] And Al Capone, who emerged in the mid–1920s as Chicago's leading but far from only bootlegger, simply maintained, "All I do is supply a public demand."[14]

There is no question that a lot of liquor was consumed in the United States while national prohibition was in effect. St. Pierre and Miquelon, the tiny French islands off the coast of Newfoundland, imported 118,600 gallons of British liquor in 1922, and it seems likely that most of it was smuggled into the United States rather than being consumed by the islands' six thousand inhabitants. By the late 1920s one million gallons of Canadian liquor was being smuggled south across the border each year. Domestic producers large and small turned out an uncertain but far greater amount, much of it of good quality. Industrial alcohol was diverted to beverage use. Doctors wrote prescriptions for legal "medicinal" liquor. California grape growers quadrupled their sales as home wine making flourished. Beer making did less well, since home brewing was difficult to conceal and "needle beer" (made by reinjecting alcohol into legal near-beer) did not taste as good. Distilling appeared to thrive, judging from references to whiskey and bathtub gin (which got its name not because it was made there but because bathtub faucets proved convenient for adding tap water to tall bottles half to two-thirds full of neutral spirits, glycerine, and juniper juice).

And yet the myth of national prohibition obscures the reality that overall drinking declined sharply. The cost of evading the law was high, in itself a discouragement to drinking. For instance, the cost of a cocktail rose from fifteen cents during World War I to seventy-five cents or more during prohibition. With average American family income well under two thousand dollars a year, only the relatively wealthy could afford such drinks. And of course not all who could afford to chose to break the law. Except in the urban areas of the North and East, liquor consumption fell significantly.

While it is difficult to measure the extent of any illegal activity, indirect indications document a significant drop in drinking during prohibition.[15] Various medical problems closely related to alcohol use, cirrhosis of the liver for instance, declined steeply once prohibition began (though later gradually rose again). Most significantly, figures on total American alcohol consumption derived from tax revenues immediately after prohibition ended show an approximately 60 percent reduction in consumption compared to the years just before prohibition. After it was again legal, annual per capita consumption was less than a gallon. Clearly, many Americans had gotten out of the habit of drinking. Indeed, per capita annual consumption did not again reach pre-prohibition levels until the 1970s. So, despite the myth, the liquor ban appears to have substantially discouraged drinking for a generation.

Why does a law which enjoys broad support and achieves significant results generate the opposition and ridicule which national prohibition came to receive? Several reasons seem worth considering. Laws, to be successful, depend far more on voluntary observance than on enforcement. No police force, however respected or feared, can deal with more than a limited number of violators. Unless there is a high degree of consensus in society that a law ought to be observed either because it makes sense or because penalties for being caught in violation are too severe to justify the risk, the police cannot isolate the offenders. Law indeed becomes a social contract, and unless most of the members of a society agree to honor the contract, it becomes unenforceable. In the case of prohibition, a very substantial number of people simply refused from the beginning to sign the contract. Drinking was an integral part of the culture of several large, cohesive, urban-centered ethnic groups, including the Irish, Italians, and Jews, and they could not be convinced that there was anything wrong with it. Even though bootlegging needed public visibility in order to function, it enjoyed sufficient social support to frustrate police efforts to squelch it. Bootleggers could not have operated, much less reaped large profits, without widespread public cooperation. So in sum, the degree of compliance with prohibition, although substantial, was insufficient to the need. The essential sense of general social endorsement of the law was never established. Worries began to be expressed that widespread and generally unpunished disregard for national prohibition would cause a withering of respect for other laws and a decline in voluntary compliance. A sort of Gresham's law would affect the social contract: a bad law would undermine the value of good laws.

Beyond this lay the issue of the proper limits of government. For all the Progressive optimism about social uplift through law, there was as well the American tradition of distaste for government. Calls for larger and larger enforcement budgets caused concern, as did evidence that police and prohibition agents took bribes to ignore violations. Efforts to enforce prohibition led federal and state police officials to claim new rights of search and seizure, to stop the automobiles of suspected bootleggers and examine them without a search warrant, to wiretap the telephones of suspected liquor smugglers. The Supreme Court upheld such procedures, considering them necessary techniques in the modern world to enforce the new constitutional mandate. But to some the bounds of privacy had been overstepped. Civil liberties were being diminished. If government could exercise such powers in order to supervise and restrict a person's diet, what other areas formerly considered private might be invaded in the name of the public interest? Many Americans, including some who had initially thought eliminating alcohol was a good idea, reacted negatively to the law in practice as ineffectual as well as an excessive government intrusion into what they still regarded as properly a private matter.

Despite disregard and dislike of the law, a general belief prevailed throughout the 1920s that nothing could be done to alter it because it had been installed in the Constitution. The amendment's author, Senator Morris Sheppard of Texas, gloated, "There is as much chance of repealing the Eighteenth Amendment as there is for a hummingbird to fly to the planet Mars with the Washington Monument tied to its tail." [16] Constitutional amending was regarded as surpassingly difficult, and removal of a previous amendment completely out of the question. A minimum of a third of the Congress and half the states would have to reverse previous positions. No wonder that no amendment had ever been repealed. So throughout the 1920s most discussion of remedies centered around increasing enforcement efforts, altering the definition of intoxicating beverage to permit beer and wine, or deliberately abandoning policing efforts, ignoring a law which could be neither removed nor enforced. None of these alternatives gave much promise of solving the problem, and all, it was feared, might further erode general respect for law. Still they all attracted serious discussion, because taking the prohibition edict out of the Constitution seemed, to use Clarence Darrow's words, "well-nigh inconceivable." [17]

Nevertheless, from the start a small group insisted that removal of the Eighteenth Amendment from the Constitution offered the only satisfactory solution. They played a critical role in coalescing support for repeal. Forming a political organization much like the Anti-Saloon League, the Association Against the Prohibition Amendment (AAPA) sought to build support for repeal on the basis that respect for law and order was needed, that the Eighteenth Amendment placed too much power in federal hands, and that prohibition was costly in terms of lost tax revenues, enforcement expenses, police corruption, and threats to civil liberties. They called for limited, socially neutral government rather than an active, reformist state which would reduce personal privacy. The AAPA grew stronger in the mid–1920s, when the du Pont brothers of Wilmington, Delaware—Pierre, Irénée, and Lammot—and their close business associate John Raskob became active in the organization and helped finance its campaign. As the Democratic party's national chairman from 1928 to 1932, Raskob strengthened that party's image as favoring repeal, which in turn attracted further working-class and ethnic antiprohibition support to the Democrats. Meanwhile, a female counterpart to the AAPA, the Women's Organization for National Prohibition Reform, was formed in 1929, grew to a claimed membership of 1.5 million, and destroyed the notion that all women supported prohibition and would therefore block constitutional change.

The unanticipated and unrelated onset of the Great Depression boosted the antiprohibition cause. If drinking were legalized, it was argued, excise taxes on liquor, which before prohibition generated nearly one-third of federal revenues, could help ease the federal budget crisis rather than merely enrich bootleggers. Furthermore, the depression produced voter hostility toward Herbert Hoover and willingness to take a chance on his less well known 1932 presidential opponent. The 1932 election returns were interpreted as a judgment on prohibition. Hoover had, after all, called it the noble experiment, while the Democratic platform advocated repeal. The Congress viewed Franklin D. Roosevelt's election as a mandate for repeal and promptly responded accordingly.

The antiprohibition organizations argued that no constitutional provision directly affecting the American people should be adopted without their specific approval. They applauded the 1930 ruling of a New Jersey federal judge that the Eighteenth Amendment had been improperly ratified because the electorate had not been directly consulted. The Supreme Court had quickly overturned the ruling, but the antiprohibitionists continued to insist that any reconsideration of prohibition should take place in state conventions with delegates specifically chosen for this purpose rather than in state legislatures whose members had been elected for a wide variety of reasons.

Convention ratification of constitutional provisions, although stipulated as one of two alternative ratification procedures, had not been employed since the ratification of the original Constitution in 1788. Congress, assuming that state legislatures would go along with their own action following the 1932 election, saw little reason to bother with an unfamiliar and apparently cumbersome procedure. Antiprohibitionists, however, fearing that dry pressure and recalcitrance in the legislatures of only a few small, rural states could thwart majority desire to end prohibition, insisted on use of the convention system. Unlike 1919, this would be an occasion when there would be no question as to whether law reflected popular preference.

Each state set up its own convention, delegate elections offered voters a clear choice between wets and drys, and between April 14, 1933, when Michigan held the first convention, and December 5, 1933, when Ohio, Pennsylvania, and Utah held theirs, the necessary thirty-six state ratifications were achieved. The conventions operated smoothly, with none taking more than a day and New Hampshire's only lasting seventeen minutes. Even more importantly, the convention system left no doubt as to the public's verdict on prohibition. In only one of thirty-seven state elections in 1933, that being South Carolina, did voters prefer to keep the Eighteenth Amendment. Altogether, 15 million out of 21 million voters chose repeal. The overall majority for repeal was 73 percent. The convention system provided one of the most prompt resolutions of any constitutional issue ever submitted to the states by Congress as well as one of the most decisive.

The emphatic rejection of national prohibition in 1933 increased doubts that the American people had ever wanted the law in the first place. The very nature of its departure fed national prohibition's myth, which may help explain why during the subsequent half century the realities and consequences of the entire episode have received so little consideration. The conference upon which this volume is based was an overdue attempt to remedy that neglect. It examined in detail prohibition's considerable impact on alcohol policy, on the economics and organizational structure of crime, and on politics, law, and constitutional attitudes. The vantage point of fifty years afforded a few general observations.

The quest for legal prohibition has dominated America's effort to deal with alcoholic beverages since before the middle of the nineteenth century. Not only did the experience with the Eighteenth Amendment lead our society to believe that drinking could not be controlled by law, at least at acceptable cost, but also the long concentration on prohibition laws directed attention away from the creative exploration of alternative legal approaches to controls on alcohol. Instead, since 1933 laws regulating access to liquor have grown more and more relaxed, while ''close-the-barn-door-after-the-horse-has-been-stolen'' statutes setting higher and higher penalties for liquor abuse have become increasingly popular. As a consequence, American society currently faces a situation in which a significant number of individuals who have a problem coping with liquor receive no personal attention until they are apprehended for driving while intoxicated, assaulting a friend or family member, or worse. The National Institute of Alcohol Abuse and Alcoholism estimates that over 7 percent of all Americans above age eighteen have an actual or potential alcohol problem. High national mortality rates for cirrhosis of the liver and drunk driving underscore the reality that in the face of an epidemic, our society has resigned itself to a legal approach emphasizing punishment rather than avoidance of the problem.

Ironically, the United States still pursues a traditional prohibitionist strategy in dealing with drugs other than alcohol. The blanket prohibition on every drug from marijuana to heroin recalls the total abstinence approach of the drys, while the inability of drug enforcement efforts to prevent a significant minority of society from obtaining a regular if costly supply recalls the limitations of the Volstead Act. The inconsistency between alcohol and drug policies suggests how little has been learned from the national prohibition episode. We have not applied in other areas prohibition's indication that laws are likely to fail if they ignore this society's cultural pluralism, its rich variety of values and habits, and try to impose a majority's will on a significant and resistent minority. And yet in regard to alcohol itself, we believe prohibition to be hopeless. Fifty years after repeal, we might consider undertaking a search for more creative legal devices which respect pluralistic values and the capacity of many persons to use alcohol sensibly and with pleasure while dealing more considerately with the problems generated by popular but potentially damaging substances.

As cautious as the prohibition myth has made us about regulating alcohol, it has led to even greater caution so far as altering the Constitution. By the early twentieth century, the gospel was widely preached and believed that the founding fathers had created a work of absolute genius. William Gladstone had described it as "the most wonderful work ever struck off at a given time by the brain and purpose of man." Prohibition heightened the perception that the nation's government could be needlessly thrown into dangerous turmoil by tampering with this eighteenth-century Constitution. This sense of risk has produced a profound reluctance to reshape it in any way to deal with twentieth-century circumstances. Since prohibition repeal no major reform in the structure of government has survived the amending process. Change has either been frustrated (as with the equal rights amendment) or has been accomplished through less direct and less democratically controllable or accountable means (the Supreme Court has fundamentally reformed government policies regarding civil rights and civil liberties; presidents, with congressional acquiescence, have centralized and obscured power). Even changes for the better rest on a shaky foundation, lacking explicit constitutional sanction and subject—as most clearly demonstrated by the Nixon and Reagan administrations—to reversal.

Rather than making us leary of tinkering with the Constitution, the prohibition episode should, after all, make us more comfortable about it. If nothing more, repeal demonstrates that constitutional mistakes can be corrected. The amending process is not, as one lawyer in the mid–1920s described it, "like the ratchet on a cog wheel. The wheel may be conveniently turned in one direction, but it cannot be reversed." [18] That hummingbird did, after all, fly to Mars with the Washington Monument tied to its tail! More importantly, however, the process by which prohibition was repealed—the convention ratification system—should make us aware that a device exists for placing fundamental political choices before the people for prompt and clear-cut decisions. Elected officials, if they wish, can thereby avoid uncomfortable choices which jeopardize their own situations without depriving the citizenry of the resolution of an issue. Of course, greater use of the amending process carries with it the risk of unwise choices and the stifling of minority interests, as prohibition should remind us. The alternative, however, seems likely to be a government of uncertain mandates and diminished democracy. Only by employing the amending process can national government structures and goals be rationally and democratically altered to suit modern circumstances.

Senator Sheppard's image of the hummingbird with the Washington Monument tied to its tail is perhaps a useful substitute for the defective and misleading myth of prohibition. Instead of the pinched, negative, one-sided national prohibition of myth, we can appreciate the strong, simple, and partially successful prohibition represented by General Washington's majestic obelisk, against which the fragile yet powerful hummingbird of personal independence and privacy strained. We can see beauty and virtue on each side, the reality of conflicting good intentions in a struggle to deal with a serious social problem. And above all, we realize that the unlikely hummingbird won the contest, though of course not easily nor immediately. That should remind and warn us (since the amending process is equally available to both sides on any contemporary issue as it was with prohibition) that our Constitution is not immobile, that some unexpected, truly extraordinary feats of amendment can be and indeed have been accomplished. The hummingbird and the monument should thus not only remind us of events a half-century past but also alert us to the ever-present possibility—for better or worse—of constitutional reform. If we are so reminded, the fiftieth anniversary observance of national prohibition's repeal will have been well worthwhile.

NOTES

1. H. L. Mencken, *Notes on Democracy* (New York: Knopf, 1926), p. 256.

2. Herbert Hoover, "Address Accepting the Nomination," August 11, 1928, *Public Papers of the Presidents of the United States: Herbert Hoover, 1929* (Washington, D.C.: GPO, 1974), p. 511.

3. Frederick Lewis Allen, *Only Yesterday* (New York: Harper, 1931), p. 204.

4. Richard Hofstadter, *The Age of Reform: From Bryan to F.D.R.* (New York: Knopf, 1955), pp. 289–90, 292.

5. Ibid., p. 289.

6. A perceptive analysis of this historical myth can be found in Ernest R. May, *"Lessons" of the Past: The Use and Misuse of History in American Foreign Policy* (New York: Oxford, 1973).

7. There is a rich and growing literature on drinking and the temperance movement in America. For what follows, I have relied particularly upon Norman H. Clark, *Deliver Us from Evil: An Interpretation of American Prohibition* (New York: Norton, 1976); Mark Edward Lender and James Kirby Martin, *Drinking in America: A History* (New York: Free Press, 1982); W. J.

Rosabaugh, *The Alcoholic Republic* (New York: Oxford, 1979); James H. Timberlake, *Prohibition and the Progressive Movement, 1900–1920* (Cambridge: Harvard University Press, 1963); and the still useful John A. Krout, *The Origins of Prohibition* (New York: Knopf, 1925).

8. A good discussion of consumption patterns is found in Lender and Martin, *Drinking in America.*

9. A fine study of this phase of the temperance crusade is Timberlake, *Prohibition and the Progressive Movement.*

10. Charles Stelzle, *Why Prohibition!* (New York: George H. Doran, 1918), p. 84.

11. This review of the adoption of the Eighteenth Amendment, together with what follows, draws, unless otherwise indicated, upon my *Repealing National Prohibition* (Chicago: University of Chicago Press, 1979).

12. New York *World,* quoted in Andrew Sinclair, *Era of Excess* (New York: Harper and Row, 1964), p. 366.

13. Edgar Dale, *The Content of Motion Pictures* (New York: Macmillan, 1935), pp. 167–69.

14. Quoted in Humbert S. Nelli, *The Business of Crime: Italians and Syndicate Crime in the United States* (New York: Oxford, 1976), pp. 211–12.

15. John C. Burnham makes a strong case for such a decline in "New Perspectives on the Prohibition 'Experiment' of the 1920's," *Journal of Social History* 2 (Fall 1968): 51–68.

16. Associated Press dispatch, September 24, 1930, quoted in Charles Merz, *The Dry Decade* (Garden City, N.Y.: Doubleday, Doran, 1931), p. 297.

17. "The Ordeal of Prohibition," *American Mercury,* August 1924, p. 419.

18. Archibald E. Stevenson, *States Rights and National Prohibition* (New York: Clark Boardman, 1927), p. 126.

2

STEVEN GOLDBERG

Putting Science in the Constitution: The Prohibition Experience

The United States Constitution is hospitable to the scientific endeavor, but it was not designed to embody judgments on controversial scientific issues. Because prohibition was based in part on just such judgments involving the medical effects of alcohol, the Eighteenth Amendment distorted the proper relationship between science and the Constitution. This aspect of the prohibition experience provides an important perspective on the current controversy concerning abortion.

Given the framers' belief in such Enlightenment ideals as the desirability of relying on empirical data rather than received authority, it is not surprising that the Constitution protects and supports science. The framers believed the rational discovery of natural laws, most dramatically demonstrated by Newton's work, could be achieved not only for natural phenomena but for human affairs as well. Indeed, to the framers the word "science" referred to knowledge generally.[1] Thus the First Amendment's protection for speech and the press was meant to prevent government suppression of the ideas of physicists as well as politicians.[2] Similarly, the First Amendment's ban on established religion was designed in part to prevent organized religion from halting the growth of systematic, empirical knowledge. Thomas Jefferson's attack on established religion is illustrative:

Galileo was sent to the Inquisition for affirming that the earth was a sphere; the government had declared it to be as flat as a trencher, and Galileo was obliged to abjure his error. This error, however, at length prevailed, the earth became a globe.[3]

The author thanks David Novak for his excellent research assistance.

The Constitution also contains provisions such as the patent clause that provide incentives for doing applied research. But the Constitution does not contain statements resolving specific controversies about the nature of the natural world. It is written on a far more general level directed toward the structure of government and the delineation of fundamental values. The Constitution provides a basic framework under which public debate takes place. It is difficult to amend and thus not designed to embody detailed judgments on the ever-changing issues of the day. As Chief Justice Marshall wrote in *McCulloch v. Maryland* in 1819, the Constitution's "nature . . . requires, that only its great outlines should be marked, its important objects designated."[4] It is unsurprising, therefore, that the Constitution contains no list of branches of science to be studied or inventions to be patented. Nor does it list substances believed to be hazardous to health. These items were not omitted because influential Americans lacked views on them. Consider, for example, Benjamin Rush, a leading physician and a signer of the Declaration of Independence, who in 1784 published his *Inquiry into the Effects of Spirituous Liquors*, an attack on "ardent spirits" that is viewed by some as the first effort to detail the physiological effects of alcohol. Rush vigorously spoke out on these matters for the rest of his life, but when, in 1787, the federal Constitution came before the Pennsylvania convention for ratification, Rush was one of its most vigorous, outspoken, and uncritical supporters. While Rush favored laws to limit the number of saloons, as well as other legislative steps to fight "ardent spirits," these were suggestions for ordinary legislation, not for inclusion in the Constitution, the fundamental framework of government.[5]

During the years following ratification of the Constitution, knowledge of the natural world grew rapidly. The natural sciences and medicine became increasingly complex and specialized, as the Enlightenment notion of the unity of all knowledge became less pervasive. This did not mean, however, that scientists and medical experts played no role in public debate. On the contrary, technical experts were often called upon to provide information and advice on public issues.[6] One of the first instances arose in 1832, when the federal government, concerned about explosions in steamboat boilers, hired a professor of chemistry to do a study that ultimately led to legislation creating the Steamboat Inspection Service.[7] Increasingly throughout the nineteenth century, scientists advised and lobbied the government on issues ranging from military preparedness to agricultural research. By the turn of the twentieth century, the medical profession, primarily through the American Medical Association (AMA), played an important role in supporting legislation such as the Pure Food and Drugs Act of 1906.[8]

Under the circumstances, it is not surprising that medical evidence played a role in the temperance movement. Expert information on how alcohol could harm the human body was relevant to the temperance cause. Moreover, while some prohibitionists, such as William Jennings Bryan, had fundamentalist beliefs at odds with modern science, many who supported the Eighteenth Amendment were Progressives with a particular affinity for science.[9] Nonetheless the use of medical evidence in the prohibition debate was in many respects unfortunate. The evidence used was distorted, divisions in the medical community were overlooked, and a controversial medical dispute was dealt with in the Constitution rather than in ordinary legislation.

Medical studies conducted in the second half of the nineteenth century indicated that alcohol consumed in significant quantities could cause cirrhosis of the liver, stomach inflammation, heart disease, and other ailments. Drys, however, often exaggerated and distorted these studies.[10] A particularly influential source of dry propaganda of this type was school texts. The department of scientific temperance instruction of the Women's Christian Temperance Union obtained legislation in many states requiring temperance instruction, and then influenced the content of the textbooks used in those courses.[11] These texts, ignoring the fact that the relevant medical studies concerned the effects of substantial drinking, referred to alcohol as "a colorless liquid poison,"[12] and sought to frighten students by alleging, for example, that "a boy once drank whiskey from a flask he had found, and died in a few hours. . . . Alcohol sometimes causes the coats of the blood vessels to grow thin. They are then liable at any time to cause death by bursting."[13] It is no wonder that modern observers have labeled these texts' use of medical evidence as "lurid pseudoscience."[14]

Other evidence used by drys was also exaggerated. Of particular importance were studies from the field of eugenics—a subject of considerable importance in American society in the pre-prohibition era. Since the inheritance of acquired characteristics was no longer scientifically accepted, some eugenicists updated old criticisms of alcohol by developing a new theory—blastophthoria—which held that alcohol in the blood could damage the germ cell and thus cause deformed offspring.[15] One proponent of this view argued that animal experiments positively demonstrated that alcohol was a "race poison" for humans. He referred to a study in which guinea pigs that inhaled alcohol fumes for years were found to have more defective offspring than those who did not.[16] He did not mention that in that experiment no abnormality had been found in the pigs' reproductive organs—the supposed source of the defects—nor did he discuss major empirical studies done by eugenicists that debunked the notion that the children of human alcoholics were genetically damaged.[17]

Wets attempted to counter the drys' misrepresentations, but the wets themselves often exaggerated medical facts, as when they referred to alcohol's food value by saying, "On the meat side, alcohol is a sort of broth prepared specially with loving care and evident skill."[18] Moreover, there was one particular piece of scientific evidence that could not easily be rebutted by the wets. The American Medical Association's June 16, 1917, resolution opposing "the use of alcohol as a beverage"[19] was an important factor in the prohibition movement. The AMA was a powerful organization long before 1917. Its resolution was cited by prohibition supporter Senator Thomas Sterling on August 1, 1917, as "one of the most valuable pieces of evidence we can find in support of the submission of this amendment to the several States of the Union."[20] A 1921 book attacking prohibition said the resolution "was of the utmost importance to the advocates of prohibition," while a modern observer has called the resolution "extremely useful to the drys."[21] Although no single statement can stand out from all the complex factors that brought about prohibition, this resolution is certainly important enough to warrant a closer look.

The usual explanation of the AMA's action is reasonably straightforward. Convinced that alcohol often caused harm, yet perhaps quietly looking forward to the money to be made by monopolizing its distribution as medicine,[22] the AMA's House of Delegates passed the 1917 resolution which read:

WHEREAS, We believe that the use of alcohol as a beverage is detrimental to the human economy, and
WHEREAS, Its use in therapeutics, as a tonic or a stimulant or as a food, has no scientific basis, therefore be it
Resolved, That the American Medical Association opposes the use of alcohol as a beverage, and be it further

Resolved, That the use of alcohol as a therapeutic agent should be discouraged.[23]

The resolution demonstrated that the medical community favored prohibition. After prohibition began, however, Congress adopted the Willis-Campbell Act, which forbade the prescription of beer as medicine and limited to one hundred the number of prescriptions for liquor that could be issued in any ninety-day period, thus restricting the freedom of many doctors. Moreover, prohibition did not appear to be reducing the number of defective newborns or otherwise dramatically improving public health. The AMA accordingly reversed itself and, by 1922, called for the liberalization of prohibition; a reversal that was used by anti-prohibition advocates in their support of repeal.[24]

While there is much truth in this version of the AMA's actions, a close look at the resolution and its aftermath reveals an additional aspect of this experience with particular implications for subsequent policy disputes involving science. The AMA's 1917 resolution did not reflect the conclusions of the medical community on a medical matter. It reflected instead the views of some members of a divided medical community on a social issue that combined controversial medical and policy considerations. The divisions within the medical community centered on whether alcohol possessed therapeutic value, an important part of the prohibition debate, since if alcohol was beneficial, people would want access to it with or without a doctor's prescription. Because the issues surrounding the therapeutic uses of alcohol were not and could not have been resolved by the 1917 resolution, use of that resolution as important evidence concerning what ought to go into the Constitution lacked justification.

The long-standing medical use of alcohol as an aid to digestion and a heart stimulant came into question in the nineteenth century. Researchers found that large quantities of alcohol interfered with digestion and depressed the heart. But they also found that small quantities of alcohol did stimulate the flow of digestive juices and indirectly accelerated the heart by partially paralyzing certain nerve centers.[25] At the time of the AMA's 1917 convention, alcohol was still used by many doctors for certain stomach and heart ailments. When the new AMA president, Dr. Charles H. Mayo, criticized the medical use of alcohol in his inaugural address at the convention, he was immediately challenged. Dr. Beverly Robinson, a prominent clinician, told the *New York*

Times that alcohol was invaluable as a "stimulant or heart tonic" and to prevent indigestion. During the same week that the AMA was considering its June 16, 1917, resolution, Dr. Robinson was criticizing Dr. Mayo and asserting that there are conditions which "absolutely demand the use of alcohol as a prominent part of medicine." [26] To this day, the use of alcohol for such purposes as aiding digestion or treating fainting remains controversial. A modern medical text states that the "proper delineation" of alcohol's "legitimate uses in medicine is sometimes difficult." [27] Under the circumstances, it is necessary to look closely at the development of the 1917 resolution to see precisely what it contained.

The resolution originated with a classic instance of a pressure group seeking to enlist scientific expertise in its cause. The National Women's Christian Temperance Union wrote to the AMA House of Delegates requesting "a warning against alcoholic liquors." The letter noted that "the medical society of Russia at its meeting in 1915 issued a notable document against alcohol. . . . Your petitioners hope for as strong and helpful an expression from the great American Medical Association as that emanating from your Russian confrères." [28] The AMA referred the letter to its Council on Health and Public Instruction, which produced a proposed resolution declaring that "it is the unanimous opinion of the Council on Health and Public Instruction . . . that alcohol has no drug value . . . as a therapeutic agent, and . . . its use as a . . . therapeutic agent is detrimental rather than beneficial to the individual." [29] The council's proposal was referred to the Committee on Legislation and Political Action. This committee reported to the House of Delegates that "since the expressions of opinion from numerous members of the House and the Association lead us to the conclusion that the status of alcohol in medicine is still undetermined," the proposed resolution should be reworded. The committee's reworded version is the resolution that was ultimately passed by the house. As noted above, the final resolution concludes simply that "the use of alcohol as a therapeutic agent should be discouraged."

Even as watered down, the resolution did not have smooth sailing. A representative of the AMA's Section on Pharmacology and Therapeutics offered a substitute resolution which had been adopted by that section:

The Section on Pharmacology and Therapeutics instructs its delegates to the House of Delegates that it is the sense of this section that the question of the therapeutic value of alcohol which has been long in dispute remains yet un-determined, and that hasty action taken in the stress of present circumstances would not be wise, and would not reflect fully the best therapeutic and phar-macologic opinions.

Furthermore, while recognizing the possible need of prohibition of the use of alcohol as a measure of public safety, it would ask that the two questions be considered separately on their respective merits.[30]

It is not surprising that a lengthy debate in the House of Delegates fol-lowed, since one would expect that the Section on Pharmacology and Therapeutics would have considerable influence on the issues in-volved. Nonetheless, the substitute resolution was ultimately voted down. Still another substitute seeking to weaken the resolution was offered, seconded, debated, and defeated before the resolution was finally passed.[31]

Whether alcohol was useful in medical therapy was obviously a controversial question turning on matters of judgment. The AMA weakened the original resolution that condemned alcohol as "detri-mental" in therapeutics, rejected a substitute that would have left the matter open, and ultimately passed a resolution that "discouraged" the use of alcohol in therapy. This quickly became an AMA endorsement of prohibition, as these distinctions were lost in the shuffle.

Under the circumstances, it is misleading to describe the medical establishment as changing its view after prohibition. It never had a clear-cut view it could change. When the New York legislature ratified the Eighteenth Amendment, the Medical Society of the County of New York passed a resolution within a month condemning ratification as "irrational" and "unscientific."[32] The AMA itself, soon pressured by increasing restrictions on the ability of doctors to prescribe alcohol, rapidly began to emphasize the difficulty of passing final medical judg-ment on the therapeutic uses of alcohol.[33] A referendum was held in which more than 30,000 physicians offered their views on whether "whiskey [is] a necessary therapeutic agent in the practice of medi-cine." The result, published in January 1922, provides little comfort to those who believe that experts agree with each other—51 percent of the doctors said yes; 49 percent said no.[34] Soon thereafter, the AMA's Council on Scientific Assembly issued a report on the therapeutic value of alcohol that concluded it was "unwise to attempt to determine moot, scientific questions by resolution or by vote."[35] A June 3, 1922, res-olution of the AMA House of Delegates referred to the referendum results and called for relaxation of the prohibition laws, arguing that the use of alcohol for therapy should not "be determined by legal or arbitrary dictum."[36] By 1926 a representative of the AMA testified before the Senate that the therapeutic use of malt liquor "was not a matter that could be settled by a vote of the organized medical profession, but was rather a scientific problem to be settled at the bedside."[37] By the time of repeal, the AMA's views had become a source of authority for those who opposed prohibition.[38]

From today's perspective, it is apparent why the AMA resolution of 1917 was not an appropriate source of support for the Eighteenth Amendment. The problem is not that science can play no role in lawmaking. There are, of course, widely agreed-upon scientific theories at any particular moment in history. For example, Albert Einstein's formula for the conversion of matter into energy, $E = mc^2$, is believed to be well-established empirically and theoretically, and, while further developments in science are always possible, it is rational for policymakers today to use that equation. For example, even taking into account practical limitations of various kinds, it may be useful for policy purposes to make judgments based on expectations of the magnitude of potential yields from nuclear energy in civilian and military contexts. While there would be no point in enacting into law the fact that $E = mc^2$, there may well be political actions, such as arms control treaties or reactor design limitations, that turn in part on the fundamental $E = mc^2$ equation.

The AMA's 1917 resolution, however, differed in two key respects from a statement of well-established scientific theory. First, as indicated above, there was no consensus on the resolution. Second, even if there had been, the resolution mixed scientific with policy considerations. It moved from the statement that alcohol as a beverage is detrimental to the conclusion that alcohol should not be used as a beverage; it similarly moved from the assertion that alcohol's use in therapeutics has no scientific basis to the conclusion that its use in therapeutics should be discouraged. In each case, the initial statement is arguably the expert opinion of at least some of the medical community, but the conclusion is a matter of social choice, not scientific necessity. For example, the majority of scientists today might believe that heavy ingestion of saccharin will increase by one percent a person's chances of getting a particular kind of cancer. Even if the scientific community is not unanimous on that point, the views of many scientists may be useful to know. But the scientists have no particular expertise on the question of whether a one-percent increase in a cancer rate justifies banning saccharin. That policy question turns on weighing the costs against the benefits of saccharin and is ultimately a value question, not a scientific one. Similarly, even if alcohol is "detrimental," the public might want to use it for the pleasure it brings, and even if alcohol's therapeutic value is unproven, the public might want to take advantage of the chance that it has value.

These kinds of limitations are well understood in a wide variety of public issues today. Policymakers are often aware of divisions in the scientific community and of the necessity of separating scientific from value judgments. When, for example, the 1983 AMA House of Delegates passed a resolution downplaying the dangers of dioxin, sharp questioning from members of Congress focusing on the uncertainty of the risks involved quickly led AMA representatives to say that a clarification of the AMA position was in order.[39] Moreover, when legislating in value-laden areas of technical uncertainty becomes necessary, it is generally recognized that decisions are not written in stone and that agency or legislative modification is quite possible as time passes. In particular, there is virtually no sympathy in any segment of society for putting judgments in areas such as nuclear energy, food additives, pesticides, and the like in the Constitution. In this respect, one of the lessons of prohibition has been learned.

In the area of abortion, however, the lesson may have to be learned again. Many activists on both sides of the abortion controversy want their views enshrined in the Constitution. Pro-abortion forces generally support *Roe v. Wade*, in which the Supreme Court found the Constitution's protection of a woman's right to privacy encompassed abortion.[40] Many abortion opponents favor a constitutional amendment protecting the fetus's right to life.[41] The Constitution may be an appropriate place to resolve this controversy one way or the other to the extent that the contending forces are concerned with fundamental values such as privacy and life. But to the extent that the contending forces place their ultimate reliance not on fundamental philosophical values but rather on supposed medical facts, the Constitution is not a sensible place to resolve the matter.

Advocates of abortion run this risk because of the way the Supreme Court has formulated the right to abortion. The Court's decision in *Roe* is based in part on the notion that after a fetus becomes viable, abortion can be limited.[42] As the Court has come to realize, however, modern technology has made viability possible at ever-earlier dates.[43] In the future, artificial wombs may move viability back to conception—a result that could severely limit abortion in a way the Court may not have intended when it chose the medical concept of viability.[44] Even beyond the viability debate, the Court has based the abortion right in part on inherently unstable grounds. The Court, in its concern that a woman's right to abortion not be unduly burdened, has been called upon to evaluate the constitutionality of an ordinance that requires that abortions done after the first trimester be performed in hospitals. The Court held this requirement unconstitutional on the ground that "present medical knowledge" establishes that such abortions can safely be performed in clinics. In reaching this conclusion, the court relied heavily and explicitly on the finding that the American Public Health Association (APHA) and the American College of Obstetricians and Gynecologists (ACOG) believed that abortions after the first trimester could safely be done in clinics. Yet, as the Court itself recognized, just a few years earlier both APHA and ACOG had taken precisely the opposite position and insisted that only hospitals be allowed to perform abortions of this type.[45] As APHA and ACOG change their views to respond to changing technology and changing attitudes, it appears that the Constitution changes with them. The similarity to shifting AMA attitudes and the constitutional status of alcohol is striking. Indeed, in abortion the Constitution is being based even more directly on even more unstable grounds.

Opponents of abortion, however, are not free of similar problems. A recurrent theme in the anti-abortion movement has been an effort to amend the Constitution to provide that human life exists from the moment of conception or fertilization. A major motivation for this proposal is the belief that scientific evidence supports this view.[46] There are two major problems with this approach. First, the "moment of fertilization" may not be a clear scientific concept. Modern texts speak of "stages of fertilization" as part of an essentially continuous process through which life is passed from one generation to the next.[47] Second, even if "fertilization" is well defined, scientists do not agree that it corresponds to the beginning of "human life" or "personhood." Prominent medical experts place the beginning of human life at various points, including fertilization, implantation, the beginning of brain waves, and viability. Many do not regard the matter as a scientific or medical issue at all.[48] Thus to the extent that anti-abortion forces succeed in putting fertilization in the Constitution on the ground that it is a medical standard for the beginning of life, they will find themselves in the same unstable position as those who rely on medical support for their constitutional views on when abortion can be performed, and those who relied, years ago, on AMA support for the constitutional ban on alcohol.

The Constitution is not timeless or infallible. It should, however, embody fundamental judgments concerning our government and our values. Putting transitory scientific matters in the Constitution serves neither science nor the Constitution.

NOTES

1. Whitfield J. Bell, *Early American Science: Needs and Opportunities for Study* (Williamsburg, Va.: Institute of Early American History, 1955), p. 8. *See also* Ernest Cassara, *The Enlightenment in America* (Boston: Twayne Publishers, 1975), pp. 15–18; Peter Gay, *The Enlightenment: An Interpretation,* 2 vols. (New York: Knopf, 1969), 2: 127–87.

2. Richard Delgado and David R. Millen, "God, Galileo, and Government: Toward Constitutional Protection for Scientific Inquiry," *Washington Law Review* 53 (1978): 354–61.

3. Thomas Jefferson, *Notes on the State of Virginia,* ed. William Peden (Chapel Hill: University of North Carolina Press, 1955), pp. 159–60. *See also* Steven Goldberg, "The Constitutional Status of American Science," *University of Illinois Law Forum,* 1979, pp. 5–6.

4. *McCulloch v. Maryland,* 4 Wheat. 316, 406 (1819).

5. David Hawke, *Benjamin Rush: Revolutionary Gadfly* (New York: Irvington, 1971), pp. 303, 347–53; Carl A. L. Binger, *Revolutionary Doctor* (New York: Norton, 1966), p. 249; Donald J. D'Elia, "Benjamin Rush: Philosopher of the American Revolution," *Transactions of the American Philosophical Society* 64 (1974): 92.

6. J. Stefan Dupré and Sanford A. Lakoff, *Science and the Nation: Policy and Politics* (Englewood Cliffs, N.J.: Prentice-Hall, 1962), pp. 4–6; Paul Starr, *The Social Transformation of American Medicine* (New York: Basic Books, 1982), pp. 140–42.

7. Don K. Price, *Government and Science* (New York: Oxford, 1962), pp. 10–11.

8. James Bordley and A. McGehee Harvey, *Two Centuries of American Medicine: 1776–1976* (Philadelphia: W. B. Saunders, 1976), pp. 364–66; Dupré and Lakoff, *Science and the Nation,* pp. 4–6.

9. George H. Daniels, *Science in American Society* (New York: Knopf, 1971), pp. 288–90; Joseph R. Gusfield, *Symbolic Crusade: Status Politics and the American Temperance Movement* (Champaign: University of Illinois Press, 1963), p. 125.

10. James H. Timberlake, *Prohibition and the Progressive Movement: 1900–1920* (Cambridge: Harvard University Press, 1963), pp. 40–52.

11. Gusfield, *Symbolic Crusade*, pp. 85–86.

12. Timberlake, *Prohibition and the Progressive Movement*, p. 49.

13. Andrew Sinclair, *Era of Excess* (New York: Harper and Row, 1964), p. 45.

14. Paul Aaron and David Musto, "Temperance and Prohibition in America: A Historical Overview," in *Alcohol and Public Policy: Beyond the Shadow of Prohibition*, ed. Mark H. Moore and Dean R. Gerstein (Washington, D.C.: National Academy Press, 1981), pp. 127–47.

15. Mark Haller, *Eugenics: Hereditarian Attitudes in American Thought* (New Brunswick, N.J.: Rutgers University Press, 1963), pp. 86–87.

16. J. E. Wallace Wallin, *Problems of Subnormality* (Yonkers-on-Hudson, N.Y.: World Book Co., 1917), pp. 445–46.

17. Michael F. Guyer, *Being Well-Born* (Indianapolis: Bobbs-Merrill, 1916), pp. 172, 179.

18. Sinclair, *Era of Excess*, p. 42.

19. *Journal of the American Medical Association*, June 16, 1917, p. 1837 (hereafter cited as *JAMA*).

20. *Congressional Record*, 65th Cong., 1st sess., 1917, p. 5646.

21. Charles Stout, *The Eighteenth Amendment and the Part Played by Organized Medicine* (New York: M. Kennerley, 1921), p. 46; Sinclair, *Era of Excess*, p. 61.

22. Timberlake, *Prohibition and the Progressive Movement*, p. 47; Sinclair, *Era of Excess*, pp. 59–62.

23. *JAMA*, June 16, 1917, p. 1837.

24. Sinclair, *Era of Excess*, pp. 404–6, 410–11; Clarence Darrow and Victor Yarros, *The Prohibition Mania* (New York: Boni and Liveright, 1927), pp. 33–35, 136–46.

25. Timberlake, *Prohibition and the Progressive Movement*, pp. 40–43.

26. *New York Times*, June 17, 1917, magazine section, p. 8. Dr. Mayo's speech was on June 6, 1917; the House of Delegates resolution was adopted June 16, 1917. The interview with Dr. Robinson was said to have taken place "the other day" in response to Dr. Mayo's speech.

27. Louis S. Goodman and Alfred Gilman, eds., *The Pharmacological Basis of Therapeutics*, 5th ed. (New York: Macmillan, 1975), p. 145.

28. *JAMA*, June 9, 1917, p. 1721.

29. Ibid., p. 1768.

30. Ibid., June 16, 1917, p. 1837.

31. Ibid. The *Journal* lists seven speakers on the motion to substitute a new resolution but does not report their comments nor the vote on the motion. The second substitute sought to strike all references to the therapeutic use of alcohol from the resolution on the floor. The *Journal* lists one speaker on the substitute but does not report his comment, nor the vote on either the substitute or the final motion.

32. The resolution was introduced on January 27, 1919. *New York Times,* January 28, 1919, p. 1. It was adopted, after a lengthy debate, by a two-to-one margin at a meeting of the medical society on February 24, 1919. *New York Times,* February 25, 1919, p. 6.

33. Sinclair, *Era of Excess,* p. 410.

34. *JAMA,* January 21, 1922, p. 210.

35. Ibid., May 27, 1922, p. 1637.

36. Ibid., June 3, 1922, p. 1709.

37. U.S. Senate, Committee on the Judiciary, *Hearings,* 69th Cong., 1st sess., April 5, 1926, p. 163 (testimony of Dr. William C. Woodward, appearing as the representative of the AMA).

38. Darrow and Yarros, *The Prohibition Mania,* pp. 33–35.

39. *Washington Post,* July 1, 1983, p. A–1.

40. *Roe v. Wade,* 410 U.S. 113, 153 (1973).

41. In 1981, for example, numerous constitutional amendments restricting abortion were proposed; a typical one provided, "The paramount right to life is vested in each human being from the moment of fertilization. . . . " Gerald Gunther, *Constitutional Law: 1982 Supplement* (Mineola, N.Y.: Foundation Press, 1982), p. 80.

42. *Roe v. Wade,* 410 U.S. 113, 163 (1973).

43. *Planned Parenthood of Central Missouri v. Danforth,* 428 U.S. 52, 64–65 (1976); *see also Colautti v. Franklin,* 439 U.S. 379, 388 (1979).

44. Carole P. Clarke, "Survey of Abortion Law: Perspectives of Viability," *Arizona State Law Journal,* 1980, pp. 128, 142–44.

45. *City of Akron v. Akron Center for Reproductive Health, Inc.,* 103 S. Ct. 2481, 2493–97 (1983). Indeed, ACOG adhered to the view that abortions after the first trimester should be done in hospitals until after the ordinance in question was passed and after the trial had been held in the case challenging that ordinance. Ibid., p. 2496, n. 26.

46. *See* U.S. Senate, Subcommittee on Separation of Powers, Committee on the Judiciary, *Hearings on the Human Life Statute,* 97th Cong., 1st sess., April 23–24, May 20–21, June 1, 10, 12, 18–19, 1981, p. 13 (statement of Dr. Gordon). These hearings were held on a bill that would provide that scientific evidence indicates that human life exists from conception. The intent of the bill, to provide the fetus with the protection of the Fourteenth Amend-

ment, is similar to the intent of many proposed constitutional amendments designed to prohibit abortion. *See* David Westfall, ''Beyond Abortion: The Potential Reach of a Human Life Amendment,'' *American Journal of Law and Medicine* 8 (1982): 99.

47. Robert G. Edwards, *Conception in the Human Female* (London: Academic Press, 1980), pp. 573–75, 1009–10. *See also Roe v. Wade*, 410 U.S. 113, 161 (1973).

48. *Hearings on the Human Life Statute*, p. 70 (statement of Dr. Mellinkoff).

Labor and Prohibition: The Unappreciated Impact of the Eighteenth Amendment

Throughout the Progressive era and the decade of the so-called Roaring Twenties, multiple forces and powerful influences worked to direct the social, economic, and political evolution of the American people. The historiography is rich with explanations of the factors operative in these first three decades of the twentieth century which have contributed significantly to our understanding of why we are where and who we are today.

The real or imagined economic prosperity of the period, a "guilt complex" among members of the American middle class, the status revolution with all of its psychological force, the "war to end all wars," the effectiveness of the anti-union and/or paternalistic programs of management in the 1920s, and even the personalities and temperaments of all the men who led the labor movement in the era were all powerful forces which helped to determine the course of American labor history. Indeed, the entire *zeitgeist* of the decades in question played its role in shaping the direction and destiny of the organized working-class movement. Prohibition was an integral part of the era, but it is rarely appreciated as a formative influence in labor history. Within the American working-class movement, prohibition was a profound force and, at least from one perspective, a force of a highly destructive nature.

From the outset of the drive to accomplish statutory prohibition, the movement presented a serious threat to labor's internal solidarity. National and local labor leaders recognized that intemperance was a genuine problem for their members, constituting a fundamental threat to the entire "uplift movement." [1] Consequently, self-interest, as well as a sincere commitment to the well-being of workers, impelled unions to adopt temperance reform. However, sensitivity to the overwhelming sentiment of the rank and file caused most to oppose statutory prohibition. [2] Making a clear distinction between "temperance" and "prohibition," most leaders of labor organizations stressed the role that poverty played in the creation of alcohol abuse, rather than the reverse. They struggled to promote the notion that the most effective way to destroy the intemperate use of alcohol among workers was the elimination of the industrial and environmental conditions which promoted poverty and its consequent despair. [3] In their minds, effective trade unions were the best mechanism for the accomplishment of a temperate way of life for workers and their families.

Samuel Gompers, founder and long-term president of the American Federation of Labor (AFL), effectively articulated this position when he wrote:

I earnestly hope that our fellow workers will practice temperate habits in all matters. I am confident that it would be to their great advantage. Of course, there is a difference of opinion in regard to regulating people's habits by law. For my own part, I would prefer to so improve the conditions of the workers that they would not be tempted to irrational or intemperate habits. To instill character, independence, and self-respect are both cause and effect for the work for the common uplift. [4]

In fact, the 1895 convention of the AFL had declared:

It is also demonstrable that the achievements of the trade union movement in the line of reduced hours of burdensome toil, an increase in wages and improved environments have done more to reduce the evils of intemperance than all the efforts from other directions. [5]

Later, Gompers would state in unequivocal terms:

There is no agency so potent to make men temperate in all their habits as the much misunderstood and misrepresented organized labor movement—a movement which brings improvement in the mental and physical status of our people and reduces to a minimum the desire, the taste, of the habit of intemperance. [6]

That this view was shared by others in the leadership is evidenced by the declaration by Matthew Woll in the *American Federationist*, the monthly publication of the AFL, that

no force in our country has been as effective in the promotion of temperance among working people as the organized labor movement. The labor movement has achieved more for the cause of temperance than all the temperance societies combined.[7]

Reasons for rank and file opposition to statutory prohibition were many and complex. The most readily identifiable were practical considerations. Most felt that thousands would lose their employment if the reform went into effect nationwide. The editors of the *Miners' Magazine*, official journal of the United Mine Workers, one of the largest AFL affiliates, spoke for most of organized labor when they wrote, "Organized labor cannot afford to give its support to a movement that will depress the labor market and make it much easier for exploiters to recruit strike breakers, when labor is engaged in conflict with a master class."[8] The *Brauer Arbeiter Zeitung*, the organ of the United Brewery Workers, stated the argument more dramatically when it declared, "An empty stomach, starving wives and children are not conducive to the furtherance of ideals."[9]

Quite obviously, the United Brewery Workers (UBW), which would be most directly impacted by the adoption of prohibition, was militantly opposed to it. But there were also many "allied trades" which would be seriously affected in an economic way. Cigarmakers, tobacco workers, glass workers, coopers, bartenders, waiters, and most of the musicians saw prohibition as a fundamental threat to their employment and joined in struggle to defeat it.[10] Members of these trade unions feared that up to "one million wage earners directly and indirectly employed will be out of work because legitimate business will be completely disarranged," perhaps even seriously impairing the entire national economy.[11]

Furthermore, the neighborhood saloon played a key social role for workers. It was, according to the Commission to Investigate Drunkenness in Massachusetts, the only place in which a poor man could be sure of "warmth, comfort and companionship."[12] The saloon keeper and his political allies might be considered the first, and for a long time the only, social welfare workers in cities. He often provided help for the immigrant, jobs for the unemployed, free lunches for the poor, and halls for union meetings. In addition, the saloon keeper had always remained hospitable to the organized labor movement itself during those times when the unions were under fire from every direction. The saloon was "practically the only place in which union-made cigars could be purchased before the adoption of the Eighteenth Amendment." [13] Saloon keepers enjoyed a virtual monopoly on small meeting places and permitted unions to use them, free of charge, for social and business meetings, confident that the men would spend their money before, during, and after the meeting. Such contributions to the welfare of the working man could not be ignored by the leaders of the organized labor movement.

But the popularity of the saloon and its product was not a complete explanation for labor's hostility to the adoption of statutory prohibition. The attitude of the great mass of laborers can be ascribed, at least in part, to a reaction against the support of the drive by employers. It had been a long-standing objective of the Anti-Saloon League of America to obtain the financial and moral backing of the nation's businessmen and industrialists. Workers saw in this support one more attack on the institutions of labor. [14]

Many workers saw the reform as an ouright attempt at class legislation. The abolition of the saloon would not hurt the employer or his middle-class friends, for their wine cellars would remain untouched. But it would surely deprive the laborer of one of the things which made life a little more endurable.

Labor was particularly hostile to the paternalism evidenced by employer support of the antisaloon cause. Working men were not convinced that prohibition was intended to benefit them as its proponents claimed. They publicly resented the attitude that seemed to indicate that employers knew enough to drink within proper bounds, but that workers were incapable of making this kind of judgment. One spokesman for labor stated, "The laboring man, like other men, objects to being treated like a child or a machine." [15] Gompers himself declared that he resented his shopmates being treated like inanimate things without feelings. [16] Hermann Schlüter, historian of the United Brewery Workers disposed of the paternalistic element by demanding that the man who really wanted to help the laborer "develop from a reformer to a revolutionist, from a prohibitionist to a Socialist." He insisted that the "battle against drunkenness can best be waged in the general class struggle of the working men and in the organizations which this class struggle produces.''[17]

Very early it was clear that the vast majority of the members of the organized working-class movement were hostile to prohibition. However, the American Federation of Labor took no official stand articulating that position. Furthermore, outstanding labor spokesmen, including members of the Executive Council of the AFL, persisted in efforts to get the organization to endorse the prohibition cause. Officials of the federation failed to publicize effectively their personal position distinguishing between support of temperance and opposition to statutory prohibition. This placed labor in an anomalous position which led to grave misunderstanding and considerable bitterness within the ranks of the national organization.[18]

As early as 1909, Charles Stelzle, a member of the powerful Machinists' Union and the director of the Department of Church and Labor of the Presbyterian Church, predicted that a time would come ''when there will be a break in the ranks of organized labor because of this issue.''[19] Samuel Gompers shared the same feeling but was determined to prevent schism.[20] Cooperating with Stelzle in the promotion of prohibition within the federation were John B. Lennon, treasurer of the AFL, Thomas Lewis, president of the United Mine Workers, and John Mitchell and James Duncan of the Executive Council.[21] Their collective efforts to get a proprohibition drive operative within organized labor were thwarted by Gompers.

In 1909 the United Brewery Workers had submitted a series of resolutions to the annual federation convention which, if adopted, would have placed the AFL squarely in the antiprohibition camp. Gompers is reported to have agreed to keep these resolutions from the floor in return for an end to Stelzle's activities. When the delegates who had presented the antiprohibition resolutions rose to ask what had become of their petitions, Gompers ruled them out of order. He insisted that discussion of all such political questions was a violation of the federation's constitution. This heavy-handed ruling angered the brewery workers and delegates of the allied trades, who never lost the feeling that they had been betrayed in their hour of need by the federation.[22]

Using all of his skill as a diplomat and a practitioner of pragmatic politics, Gompers managed to continue to keep the issue off the floor of the annual meetings. As late as April 1919, he successfully withstood pressure to have the convention address the problem, warning,

"There are enough efforts made to divide labor without my adding to their number." [23] So, in spite of their best efforts and great need, the antiprohibition forces within labor were unable to get a resolution of opposition before the convention until it was too late.

Parenthetically, it must be pointed out that Samuel Gompers personally came out against prohibition as early as 1915 and 1916.[24] He actually traveled around the country in cooperation with the program of opposition devised by the United Brewery Workers and the brewing industry trade association, but always attempted to make it clear that he did so in his capacities as private citizen, cigarmaker, and vice president of the Cigarmakers, which had sanctioned the opposition by national convention.

Such personal efforts by Gompers were not enough to dilute the bitterness felt by the unions most directly threatened by the reform.[25] The hotel and restaurant workers faced a mutiny of the bartenders over the issue. This element in the international threatened to withdraw and affiliate with the brewery workers because of the failure of the American Federation of Labor to fight prohibition nationally.[26] The editors of both the *Brewery Workers Journal* and *Mixer and Server*, the newspaper of the hotelmen, regularly complained of the total lack of understanding of the desperate plight of liquor industry unions and the acute ignorance within organized labor of the interdependence of modern industry which meant that all workers would pay a price for the demise of any element in the economy. To their minds, these failures bred indifference on the part of their brothers in the movement to the fate of members of unions dependent on the liquor industry and indirectly to their own fate.[27]

Jere Sullivan of the restaurant workers expressed the bitterness of all labor's opposition when he wrote in the *American Federationist* that it was the "flood of votes cast by men and women, no different than our own members, workers for wages, willingly and knowingly increasing the numberable strength of the army of unemployed, adding to the hundreds of thousands of seekers for jobs, for the fight to labor and compensation therefore" which had created the problem for those he represented. "Few Internationals," he insisted, "have had to stand on seeing approximately 10,000 on their way through the hole left in the ship by rocks created by folks who thought they were exercising their right to place those rocks where they accomplished the damage referred to."[28] The entire Hotel and Restaurant Workers International was long pervaded with the conviction that labor—leadership and rank and file—had abandoned them, in violation of the fundamental principles of working-class solidarity.

Needless to say, this anger was shared by the members of the United Brewery Workers. The twenty-second convention, meeting in 1920, faced a resolution calling for withdrawal from the American Federation of Labor because that organization had "proved itself reactionary and an opponent of the progressive working classes."[29] A substantial number of the brewery men were convinced that the AFL had not done its duty in the fight against prohibition, that "part of the workers helped their exploiters to deprive them of the things which make life, at least in part, a little more endurable to the men and women who produce all [wealth]."[30] The move to disaffiliate from the federation was not easily turned back.

The prohibition movement affected the general labor movement in other, more subtle ways.[31] It did not help the image of labor, at a crucial time in its history, when in March of 1919 the chief spokesman for organized labor in New York City called for the organization of a militia to "protect our city [from prohibition] until a United States Constitutional Convention can be called to decide the fundamental issues involved." Others jeopardized labor's hard-won respectability when they insisted that the nullification of the Fifteenth Amendment by the South was ample precedent for New York City to nullify the Eighteenth, or asserted that Wilson's Fourteen Points had established the precedent that Washington could not coerce a community bent on self-determination.[32] As it became clear that the Volstead Act would be enforced without modification to allow for light wines and beer, the increasingly fanatic and quixotic atmosphere surrounding labor-endorsed and labor-sponsored rallies of protest in the first five months of 1919 served to give organized labor an unstable image in the public mind. Some even saw a Bolshevik tinge.[33]

The efforts of organized workers in New York City and its vicinity added to the problem. Under the leadership of Ernest Bohm, the Central Trades and Labor Council laid plans for a national general strike if beer was included under the Prohibition Enforcement Act. On February 8, 1919, the New York body adopted a resolution which declared that in spite of "noble wartime sacrifice of life, limb, tax dollars and bond drives," the appeal of its 350,000 members "fell upon deaf ears, and while giving us the glad hand, the knife was poised to be buried to the hilt in our vitals'' by the very people who had demanded the sacrifices.[34] The resolution went on to ask that each member of organized labor submit his "free and unbiased" declaration on the proposal: "THAT IF THE BONE DRY PROHIBITION LAW IS REALLY ENFORCED ON JULY 1, 1919, TO THEN CEASE WORK UNTIL THIS LAW IS ANNULLED."[35]

Sentiment for such a general strike spread quickly to Newark and Essex, New Jersey. Almost immediately support came from longshoremen, the building trades councils in the area, shipbuilders, iron workers, stationary firemen, engineers, pavers and hammermen, and hatters. The Letter Carriers Association pledged moral support because its members could not strike. Within weeks, fully half a million had endorsed the New York call for a general strike through referendum in their locals.[36]

For the general public, and also for Samuel Gompers, a general strike was a frightening proposition for it constituted an insurrection. And within the context of 1919, it was a particularly threatening specter. The *Literary Digest,* reflecting middle-class sentiment in the nation, reported that the proposal had stirred up "indignation and denunciation" of the entire labor movement.[37] Other reports noted that the general strike movement was the reaction of "all of organized labor" to the pending Volstead Act, in spite of the fact that it had been roundly and publicly condemned by Gompers and other responsible federation spokesmen.[38] But it served to warn such leaders that their fear of "Bolshevik reactions" was more than mere rhetoric.

In still another way, the impact of prohibition on organized labor was so dramatic that a serious scholar can legitimately suggest that the course of American labor history could have been substantively different if the Eighteenth Amendment had never been added to the Constitution. Prohibition destroyed or effectively circumscribed elements within the labor movement which, if they had been given free reign, might well have pressured the American Federation of Labor to move sooner in directions that it would ultimately choose. Granting that it is exceedingly difficult to make a case for that which was not there, it can be asserted that the absence of a powerful countervailing force driving a movement in a different direction can well have a high degree of validity as an explanation for the course of actual developments.

The adoption of the prohibition amendment and the subsequent passage of the "bone-dry" Volstead Act severely circumscribed the power, influence, and vitality of one of the most positive and dynamic units within the "House of Labor," the United Brewery Workers. In so doing, it destroyed, to all extents and purposes, one of the most effective internal forces for progress and reform and helped to determine that organized labor would remain for at least a generation, if not more, devoted to the status quo—as much committed to things as they were as any other element in the so-called establishment.

When prohibition took its terrible toll on the liquor industry, brewing was one of the most completely and effectively organized trades in the nation. What was done to the industry proper was equally visited upon the workers and their representative organization. If the UBW had any special role to play in the working-class movement, or in American society at large, its capacity to realize that role was destroyed by the adoption of the Eighteenth Amendment.

The United Brewery Workers was one of the earliest affiliates of the American Federation of Labor. By 1890–95 this cohesive union had worked out a relatively harmonious relationship with management which might well have become a model for American industry in general. Fully 90 percent of the workers in brewing were covered by collective bargaining agreements, with binding arbitration.[39] This gave the international an early stability and an extraordinarily sound financial position. In short, the UBW was one of the richest and most powerful of the affiliates of the AFL as the twentieth century dawned. In addition, the organization was never reluctant to use its wealth and power to promote the interests of the brotherhood of all workers and fundamental issues of social justice.

The history of the UBW began with the Knights of Labor. Workers in brewing for the most part shared a common German socialist background and were most comfortable with the high ideals of that pioneering working-class organization. Particularly attractive were the Knights' commitments to the promotion of the brotherhood of all men and the principles of racial and sexual equality. These were ideals to which the brewery workers remained faithful long after the Knights of Labor had faded from the American scene.

The tenacity of their commitment is reflected in the extraordinary support given by the United Brewery Workers to the cause of racial equality in 1902. In that year, the Longshoremen went out on strike against the management of the docks in New Orleans over its refusal to give equal pay for equal work and equal job opportunity to black members. The UBW was the only union in the city to support that effort.[40] In addition, the controversial Mother Mary Jones was employed to organize women for the UBW when they were added to the payrolls as bottlers in Milwaukee.[41] Her efforts to expose and eliminate the sexism and outright indignities to which such women were subjected by foremen, simply because they were women, received consistent public and financial support from the international. And this was done despite the fact that women were an extremely minor element in the brewery workforce and therefore in the union.

A further attraction of the Knights of Labor was its constitution, which permitted the establishment of affiliates in a manner entirely compatible with the realities of the brewing industry. Unlike the dominant organizational approach of the younger American Federation of Labor, the Knights allowed for the creation of a national affiliate along purely industrial lines. Brewing was an industry which required very few highly skilled artisans. A brewmaster, backed up by a handful of skilled and experienced workers, could keep a plant in operation in the face of a strike. Regular employees could be readily replaced by unskilled strikebreakers because the need for true craftsmen was so limited. Indeed, in the very first efforts to improve the scandalous terms and conditions of employment which had characterized the early American brewing industry, organizers of the union had learned to their sorrow that the exclusion of such unskilled fellow workers as teamsters and common laborers from the cause was a fatal error.[42] Very quickly, the United Brewery Workers adopted an unalterable commitment to the industrial structure of organization, incorporating it into the constitution at the second national convention.[43] Thereafter every person employed in the brewery in a nonmanagerial position was welcomed to membership.

But this approach to organization ran contrary to the conventional wisdom of the American Federation of Labor. The overwhelming majority of its affiliates were militantly devoted to the narrower craft philosophy of structure. By the turn of the century, the United Mine Workers (which had developed an industrial structure for very different reasons) and the United Brewery Workers were the only truly industrial organizations in the labor movement—the only ones willing to welcome the unskilled and share with them power and negotiated benefits. Indeed, the hostility of the majority in the federation to this approach to organization was so intense that it was only the wealth and power of the two giants which kept them within the ranks. Throughout its history the UBW would find itself engaged in a series of intense and often violent jurisdictional disputes with the International Brotherhood of Teamsters, among others, which threatened its relationship with the parent organization.

More than once in the two decades before the adoption of the "noble experiment," Samuel Gompers had to intervene with the Executive Council of the American Federation of Labor to prevent the total alienation or the expulsion of the United Brewery Workers from the "House of Labor" over this issue.[44] Gompers, who had little love for industrial unions in general and even less for the UBW in particular,[45] felt impelled to utilize his personal influence with his colleagues on the council and even in the annual conventions because of his overriding fear of "dual unionism" and his unwaivering commitment to unity in the labor movement. It is clear from his action and his correspondence that the father of the American working-class movement felt that the United Brewery Workers, at least in these years before national prohibition, was too powerful and too wealthy to allow it to separate from the movement in spite of its "heretical" structure and almost "criminal" devotion to foreign ideologies. There is some evidence to suggest that many delegates to the annual meetings shared this conviction because they felt that they might need the support of the powerful UBW at some future date when their own interests were at stake. They were therefore loathe to antagonize it.[46]

The cohesion and strength of the United Brewery Workers in these crucial years was significantly enhanced by the fact that its membership was remarkably homogeneous. With few exceptions, most notably among affiliates of the ale and porter wings of the industry, UBW locals were overwhelmingly German in ethnic origin. So pervasive was this domination of the organization that until 1944 its constitution required that the elected president be German-speaking.

Each year in its early history brought new immigrants to the ranks who had been infused with the social justice principles and ideology of the German socialist movement. These newcomers served to reinforce the already real predisposition of the international to promote the ideals of socialism in the new "fatherland" with the result that the United Brewery Workers were overtly and enthusiastically socialist. The

1912 rank and file rejection of an industry-wide pension plan because it was proposed by management and therefore suspect is clear evidence of the class struggle.[47]

Annually, members were exhorted to take out citizenship papers at the earliest opportunity so that they could support endorsed socialist candidates at the polls. The minutes of both the local affiliates and the national organization report regular and substantial contributions to the war chests of such candidates and parties. The editor of the *Brauer Arbeiter Zeitung*, Charles Trautman, was a founding member and officer of the Industrial Workers of the World (IWW). He was also one of its leading theoreticians. In fact, at the founding convention of the IWW, the United Brewery Workers were second only to the Western Federation of Miners in terms of numerical strength.

The militant involvement of the UBW in the socialist and IWW causes makes Samuel Gompers's support of their continued affiliation with the American Federation of Labor all the more remarkable. He was, after all, almost pathologically opposed to both positions as anathema to the health and well-being of the American working-class movement. Only the wealth and strength of the international in the pre-prohibition decades can explain the continued support of its affiliation by this masterful practitioner of *realpolitik*.

As the tide of popular support for prohibition rose, the United Brewery Workers found itself impaled on the double horns of the proverbial dilemma. Here was a committed socialist organization, devoted to militant class warfare, unalterably committed to the principle that the capitalist class must be eliminated and American industry nationalized. But national prohibition, if enacted, would destroy the livelihood of the members before any of these great goals could be accomplished. Members were forced to rationalize a compromise with their ideology and adopt a course of action which caused them to devote large parts of their considerable financial resources and energies to support of the capitalists. They were caught: holding their socialist ideals, devoted to the class struggle, they found themselves in a new war, fighting not to defeat but to save the investments of the "exploiters." Militancy in the class struggle could not long survive complete cooperation with the enemy, no matter how necessary such cooperation might be.

The merging of interests between the workers and the industrialists in brewing began as early as 1913. The United Brewery Workers joined with the United States Brewers Association, the national trade association for the industry, in the financing of so-called Liberal Leagues and the Trades Union Liberty Leagues.[48] In such arrangements, each partner contributed 50 percent of the cost of the program. Officers of UBW locals headed up committees of this nature, which continued operations down through the repeal of the Eighteenth Amendment in 1933.

Karl Feller, president of the United Brewery Workers at the time of its absorption by the Teamsters, stated that the joint efforts in opposition to prohibition "strengthened the ties between our Union and the industry and did much to improve what we feel is one of the best collective bargaining relationships in the country today."[49] Feller could be interpreted as suggesting that it was the prohibition struggle, requiring cooperation between labor and management for their mutual survival, which contributed significantly to the destruction of the class-conscious militancy and tenacious devotion to socialist principles which had been the hallmark of the organization in its youth.

Prohibition also served to destroy the internal cohesion of the UBW. In response to its declining numerical strength, the AFL allowed expansion of its jurisdiction to permit the organization within its ranks of persons in the flour, cereal, soft drink, and distillery industries. Most of the laborers in these new areas of organizational activity were not German. They did not share the common cultural or ideological heritage of the original organization's members. For example, in the effort to unionize the flour workers of Buffalo, New York, in the 1920s, the international had to hire organizers who were fluent in eleven different languages.[50] Dilution of the heavy German membership of the UBW in Texas seriously undermined the efforts of reformers seeking to repeal the onerous poll tax in that state.

Declining membership also meant declining wealth and a commensurate reduction of power within the American Federation of Labor. Dramatic evidence of this comes from even a superficial survey of the history of the painful jurisdictional disputes between the United Brewery Workers and the International Brotherhood of Teamsters. In spite of the fact that the UBW had loaned money and organizers to help the Teamsters create a union back in the late 1880s, the brotherhood was determined to wrest the teamsters employed in breweries from the UBW. Throughout the pre-prohibition era, the United Brewery Workers were uniformly successful in maintaining their industrial structure inviolate, AFL hostility and repeated raids by the Teamsters notwithstanding.[51] However, after the adoption of the Eighteenth Amendment, the Teamsters were almost uniformly successful in defeating the UBW in such disputes. So successful was the brotherhood in these efforts that the UBW lost its separate identity and was absorbed into the Teamsters, becoming a department of that organization in 1968.[52] Because of what prohibition did to the United Brewery Workers it is not much of an exaggeration to suggest that the ''noble experiment'' contributed significantly to the unfortunate ascendancy of the International Brotherhood of Teamsters because it effectively destroyed the one obstacle to that end.[53]

When national prohibition struck, the United Brewery Workers stood almost alone in the organized working-class movement as a powerful force for values which eventually became accepted as American values. The UBW was an industrial union in a movement overwhelmingly hostile to sharing power with the unskilled. Perhaps if the UBW had remained whole and powerful, the ultimate acceptance of industrial unionism might have been accomplished with greater rapidity and without the internal wrenching and bloodshed which divided the ''House of Labor'' over that fundamental reform throughout the 1930s and 1940s.

While it is highly doubtful that the American labor movement would ever have adopted the militant class warfare ideology of the United Brewery Workers it is entirely conceivable that the labor movement might have developed a much sharper class consciousness than has characterized it, with a consequent commitment to the principles of racial and sexual equality, if the UBW had not been circumscribed by the impact of the Eighteenth Amendment. If the UBW had not been weakened, organized labor in the United States might well have led, not followed, the civil rights movement of the 1960s.

Uncompromised, the power and place of the United Brewery Workers could have contributed significantly to the development early on of a true devotion to social justice, placing organized labor in the forefront of struggles for the minimum wage, social security, and other exceedingly belated efforts to ameliorate the impact of the industrial revolution in America. What anachronistic attitudes might have disappeared if prodded by a powerful UBW? Perhaps there might have been a true American labor party patterned after the English Labor or the German Social Democratic parties. Perhaps not, but without the divisions and destruction in the labor movement provoked by national prohibition, a different course for American unionism during and after the 1920s can certainly be imagined.

4

A Dubious Constitutional Experiment

The phenomenon in American life that John D. Hicks once called the Populist Revolt set in motion a series of state and national reforms that in at least two respects seemed to reach a peak in the Eighteenth Amendment to the Constitution of the United States. On the one hand, the amendment was part of a series of constitutional changes which marked the climax of the Progressive movement. The income tax amendment took effect in February 1913, and the provision for the popular election of U.S. senators followed in May of the same year. The prohibition amendment was proclaimed as ratified on January 16, 1919, and was declared in effect the following January, while the women's suffrage amendment won adoption in August 1920. Thus, in little more than seven years, four major objectives of reformers from the early Populists to the age of Woodrow Wilson's New Freedom had presumably been graven in stone as the law of the land. On the other hand, both the reform movement and the improbable coalition of agrarians and urban social forces that had provided its momentum appear to have spent their energies in these constitutional accomplishments of the second decade of the twentieth century. It is worth noting that the coalition broke up in the attempt to win the fifth objective of the Progressives—the proposed child labor amendment, which came a cropper in the third decade of the century.

While it is increasingly argued by political historians that the rural origins of the reform movement in general, and of prohibition in particular, are not as significant as they were once thought to be, the fact remains that the agrarian stereotype (the "log cabin syndrome") continued to color national thought and behavior for a long period of the twentieth century. The problem of "rotten boroughs" of overrepresented and underpopulated sections of America was not addressed until the malapportionment cases of the 1960s; and the yeoman image of the native American still lingers in many of our urban mannerisms. On the other hand, the future was also discernible in the Progressive era reform amendments of the first quarter of the present century.

The tendency of the American people to turn to the Constitution as a repository for a variety of social and economic (as distinct from governmental) criteria traces its beginnings to the messianic zeal of the period 1900–20. In most cases, this was essentially a tactical option when efforts to secure legislative endorsement of the criteria had fallen short of the reformers' goals. As the subsequent history of many of these constitutional alternatives was to demonstrate, the campaign to amend the Constitution simply introduced a much more intense judicial struggle over scope and implementation.

It is also worth noting that the three principal amendments of the reform era—the Seventeenth, Eighteenth, and Nineteenth—were the culmination of a grass roots movement which had begun in the previous generation. By the age of Wilson, in a number of states democratic forces had legislated a type of preferential, even though nonbinding, senatorial primary to challenge the courthouse lobbies which had so long dominated state assemblies' choices for these federal offices. (For that matter, the voice of the electorate had been decisive in such questions on earlier occasions; it should be remembered that the famous Lincoln-Douglas debates of 1858 had been an appeal to voters for one or another candidate for the Illinois state legislature, which would in turn select the person who would have the next Senate term.) In a comparable grass roots movement, the concept of women's suffrage had spread slowly through state constitutional channels following its introduction into the Wyoming constitution of 1889.

In this context, perhaps the most remarkable of the Progressive era amendments was the Eighteenth, which, while it had gradually broadened its state constitutional base, had never won the formal endorsement of a major national political party. This amendment reflected, more than its companion amendments of the time, the fundamentalist and relatively simplistic democratic faith which had aroused such fervor in the last quarter of the nineteenth century. That faith was rooted in the value system of an agrarian America which was already passing from its period of dominance in national life; indeed, the temperance movement's final success was in part due to its reinforcement from the urban-oriented Anti-Saloon League. The census of 1920 marked the first time that the statistical balance of population shifted to the urban sector, and the decade to follow—which was the decade of prohibition—steadily diminished the force of the agrarian value system.

This demographic phenomenon, accentuating the general change in American character precipitated by World War I, may be taken as a primary factor in foredooming the experiment in national prohibition. For experimental the Eighteenth Amendment certainly was, however fond were the hopes and assumptions of those who saw it through Congress and the ratification process. It was then, and remains to date, the only constitutional attempt to incorporate a sumptuary provision into the fundamental law of the land. Sumptuary laws—statutory attempts to control individual behavior in personal areas such as apparel and consumption—had been a phenomenon of the Middle Ages, and its vestigial legislation had been steadily atrophying since the time of the Puritans. Whether such subjects could be properly treated in the Constitution was disputed by some opponents of the prohibition amendment both before and after enactment, as shown in the several efforts to offer evidence that the subject matter was *ultra vires* the Constitution. The *ultra vires* position—the argument that the subject was beyond the function or nature of the legal instrument—might have, if judicially accepted, put an effective brake on the trend toward incorporating social and economic standards into the Constitution. Even though judicial history set its face against these arguments, the chilling effect of the Eighteenth Amendment experience upon comparable constitutional experiments—possibly child labor and the equal rights amendment—should not be overlooked as completely as it has been.

The pivotal fact, in any event, is that a once dominant theme in national life—the husbandman as the prototypical American—had been steadily diminishing after the opening of the twentieth century and became permanently subordinated after the mobilization of national economic effort in the course of World War I. Sumptuary laws, in general, from the medieval period to the time of the Puritans and later the Victorians, have been the articulated standards of behavior of dominant (though not necessarily majority) elements in a society. When the dominance of these elements passes to others, as from rural to urban, it is an all but foregone conclusion that the bases of support for the standards themselves will be weakened or eliminated. While the detailed analysis of this subject may be more properly the province of the social historian rather than the constitutional lawyer, it requires to be taken into account in any review of the constitutional experiment that failed.

THE ANOMALIES OF DRAFTING AND CONSTRUCTION

The subject matter of the national prohibition amendment had been previously unknown to American constitutional law (except for the "unbroken package" doctrine of the commerce clause, which bred its own share of anomalies). In 1890 Chief Justice Fuller in *Leisy v. Hardin* had declared, for a divided Court, that a sealed package, e.g., liquor, was exempt from state prohibition laws while moving in interstate commerce.[1] Yet even in that period, the doctrine was substantially qualified. This may account for some of the confusion in draftsmanship, both in the amendment and in its implementing legislation, the Volstead Act. The amendment was organized in three sections, each subsequently tending to compound the uncertainties of the courts in construing the whole.

The opening section of the amendment was a recognition of the cataclysmic impact of nationwide prohibition, viz.:

After one year from the ratification of this article the manufacture, sale or transportation of intoxicating liquors within, the importation thereof into, or the exportation thereof from the United States and all territory subject to the jurisdiction thereof for beverage purposes is hereby prohibited.

The amendment passed the Senate on December 18, 1917, and the House the previous day, with the first state ratifying on January 8, 1918, and the needed thirty-sixth state on January 16 of the following year. By the terms of Section 1, it was not legally in effect until January 1920. This is the only amendment passed to date containing such a tolling provision, i.e., suspending or postponing the date when the amendment was to take effect. The addition of this provision to the text of the amendment in the course of the floor debate was a sign of the substantial proportion of the industrial economy made up of liquor manufacture and sales. Critics of the provision insisted that it qualified the implied process of the original Constitution—that an amendment should go into effect immediately upon ratification. While this was perhaps literally true, the Thirteenth Amendment of 1865 had introduced the analogous provision that "Congress shall have power to enforce this article by appropriate legislation"—even though, in the case of that amendment, its preceding language could be treated as self-executing.

The fact that most, though not all, subsequent amendments had such an "appropriate legislation" provision suggested that such amendments went into effect for practical purposes only when implemented by statute. In the case of the prohibition amendment, the Volstead Act treated the amendment as absolute and its own legislative character as declaratory and procedural rather than substantive. This in turn tended to frustrate the efforts of Congress in the latter part of the decade to deal with the practical problems of enforcement by making the statute itself less absolute. In the face of that theory of statutory construction of the constitutional language, the congressional option was limited to repeal of the amendment itself.

Section 2 of the draft amendment added to the confusion. While it included an "appropriate legislation" provision, it added an apparent qualification, viz.:

The Congress and the several States shall have concurrent power to enforce this article by appropriate legislation.

The confusion was double-edged: vis-à-vis the amendment itself, it introduced a cloud on the "appropriate legislation" concept because, under the Volstead Act's premise that the prohibition was absolute and the implementing statute was merely declaratory of that fact, the only appropriate legislation which the states could enact under the "concurrent power" language would have to be equally absolutist in theory and declaratory in language. State laws could therefore either (1) echo the congressional statute, (2) provide prohibition penalties which exceeded the federal provisions, or (3) decline to exercise concurrent power and repeal their own legislation on the subject. The last of these options, which various states in fact exercised, not only threw the entire enforcement burden on the federal administration but also created an unholy muddle between state jurisdictions, which no longer recognized the subject as criminal, and federal jurisdiction, which did. (This may be a prospective development in certain states which have recently decriminalized the growing, processing, sale, or use of marijuana in contrast to the existing federal criminal statutes on the subject.)

The "concurrent power" language came before the courts for clarifiction almost immediately, in the *National Prohibition Cases* in 1920.[2] The Supreme Court quickly disposed of the matter in its own fashion. "Concurrent" was distinguished from "joint" power. The latter would have made enforcement depend entirely upon reciprocal administration and thus would have substantially "federalized" the state power. Although it avoided jurisprudential semantics, the Court emphasized that it was seeking to carry out the intent of the draftsmen of the amendment investing equal enforcement powers in both state and federal courts. "Concurrent" power was thus judicially defined as "separate" though "equal"; on the other hand, "joint" power would have compelled the state courts to participate in the enforcing process of the federal courts. The Coolidge administration did in fact attempt such a deputizing of state enforcement officials as the difficulties of federal administration increased in the mid–1920s, but this provoked such a political and legal outcry that the program was quietly discarded. Meantime, in 1921 a Connecticut court held that state legislation, to be "appropriate," might differ in procedure but had to set a standard of liability at least as great as the federal law.[3]

As a final feature of innovative draftsmanship, Section 3 of the Eighteenth Amendment introduced for the first time a limit to the period in which a proposed amendment could be considered open for ratification. This so-called seven-year limit was subsequently included in the Twentieth ("lame duck"), Twenty-first (prohibition repeal) and Twenty-second (two-term presidency) Amendments, but not in any others to date. (The proposed equal rights amendment repeated some of the anomalies of the Eighteenth by including a two-year stay on going into effect. The seven-year limit was set not by language of the amendment but by congressional resolution, and when a subsequent resolution extended the time period to ten years, some very substantial legal doubts were raised. These matters, of course, became moot with the end of the ERA ratification campaign.)

THE DECADE OF ATTEMPTED ENFORCEMENT

The defeated anti-amendment forces took to the courts almost at once, raising a series of rather esoteric constitutional questions which revealed their last-ditch position. The first challenge was raised in Ohio, where the state constitution provided for a referendum on actions of the legislature. Since a 1919 referendum disapproved legislative ratification of the prohibition amendment, it was argued that ratification itself was invalid. The Supreme Court dismissed the case on appeal on the ground that a referendum could be required only for state legislative acts, whereas the state legislature, in following a ratification method prescribed by Congress, had been discharging a national legislative act.[4]

If the Supreme Court's rationale was highly technical, the next argument to come before it was theoretically "far-out." In the *National Prohibition Cases*, half a dozen states sought an injunction against the executive department to prevent enforcement of the Eighteenth Amendment on the ground that its subject matter was *ultra vires* the Constitution. They argued that the Constitution viewed as a whole was simply a "great legal process, warrant, or commission" defining the nature and powers of government. Any amendment, therefore, should be an amendment of the process and not deal with subject matter unrelated to the process. The Court did not yield to the temptation to ruminate upon constitutional theory, simply dismissing the petition for the injunction.[5] It could, had it so chosen, have pointed out that the petitioners' argument that the Constitution was merely a charter of government had been negated almost from the outset by adoption of the Bill of Rights, thereby removing any doubt that the Constitution by amendment could embrace any subject matter.

As the decade of attempted enforcement went on, however, a number of more serious constitutional problems had to be addressed. In an effort to control the flow of foreign intoxicants into the United States, the government undertook to negotiate with cooperating foreign powers a series of so-called rum treaties which provided that the contracting states would "raise no objection" to searches and seizures of private shipping under their flags whenever there should be "reasonable cause for belief that the vessel has committed or is committing an offense against the laws of the United States . . . prohibiting the importation of alcoholic beverages." Unprecedented as this provision was, the treaties went further and, instead of confining the authority for search and seizure to the three-mile limit of sovereignty or the twelve-mile limit for customs purposes, extended the jurisdiction of the Coast Guard to such a distance from the coast as "can be traversed in one hour."

This adaptation of the international law doctrine of "hot pursuit"— the theory that a legal chase already in progress may continue for a reasonable time and distance within the sovereign territory of a particular state—could create a myriad of problems, as was demonstrated in the 1929 incident involving the Canadian-registered power boat *I'm Alone*. The fact that the vessel was found some five hundred miles off course when it had cleared from British Honduras for Bermuda was certainly reasonable cause for the Coast Guard to hail it. However, the pursuit began at a distance of two hundred miles from the Louisiana coast and continued for forty-eight hours before converging Coast Guard cutters opened fire on the fugitive and eventually sank her. All but one of the crew were rescued and taken to New Orleans, where a six-year battle in the courts got under way. In 1935, after the prohibition amendment itself had been repealed, an international inquiry commission found the United States liable for an indemnity of $50,000.

Meantime, back on the domestic front, a profound admixture of law and morals was presented in the renowned case of *Olmstead v. United States*.[6] Here, ironically enough, the prosecution was directed against a "conscientious" bootlegger who sought to import high-quality Canadian liquor (as against the increasingly noxious and adulterated brews being distributed by the underworld) and sell it at reasonable prices in undiluted quality. Olmstead, prosecuted on the basis of evidence gained from a wiretap on his telephone, relied on his own constitutional immunities under the Fourth Amendment protection against unreasonable searches and seizures and the Fifth Amendment provision against self-incrimination. Against these defenses, the prosecution argued that the absolutist nature of the Eighteenth Amendment, implying a modification of the "search and seizure" clause of the Fourth Amendment, had already been upheld in the rum treaties, while the Fifth Amendment defense against self-incrimination did not extend to the gathering of evidence by wiretapping.

The constitutional morality of wiretapping, as an undermining of the ultimate values on which the Constitution as a whole was based, was raised in a dissent in the intermediate Court of Appeals, which sustained Olmstead's conviction. Judge Frank Rudkin's minority opinion said of wiretapping, "If such ills as these must be borne, our forefathers signally failed in their desire to ordain and establish a government to secure the blessings of liberty to themselves and their posterity."[7]

Chief Justice William Howard Taft, for whom the final disposition of the case would also mark the last major constitutional opinion of

NOTES

1. John Koren, *The Economic Aspects of the Liquor Problem* (1899; reprint, New York: Arno Press, 1981), pp. 26–37; Raymond Calkins, *Substitutes for the Saloon* (Boston: Houghton, Mifflin, 1901), pp. 308–10; James H. Timberlake has carefully analyzed the dilemma of the labor organizations in *Prohibition and the Progressive Movement, 1900–1920* (Cambridge: Harvard University Press, 1963), pp. 67–99.

2. Timberlake, *Prohibition and the Progressive Movement*, p. 82.

3. Mathew Woll, "Thou Shalt Not," *American Federationist* 26 (July 1919): 619; *see*, for example, *United Mine Workers' Journal* 16 (December 28, 1905): 8; 17 (October 4, 1906): 7; 22 (February 1, 1912): 6; *Coast Seaman's Journal* 26 (December 11, 1912): 6; *Brauer Arbeiter Zeitung* 29 (February 28, 1914): 1; *Mixer and Server* 28 (September 15, 1919): 42; Hermann Schlüter, *The Brewing Industry and the Brewery Workers Movement in America* (Cincinnati: International Union of United Brewery Workmen of America, 1910), p. 303; U.S. Senate, Subcommittee of the Judiciary, *Hearings on the Bills to Prohibit the Liquor Traffic and to Provide for the Enforcement of Such Prohibition and the War Prohibition Act,* 66th Cong., 1st sess., 3 parts (Washington, D.C.: GPO, 1919), pt. 1, p. 24; John G. Wooley and William Johnson, *Temperance Progress in This Century* (Toronto: Macmillan, 1905), p. 204; John R. Commons and Associates, *History of Labour in the United States,* 2 vols. (New York: Macmillan, 1926–35), 1: 17; 2: 476–79; American Federation of Labor, *Proceedings, 1895,* p. 61; Samuel Gompers to Benjamin Johnson, February 25, 1917, in *Cigarmakers' Official Journal* 41 (April 1917): 11; Woolley and Johnson, *Temperance Progress,* pp. 402–3.

4. Gompers to Ernest Page, February 16, 1903, Gompers Letterbook 147, p. 193, Library of Congress.

5. AFL, *Proceedings, 1895,* p. 61.

6. Gompers to Benjamin Johnson, February 24, 1917, in *Cigarmakers' Official Journal* 41 (April 1917): 11.

7. Woll, "Thou Shalt Not."

8. *Brauer Arbeiter Zeitung* 25 (May 15, 1910): 1.

9. Ibid., 28 (September 6, 1913): 1.

10. *Cigarmakers' Official Journal* 40 (April 1916): 8–9; 41 (April 1917): 11; *American Flint* 9 (November 1917); 6; *Miners' Magazine* 9 (May 1908): 5; 11 (May 1910): 6; 15 (June 18, 1914): 4; *Shoe Workers' Journal* 18 (July 1915): 1; 24 (March 6, 1909): 1; 25 (October 11, 1910): 1; *Literary Digest* 44 (November 21, 1914): 997–98. *See also* Prohibition Petitions and Brewery Propaganda, Records of the U.S. Senate and House of Representatives, National Archives, Washington, D.C.

11. Prohibition file, June 21–28, 1917, Records of the 65th Senate, National Archives.

12. Commission to Investigate Drunkenness in Massachusetts, *Report* (Boston: Wright and Potter Co., State Printers, 1914), p. 34.

13. Matthew Josephson, *Union House and Union Bar: The History of the Hotel and Restaurant Employees' & Bartenders' International Union, AFL–CIO* (New York: Random House, 1956), p. 93; Charles Stelzle, *A Son of the Bowery: The Life Story of an East Side American* (New York: George H. Doran, 1926), p. 199.

14. Cecil Shirley, *Fetters on Freedom* (London: Saint Martins, 1920), pp. 23–24; Joseph Pinebustle, "Brewery Worker's International Union," *American Federationist* 23 (September 1916), p. 789.

15. Charles Wood, ed., *A Criticism of National Prohibition* (Washington, D.C.: Association Against the Prohibition Amendment, 1926), p. 44.

16. Ernest H. Cherrinton, ed., *Standard Encyclopedia of the Alcohol Problem* (Westerville, Ohio: American Issue Publishing Co., 1925–30), 1: 154.

17. Schlüter, *Brewing Industry*, p. 307.

18. Prohibition file, June 21–28, 1917, Records of the 66th Senate, National Archives.

19. Charles Stelzle, "Temperance and Labor," in National Conference of Charities, *Proceedings, 1911*, pp. 123–25.

20. U.S. Senate, Committee on the Judiciary, *Brewing and Liquor Interests and German and Bolshevik Propaganda*, 65th Cong., 2nd and 3rd sess., and 66th Cong., 1st sess., 4 vols. (Washington, D.C.: GPO, 1919), p. 383; Gompers to Jerome Jones, April 14, 1913, Gompers Letterbook 198, p. 142.

21. *Literary Digest* 39 (December 18, 1909): 1119; 78 (June 23, 1923): 32; Calkins, *Substitutes*, pp. 303–13; J. S. Billings et al., *The Liquor Problem: A Summary of Investigations Conducted by the Committee of Fifty: 1893–1903* (Boston: Houghton, Mifflin, 1905), pp. 130–31; Koren, *Economic Aspects*, pp. 36–37; Railway Engineers Brotherhood, *Proceedings, 1915*, pp. 375–76, 602.

22. Stelzle, *Son of the Bowery*, pp. 197–99; idem., "Temperance and Labor," pp. 121–22; *Brauer Arbeiter Zeitung* 24 (November 20, 1909): 2.

23. Samuel Gompers to James Knox, April 12, 1919, Records of the 66th Senate, National Archives.

24. Nuala M. Drescher, "Organized Opposition to Prohibition, 1900–1919: A Social and Institutional Study," Ph.D. diss., University of Delaware, 1964, pp. 279–85.

25. Karl Feller, president of the United Brewery, Flour, Cereal, Soft Drink and Distillery Workers International, to the author, April 17, 1983; Senate, *Brewing and Liquor Interests*, 1: 833.

26. Cincinnati Hotel and Restaurant Employees International Alliance and Bartenders International League of America, *Proceedings of the General Convention, 1919*, p. 48; Josephson, *Union House and Union Bar*, p. 48; J. Rubin

and Michael Obermeier, *The Growth of a Union: The Life and Times of Edward Flore* (New York: Historical Union Association, 1943), p. 153.

27. Cincinnati International Union of United Brewery, Flour, Cereal, and Soft Drink Workers of America, *Proceedings, 1920,* p. 16; *American Federationist* 26 (September 1919): 810; United Brewery Workers International, *Proceedings, 1914,* p. 142.

28. Jere Sullivan, "Labor's Progress Onward and Upward," *American Federationist* 23 (September 1919): 779.

29. International Union of United Brewery, Flour, Cereal, and Soft Drink Workers, *Proceedings, 1920,* p. 16.

30. *American Federationist* 26 (September 1919): 810.

31. *New York Times,* January 22, 1919, pp. 5, 12.

32. Ibid., March 17, 1919, p. 5.

33. Ibid., January 22, 1919, p. 5; May 25, 1919, p. 3.

34. Drescher, "Opposition to Prohibition," pp. 292–94.

35. Un-American Propaganda, Records of the Judiciary Committee, Records of the 66th Senate, National Archives.

36. *New York Times,* February 8, 1919, p. 1; February 12, 1919, p. 1; February 13, 1919, p. 9; February 22, 1919, p. 1; March 3, 1919, p. 8; March 8, 1919, p. 9; *Literary Digest* 60 (March 1, 1919): 17.

37. *Literary Digest* 60 (March 1, 1919): 17.

38. Ibid.; Cherrington, *Standard Encyclopedia,* 1: 154.

39. A representative sample of such agreements is to be found in the Archives of the New York State School of Industrial and Labor Relations, Cornell University, Ithaca, New York.

40. *Brauer Arbeiter Zeitung,* April 1902.

41. Mother Mary Jones Papers, Archives, Catholic University of America, Washington, D.C.; *The Appeal to Reason*, March 1910.

42. *New York Times,* July 26, 1886, p. 8; December 31, 1886, p. 8; March 8, 1889, p. 2.

43. Copies of the UBWI constitutions can be found in the Industrial and Labor Relations Archives, Cornell University.

44. See the Executive Council minutes and related correspondence, 1902–1910, in the John Mitchell Papers, Archives, Catholic University of America, for the most graphic of these developments.

45. R. L. Grant, secretary to Samuel Gompers, to F. D. L. Squires, April 14, 1913, Gompers Letterbook 184, p. 621; Gompers to G. P. Crandill, editor of the *National Liberty Herald,* April 24, 1914, Gompers Letterbook 193, p. 748.

46. Stelzle, *Son of the Bowery,* pp. 200–201; Timberlake, *Prohibition and the Progressive Movement,* p. 95.

47. Nuala M. Drescher, Workmen's Compensation and Pension Proposal

of the Brewing Industry, 1910–1912: A Case Study of Conflicting Self-Interest, *Industrial and Labor Relations Review*, October 1970, pp. 32–46.

48. Nuala M. Drescher, "Organized Labor and the Eighteenth Amendment," *Labor History* 8 (Fall 1967): 280–99.

49. Karl Feller to the author, April 17, 1983.

50. Jean Spielman Papers, Minnesota Historical Society, St. Paul, Minnesota.

51. See the AFL Executive Council minutes in the John Mitchell Papers. No issue of the office publications of either the International Brotherhood of Teamsters or the UBW in these years reports on jurisdictional conflict between the two.

52. *New York Times*, August 3, 1972, p. 67; December 20, 1972, p. 18; October 24, 1973, p. 53.

53. Evidence of the impact of prohibition on the strength of the United Brewery Workers can be found as early as 1910, when the international reported substantial loss of membership due to local option campaigns in several states. In October of that year, it reported that fourteen locals and ten branches of the UBW had surrendered charters. *Brauer Viteum* 22 (October 21, 1907): 1; 24 (March 6, 1909): 1; 25 (October 1, 1910): 1. After the adoption of the Eighteenth Amendment, only the expansion of the organization's jurisdiction by the American Federation of Labor to include flour, cereal, and soft drink workers enabled it to survive through repeal.

A Dubious Constitutional Experiment

The phenomenon in American life that John D. Hicks once called the Populist Revolt set in motion a series of state and national reforms that in at least two respects seemed to reach a peak in the Eighteenth Amendment to the Constitution of the United States. On the one hand, the amendment was part of a series of constitutional changes which marked the climax of the Progressive movement. The income tax amendment took effect in February 1913, and the provision for the popular election of U.S. senators followed in May of the same year. The prohibition amendment was proclaimed as ratified on January 16, 1919, and was declared in effect the following January, while the women's suffrage amendment won adoption in August 1920. Thus, in little more than seven years, four major objectives of reformers from the early Populists to the age of Woodrow Wilson's New Freedom had presumably been graven in stone as the law of the land. On the other hand, both the reform movement and the improbable coalition of agrarians and urban social forces that had provided its momentum appear to have spent their energies in these constitutional accomplishments of the second decade of the twentieth century. It is worth noting that the coalition broke up in the attempt to win the fifth objective of the Progressives—the proposed child labor amendment, which came a cropper in the third decade of the century.

While it is increasingly argued by political historians that the rural origins of the reform movement in general, and of prohibition in particular, are not as significant as they were once thought to be, the fact remains that the agrarian stereotype (the "log cabin syndrome") continued to color national thought and behavior for a long period of the twentieth century. The problem of "rotten boroughs" of overrepresented and underpopulated sections of America was not addressed until the malapportionment cases of the 1960s; and the yeoman image of the native American still lingers in many of our urban mannerisms. On the other hand, the future was also discernible in the Progressive era reform amendments of the first quarter of the present century.

The tendency of the American people to turn to the Constitution as a repository for a variety of social and economic (as distinct from governmental) criteria traces its beginnings to the messianic zeal of the period 1900–20. In most cases, this was essentially a tactical option when efforts to secure legislative endorsement of the criteria had fallen short of the reformers' goals. As the subsequent history of many of these constitutional alternatives was to demonstrate, the campaign to amend the Constitution simply introduced a much more intense judicial struggle over scope and implementation.

It is also worth noting that the three principal amendments of the reform era—the Seventeenth, Eighteenth, and Nineteenth—were the culmination of a grass roots movement which had begun in the previous generation. By the age of Wilson, in a number of states democratic forces had legislated a type of preferential, even though nonbinding, senatorial primary to challenge the courthouse lobbies which had so long dominated state assemblies' choices for these federal offices. (For that matter, the voice of the electorate had been decisive in such questions on earlier occasions; it should be remembered that the famous Lincoln-Douglas debates of 1858 had been an appeal to voters for one or another candidate for the Illinois state legislature, which would in turn select the person who would have the next Senate term.) In a comparable grass roots movement, the concept of women's suffrage had spread slowly through state constitutional channels following its introduction into the Wyoming constitution of 1889.

In this context, perhaps the most remarkable of the Progressive era amendments was the Eighteenth, which, while it had gradually broadened its state constitutional base, had never won the formal endorsement of a major national political party. This amendment reflected, more than its companion amendments of the time, the fundamentalist and relatively simplistic democratic faith which had aroused such fervor in the last quarter of the nineteenth century. That faith was rooted in the value system of an agrarian America which was already passing from its period of dominance in national life; indeed, the temperance movement's final success was in part due to its reinforcement from the urban-oriented Anti-Saloon League. The census of 1920 marked the first time that the statistical balance of population shifted to the urban sector, and the decade to follow—which was the decade of prohibition—steadily diminished the force of the agrarian value system.

This demographic phenomenon, accentuating the general change in American character precipitated by World War I, may be taken as a primary factor in foredooming the experiment in national prohibition. For experimental the Eighteenth Amendment certainly was, however fond were the hopes and assumptions of those who saw it through Congress and the ratification process. It was then, and remains to date, the only constitutional attempt to incorporate a sumptuary provision into the fundamental law of the land. Sumptuary laws—statutory attempts to control individual behavior in personal areas such as apparel and consumption—had been a phenomenon of the Middle Ages, and its vestigial legislation had been steadily atrophying since the time of the Puritans. Whether such subjects could be properly treated in the Constitution was disputed by some opponents of the prohibition amendment both before and after enactment, as shown in the several efforts to offer evidence that the subject matter was *ultra vires* the Constitution. The *ultra vires* position—the argument that the subject was beyond the function or nature of the legal instrument—might have, if judicially accepted, put an effective brake on the trend toward incorporating social and economic standards into the Constitution. Even though judicial history set its face against these arguments, the chilling effect of the Eighteenth Amendment experience upon comparable constitutional experiments—possibly child labor and the equal rights amendment—should not be overlooked as completely as it has been.

The pivotal fact, in any event, is that a once dominant theme in national life—the husbandman as the prototypical American—had been steadily diminishing after the opening of the twentieth century and became permanently subordinated after the mobilization of national economic effort in the course of World War I. Sumptuary laws, in general, from the medieval period to the time of the Puritans and later the Victorians, have been the articulated standards of behavior of dominant (though not necessarily majority) elements in a society. When the dominance of these elements passes to others, as from rural to urban, it is an all but foregone conclusion that the bases of support for the standards themselves will be weakened or eliminated. While the detailed analysis of this subject may be more properly the province of the social historian rather than the constitutional lawyer, it requires to be taken into account in any review of the constitutional experiment that failed.

THE ANOMALIES OF DRAFTING AND CONSTRUCTION

The subject matter of the national prohibition amendment had been previously unknown to American constitutional law (except for the "unbroken package" doctrine of the commerce clause, which bred its own share of anomalies). In 1890 Chief Justice Fuller in *Leisy v. Hardin* had declared, for a divided Court, that a sealed package, e.g., liquor, was exempt from state prohibition laws while moving in interstate commerce.[1] Yet even in that period, the doctrine was substantially qualified. This may account for some of the confusion in draftsmanship, both in the amendment and in its implementing legislation, the Volstead Act. The amendment was organized in three sections, each subsequently tending to compound the uncertainties of the courts in construing the whole.

The opening section of the amendment was a recognition of the cataclysmic impact of nationwide prohibition, viz.:

After one year from the ratification of this article the manufacture, sale or transportation of intoxicating liquors within, the importation thereof into, or the exportation thereof from the United States and all territory subject to the jurisdiction thereof for beverage purposes is hereby prohibited.

The amendment passed the Senate on December 18, 1917, and the House the previous day, with the first state ratifying on January 8, 1918, and the needed thirty-sixth state on January 16 of the following year. By the terms of Section 1, it was not legally in effect until January 1920. This is the only amendment passed to date containing such a tolling provision, i.e., suspending or postponing the date when the amendment was to take effect. The addition of this provision to the text of the amendment in the course of the floor debate was a sign of the substantial proportion of the industrial economy made up of liquor manufacture and sales. Critics of the provision insisted that it qualified the implied process of the original Constitution—that an amendment should go into effect immediately upon ratification. While this was perhaps literally true, the Thirteenth Amendment of 1865 had introduced the analogous provision that "Congress shall have power to enforce this article by appropriate legislation"—even though, in the case of that amendment, its preceding language could be treated as self-executing.

The fact that most, though not all, subsequent amendments had such an "appropriate legislation" provision suggested that such amendments went into effect for practical purposes only when implemented by statute. In the case of the prohibition amendment, the Volstead Act treated the amendment as absolute and its own legislative character as declaratory and procedural rather than substantive. This in turn tended to frustrate the efforts of Congress in the latter part of the decade to deal with the practical problems of enforcement by making the statute itself less absolute. In the face of that theory of statutory construction of the constitutional language, the congressional option was limited to repeal of the amendment itself.

Section 2 of the draft amendment added to the confusion. While it included an "appropriate legislation" provision, it added an apparent qualification, viz.:

The Congress and the several States shall have concurrent power to enforce this article by appropriate legislation.

The confusion was double-edged: vis-à-vis the amendment itself, it introduced a cloud on the "appropriate legislation" concept because, under the Volstead Act's premise that the prohibition was absolute and the implementing statute was merely declaratory of that fact, the only appropriate legislation which the states could enact under the "concurrent power" language would have to be equally absolutist in theory and declaratory in language. State laws could therefore either (1) echo the congressional statute, (2) provide prohibition penalties which exceeded the federal provisions, or (3) decline to exercise concurrent power and repeal their own legislation on the subject. The last of these options, which various states in fact exercised, not only threw the entire enforcement burden on the federal administration but also created an unholy muddle between state jurisdictions, which no longer recognized the subject as criminal, and federal jurisdiction, which did. (This may be a prospective development in certain states which have recently decriminalized the growing, processing, sale, or use of marijuana in contrast to the existing federal criminal statutes on the subject.)

The "concurrent power" language came before the courts for clarifiction almost immediately, in the *National Prohibition Cases* in 1920.[2] The Supreme Court quickly disposed of the matter in its own fashion. "Concurrent" was distinguished from "joint" power. The latter would have made enforcement depend entirely upon reciprocal administration and thus would have substantially "federalized" the state power. Although it avoided jurisprudential semantics, the Court emphasized that it was seeking to carry out the intent of the draftsmen of the amendment investing equal enforcement powers in both state and federal courts. "Concurrent" power was thus judicially defined as "separate" though "equal"; on the other hand, "joint" power would have compelled the state courts to participate in the enforcing process of the federal courts. The Coolidge administration did in fact attempt such a deputizing of state enforcement officials as the difficulties of federal administration increased in the mid–1920s, but this provoked such a political and legal outcry that the program was quietly discarded. Meantime, in 1921 a Connecticut court held that state legislation, to be "appropriate," might differ in procedure but had to set a standard of liability at least as great as the federal law.[3]

As a final feature of innovative draftsmanship, Section 3 of the Eighteenth Amendment introduced for the first time a limit to the period in which a proposed amendment could be considered open for ratification. This so-called seven-year limit was subsequently included in the Twentieth ("lame duck"), Twenty-first (prohibition repeal) and Twenty-second (two-term presidency) Amendments, but not in any others to date. (The proposed equal rights amendment repeated some of the anomalies of the Eighteenth by including a two-year stay on going into effect. The seven-year limit was set not by language of the amendment but by congressional resolution, and when a subsequent resolution extended the time period to ten years, some very substantial legal doubts were raised. These matters, of course, became moot with the end of the ERA ratification campaign.)

THE DECADE OF ATTEMPTED ENFORCEMENT

The defeated anti-amendment forces took to the courts almost at once, raising a series of rather esoteric constitutional questions which re-

his career, saw the moral issue to be not the jeopardy to the Fourth and Fifth Amendments in implementing the Eighteenth but the absolute prohibition written into the Constitution by the Eighteenth itself. While he had personally expressed strong doubt about the proposed amendment before it was adopted and before he came onto the bench, it was now a part of the law of the land. Taft felt that more damage would be done to an orderly society by failing to uphold the legality of strict enforcement. This was "only adapting old principles and applying them to new conditions created by the change in national policy which the Eighteenth Amendment requires," he had written earlier in *Carroll v. United States*.[8]

In both the *Olmstead* and *Carroll* cases, the prohibition of unreasonable searches and seizures was readily offset at that time by the counterargument of probable cause, based on the prohibitory absolutism of the Eighteenth Amendment. Although in the later Court under Chief Justice Warren, "reasonableness" tests were to be much more sternly scrutinized by the judiciary, in the age of prohibition the reasonableness of the search was determined by the probability of violation under the circumstances.

The Olmstead conviction was upheld by a five-to-four majority of the Court, but Justice Louis D. Brandeis in dissent posed the fundamental moral issue in the admission of wiretapping evidence. "If the government becomes a lawbreaker," he warned, "it breeds contempt for the law."[9] This, as much as any judicial pronouncement, passed the ultimate judgment on the concept of prohibition as a constitutional subject.

REPEAL

As the manifest cost in lawbreaking, public moral values, and the expenses of enforcement efforts mounted in the closing years of the decade, talk of repeal of the Eighteenth Amendment began to grow. At the outset, the dry forces advanced theoretical arguments as esoteric as those of the opposing wets at the beginning of the prohibition era. No less a personage than Woodrow Wilson's son-in-law and former secretary of the treasury, William Gibbs McAdoo, told a state bar association in 1927 that in the Volstead Act, Congress had performed the "affirmative duty imposed by the Eighteenth Amendment," implementing the absolute prohibition stipulated in the amendment, and that any attempt to repeal the statute was an attempt to repeal the amendment itself. The courts, McAdoo concluded, would have no recourse but to invalidate the statute as an unconstitutional attempt to deny what was immutably written into the Constitution.[10]

Underlying this theory was the assumption that constitutional language was not only immutable but infallible. It was, of course, a perversion of Chief Justice John Marshall's famous description of the Constitution as an instrument "intended to endure for ages to come." It also disregarded the common experience of state constitutions, which not only repealed all manner of provisions originally written into their documents but replaced the documents themselves. For that matter, the Thirteenth Amendment had rejected the original Constitution's recognition of slavery as an inviolable property right.

The floundering amid theories to support the proposed repeal of the Eighteenth Amendment led even respected jurists such as District Judge William Clark into deep waters. In a decision which he confessed would almost certainly meet with "a cold reception in the appellate courts," Judge Clark challenged the legislative ratification provision of the original amendment, declaring in *United States v. Sprague* that since prohibition was a novel instance of government control over private and personal conduct, it should only have been ratified by the people themselves. The Supreme Court promptly overturned the judgment by reiterating, as in the *Hawke* case of 1920, that Congress had the exclusive power to determine the means of ratification of any proposed amendment.[11]

But when the Twenty-first Amendment finally became a reality, it could not mean a return to the America which had existed before 1920. The nation had entered World War I in the fading afterglow of the frontier, with an agrarian, yeoman image of itself. By 1933 the disaster visited upon the urban industrial system by the Great Depression had begun a cataclysmic change in the way Americans viewed their own economic and political system. Change, the experimental nature of constitutional efforts in general, and the gradual recognition that— to quote Chief Justice Vinson's conclusion—all guarantees are relative in terms of circumstances[12] suggested the futility of thinking of any system of government as immutable or infallible. If the prohibition amendment precipitated a succession of tenuous theories of constitutional law, this concluding principle born of harsh experience was perhaps the only viable one.

The Twenty-first Amendment did not simply repeal the Eighteenth but also attempted to revive some of the interstate liquor controls first introduced in the Webb-Kenyon Act of 1913, the constitutionality of which was upheld in 1917.[13] The provision of Section 2 of the Twenty-first Amendment, prohibiting the importation of intoxicants into states where local law prohibited them, was essentially a revival of the general philosophy, if not the letter, of the "unbroken package" doctrine of *Leisy v. Hardin* in 1890. Thus the later amendment became a breeding ground for constitutional issues of its own, with the courts compelled, after originally denying the fact,[14] to concede that Section 2 did in fact permit a broad area for state legislation for the purposes of subject matter jurisdiction within the normal reach of the commerce clause. This determination was made in 1966 in the leading case of *Seagram & Sons v. Hostetter*.[15] Ten years later the Supreme Court declared explicity in *Craig v. Boren* that the repeal amendment's Section 2 "created an exception to the normal operation of the commerce clause."[16]

The ultimate product of the constitutional law pronounced by the courts under both the Eighteenth and Twenty-first Amendments is as significant as it is subtle. The obvious fact that a national loss of innocence occurred in the decade between World War I and the Great Depression—and that a far greater social revolution has followed World War II—has tended to blend the innovative elements of prohibition era law into the sweeping constitutional doctrines of the past thirty years. The broadening of the jurisdiction of the commerce clause, encouraged in the prohibition and repeal cases, has been amplified in more definitive causes affecting other aspects of national life—e.g., equal opportunity and protection for all groups in society. But this is only to say that the relatively ephemeral issues of the prohibition era were at least some straws in the wind. The modern constitutional posture is one of concurrent state and federal responsibilities undreamed of in the second section of the Eighteenth Amendment: witness, as a single example, the growth of the abstention doctrine.

The abstention doctrine, which was introduced into constitutional law in 1941 in *Railroad Comm. v. Pullman Co.*,[17] was seized upon by the U.S. District Court in 1976 as applicable to Section 2.[18] This doctrine provides that where a state law is challenged for possible conflict with the federal Constitution, a federal court may abstain from a "premature constitutional determination" by remanding to the states for possible resolution of the statutory question on state grounds, thus "moot-ing the federal constitutional issues."[19] However, where the federal court finds, as in *Vintage Imports*, that the state law is unavoidably in conflict with the due process clause of the Fourteenth Amendment—in this instance, being void for vagueness—the abstention doctrine ought not to apply. Be that as it may, the doctrine may offer a reasonable accommodation of the various state-federal issues that have risen with fair regularity under Section 2 of the repeal amendment.

LESSONS OF THE EIGHTEENTH AND TWENTY-FIRST AMENDMENTS

Prohibition as a constitutional experiment was a gaudy failure, rather obviously because it undertook to establish an absolute, uniform rule of conduct based on an orthodox social standard which simply became irrelevant under the cataclysmic changes in national life which fol-lowed its enactment. The costly lessons it taught—in terms of the weakened tendency to obey such a law, leading it to be modified or repealed—are certainly worth remembering today, when fresh propos-als for behavioral and attitudinal control by constitutional amendment are gaining some momentum with every indication of comparable con-sequences. The self-righteously denominated "right to life" proposals and the compulsory school prayer proposal are the most conspicuous examples of the moment. Whatever the merits of the subject matter itself, the theoretical and practical consequences of attempting to im-pose these viewpoints by constitutional fiat should be sufficient argu-ment against them.

It may also be worth noting that the constitutional issue of child la-bor was ultimately resolved by judicial construction rather than by par-ticular amendment. From *Hammer v. Dagenhart* in 1917 to *United States v. Darby* in 1941, judicial construction of the commerce clause was broadened to legitimatize congressional uses of the clause—and the proposed child labor amendment passed into oblivion. Segregation un-der *Plessy v. Ferguson* in 1896 became desegregation under *Brown v. Board of Education* in 1954. If the standard charge of "judicial leg-islation" is raised against the more recent doctrines, it must be equally directed to the earlier doctrines. The ultimate point is that constitu-tional law is more often than not a matter of reading the language of the instrument in the context of the present. Where the language is absolute, as in the case of the prohibition amendment, it is in danger of becoming unenforceable. To ignore the lessons of that experience is to risk repeating it.

NOTES

1. 135 U.S. 100 (1890).
2. 253 U.S. 350 (1920).
3. *State of Connecticut v. Coriani*, 113 Atl. 316 (1921).
4. *Hawke v. Smith*, 253 U.S. 221 (1920).
5. *Rhode Island v. Palmer*, 253 U.S. 350 (1920).
6. 277 U.S. 438 (1928).
7. 19 Fed. 2nd, 842, 850 (1927).
8. 267 U.S. 132 (1925).
9. *Olmstead v. U.S.*, 277 U.S. 438, 485 (1928).
10. *American Bar Association Journal* 13 (March 1927): 117.
11. 282 U.S. 117 (1931).
12. *Dennis v. U.S.*, 341 U.S. 494 (1951).
13. *Clark Dist. Co. v. Western Md. R. Co.*, 242 U.S. 311 (1917).
14. *Young's Market v. Calif. Board of Equalization*, 299 U.S. 59 (1936).
15. 384 U.S. 35 (1966).
16. 429 U.S. 190 (1976).
17. 312 U.S. 496 (1941).
18. *Vintage Imports v. Seagram & Sons*, 409 F.S. 497 (1976).
19. 312 U.S. 496 (1941).

Societal Morality and Individual Freedom

I would like to attempt a rather broad and sweeping overview of the phenomenon of national prohibition as it applies to changing attitudes toward the law and toward morality. At the same time, I would like to include consideration of where the emergence of civil liberties fits into this process, and what lessons for constitutionalism and civil liberties the process taught. I realize this is a big order, and my conception may be quite personal and idiosyncratic. But I would hope to stimulate discussion, and dissent, in order to bring into better view where prohibition belongs regarding the whole question of societal morality and individual freedom.

The proper relationship of law and morality was hardly a new one in Progressive America. In fact, as David Flaherty has pointed out so well,[1] law's principal function in the colonial period turned around the enforcement of morals, which at that time entailed issues of the complex relationship between sin and crime, between divine law and secular law, and above all, between moral law and the criminal law. In an earlier era all of these were closely intertwined. And the habit in colonial America, starting with the Massachusetts Code of 1648, was to criminalize immoral behavior. Drunkenness was a frequent example. This inevitably resulted in a new role for the state. To label behavior as criminal meant government would punish that behavior at its own initiative and expense. By contrast, criminal law in the Progressive period and now expresses more than current standards of morality. It is a vehicle for economic and social planning and an index to the community's division of power.

The earlier colonial view was sharply modified in nineteenth-century America. Then the use of the law to enforce morality gave way, in a variety of circumstances, to a more laissez-faire attitude. Generally, the majority in those years felt it inappropriate for the government to attempt to control behavior that had no substantial significance except as to the morality of the actor. Such matters, it was felt, were best left to religious, educational, and other social influences that are informal forms of social control. Hostility toward statism and ongoing commitment to the principles of limited government ran high in those years, as did the feeling that the local community could and would deal with immorality in its own way.

Progresive America, to some degree, was a throwback to the earlier times. Society had become not only complex but evil and filled with sin. The individual was in many ways at the mercy of a variety of massive and relentless forces which he or she could not individually control. Hence the concept of stewardship and the moral responsibility of natural leaders within the society burgeoned. To the stewards, moral uplift and a more efficient functioning of society could best be achieved by a responsible upper class of generally Waspy talent and wealth, conscious of the need for imposing stable policies in order to hold together a turbulent, threatening-to-disintegrate, and distressingly changing society. A Durkheimian sense of anomie ran strong. This perception assumed the desirability of a kind of social engineering which would create, through law, improved conditions under which morality could, and, it was hoped, eventually would, emerge.

But the legal and constitutional implications of this shift were startling to a generation raised on laissez-faire and an apprehension over even the faltering beginnings of public regulation. To embrace such a view of positive government constituted necessary rethinking, particularly of constitutional roles, and of the relationship of the federal government to the states as well as to the individual. More precisely, this meant rethinking the old concept of police power, which prior to this time had solely been a justification for action at the state level.

The concept of police power went back to the days of John Marshall. It entailed the rights of the community in promoting the general welfare to use public law to ensure the health, safety, and morals of citizens. Indeed, Roger B. Taney, chief justice of the United States, had argued in 1837 that "the object and end of all government is to promote the happiness, and prosperity of the community by which it is established."[2] With the advent in the Progressive era of what Roscoe Pound called sociological jurisprudence,[3] the role of police power was broadened to include and to constitutionally legitimate federal action in this area. And in those years, this resulted in laws seeking to proscribe and limit evil behavior damaging to the broader society—behavior which was now of such a national scope that the states could no longer deal with it effectively. By making criminal everything from commerce in narcotics, to the movement of women across the state lines for immoral purposes, to the closing of immigration to alien anarchists, to the exclusion from the federal mails of obscene material, to the consumption of alcohol, it was felt that a moral purpose could be achieved. This could produce sigificant steps toward attaining the perfectability of man. This did imply saving people from themselves, with their acquiescence irrelevant. It further implied that the rights of the community and the welfare of the broader society constituted a far higher priority than the freedom of the individual being legally coerced. It also rejected as irrelevant any pluralistic concepts entailing differences in individuals' circumstances, backgrounds, and above all, ultimate desires. The fact, for example, that some immigrant and ethnic groups came out of cultures in which beer and wine were natural and integral parts of social and even family activities carried little weight in an era which placed heavy emphasis upon the melting pot and the removal of undesirable ethnic traits from those who would be true Americans.

There would seem to have been other implications regarding law and morality. Little public thought in this era conceived of "drink" as a victimless crime—behavior labeled criminal which involves consenting adults engaging in activity which causes no clear or direct harm either to themselves or others and therefore involves no complainants. There was too strong a puritanical thrust among the moral stewards of society, who felt that drink was not such an individual matter. It was a social problem. Drink brought about social disintegration. It threatened the common morality. In a position strikingly similar to that taken by Lord Devlin years later, Progressives held that if the common morality collapsed, the state would crumble.[4] This would lead to the dissolution of moral and other central social values. Criminalizing drink would thus serve the common morality and make law its guardian, as would criminalizing gambling, pornography, drug abuse, prostitution, and laws against certain kinds of private sexual expression.

This left little room for a civil libertarian view that drink, like other forms of individual behavior, should be a matter of freedom of choice, and that the individual should be responsible for his or her own behavior in this area. Also involved were concepts of capacity and incapacity. Lesser individuals, the undeserving, did not have a high enough quotient of social responsibility to make personal decisions regarding many aspects of their behavior in a modern, industrial, but also wicked and cruel, world. Free choice could only responsibly be extended to those citizens who had demonstrated by both their attitudes and their behavior that they were prepared to utilize their freedom in positive and constructive ways. Such decisions as to whether a person deserved to have his or her civil liberties formally protected had to be made by those responsible elements within the society knowledgeable in the proper use of personal freedom. Liberty, in short, was a condition conferred by the community at its discretion, usually only to people who had earned it. Those tempted by alcohol hardly needed freedom. They needed to be protected, and the community needed to be protected from them, through the removal of the temptation which they were not strong enough to resist.

In this regard, the prohibition movement was of a piece with other movements of the Progressive period. As I have tried to point out in a recent book, everything from expanded censorship laws and antiprostitution and drug laws to espionage legislation, criminal syndicalism statutes, sedition laws, and other restraints on individual rights were all designed to protect the community or the nation from forces and individuals threatening its moral preservation and social health.[5]

These values certainly emerge from Supreme Court rulings of this period. When labor troubles exploded into strikes and threats of violence, and a governor declared martial law and suspended habeas corpus for a labor leader, the Court, speaking through Justice Oliver Wendell Holmes, Jr., sustained the suspension, arguing that in times of public danger, the judicial process and the ordinary rights of citizens must yield to the executive and his perception of the public good.[6] When a Massachusetts citizen protested, for religious reasons, against submitting to compulsory smallpox vaccination as required by state law and argued that the state was invading his liberty and his inherent right as a free person to care for himself, Justice John Marshall Harlan rejected his claim, contending that ''liberty secured by the Constitution . . . to every person within its jurisdiction, does not import an absolute right in each person to be . . . freed from restraint. There are manifold restraints to which every person is necessarily subject for the common good. . . . ''[7] And when a Colorado editor launched a newspaper campaign against alleged corruption in the state supreme court and was cited by that body for contempt and libel, the U.S. Supreme Court, again speaking through Oliver Wendell Holmes, Jr., sustained his conviction, contending that libel was a local issue and that even the assumption that freedom of speech and press are protected from abridgment by the states does not preclude subsequent punishment for statements deemed to be contrary to the public welfare.[8]

This value system, which placed the needs of society above the liberty of the individual, continued in the post–World War I period. Test cases raised constitutional questions regarding the federal government's massive sedition program in which it had criminalized certain forms of expression, belief, and association and arrested thousands of individuals for criticizing the government or belonging to groups that did. But in all, the national community's security came first, and the individual dissenter had to give way. Societal morality, even if produced by questionable vigilante tactics and the denial of First Amendment freedoms, had a higher priority than individual liberty. Thus, it is clear that as yet there was no broadly held view of the individual's right against the state. People had not begun to think in civil liberties terms except in the abstract sense that in some respects freedom from government was desirable for responsible individuals.

On the other hand, it is significant that World War I saw the emergence for the first time in American history of an organized civil liberties movement based upon an opposite series of assumptions. These were far closer to John Stuart Mill than to Lord Devlin. Mill had argued that the law must not interfere with individual's behavior

for their own good, whether that be physical or moral. He cannot rightfully be compelled to do or forbear because it will be better for him to do so, because it will make him happier, because in the opinions of others, to do so would be wise or even right. . . . The only purpose for which power can rightfully be exercised over any man of a civilized community against his will is to prevent harm to others.[9]

The position, reminiscent of statements a century and a half earlier by Thomas Jefferson, came close to questioning punishment of victimless crime.

From a legal standpoint, there were also important inferences. Civil liberties spokesmen argued, particularly out of the offices of the American Civil Liberties Union in New York, that there should be legal remedies to which a citizen might turn when forms of Progressive social control became overly restrictive of individual freedom. The Red Scare of 1920 and the excesses which it produced, particularly arbitrary arrest, unreasonable search and seizure, and massive, heavy-handed, and insensitive use of federal authority, played into the picture. It tended to turn the public mind toward considering at least the potential for damage to the individual which too aggressive a federal policy, in the name of the general welfare and community morality, could produce.[10]

The 1920s is an interesting decade from a civil liberties standpoint, particularly as those views began at that time to garner some support from divergent freedom-oriented groups and individuals. And to the extent that prohibition itself was a form of coerced societal morality which had little concern for individual rights, it became a part of that scene. It produced civil liberties concerns, at least to the degree that it was perceived as parallel with such developments as the now expired wartime restrictive laws curtailing free speech, press, and association.

Civil liberties concerns in the 1920s went far beyond the abstract issue of massive central government turning to a federal police power to impose its statist will on free individuals. That view, however, was normally the starting point. When a group of prominent American businessmen and political leaders met in Washington in December 1927 in the home of Senator James Wadsworth to discuss repeal of the Eighteenth Amendment, a central consensus was that national prohibition represented a major expansion of the scope of the federal government, particularly in regard to individual behavior, and was based upon assumptions which might logically lead to further growth of federal authority.[11] During the decade, Republican leader James Beck assailed the Eighteenth Amendment as destroying the basic principle of local self-government and infringing individual rights. But Beck was also concerned that if the Republican party continued to sell its soul to the fanatical drys (and I will resist the temptation to draw contemporary parallels), it was rapidly going to lose its political credibility. For him, then, the party was central, clearly more central than concrete civil liberties considerations.[12] When Captain William H. Stayton became interested in the prohibition amendment early in its history in

Wilsonian days, he was troubled that discussions about controlling the public morals seemed to Wilson administration leaders more important than the war effort. But in the long run, it was Stayton's strong view that the loss of individual community decision-making power was the real danger. The Constitution, he argued, was no place for prohibition. That was a local question.[13] As for Senator Wadsworth, he campaigned for reelection in New York by declaring that civil liberties and the traditional forms of government were endangered by a centralizing, personally interfering national prohibition. The Eighteenth Amendment, he contended, was putting a restriction on individual behavior in the Constitution. "We shall continue to suffer," he argued, "just so long as that 'Thou shalt not' remains in the Constitution."[14]

Running through such professed civil liberties concerns was a fairly uniform consensus that the enjoyment of civil liberties was equated with local control and that the enemy of civil liberties was national statism. The idea that states or communities might be capable of denying civil liberties seems not to have occurred to such spokesmen.

The small but growing band of civil libertarians in the 1920s expressed other kinds of concerns. Particularly troubling to them was the fact that a majoritarian, legislative constitutionalism which seemed to be generally in place where the rights of minorities were concerned was not reviewable in the courts. The Supreme Court, under Chief Justice William Howard Taft, generally turned a totally deaf ear to cases involving individual rights in the decade. And while Justices Holmes and Brandeis increasingly deplored what they considered a double standard of the Court protecting economic rights of the wealthy and powerful but dismissing liberty claims of the weak and those of a minority status, little was done by the courts to offer much hope to those seeking to establish individual claims involving personal freedom.[15]

But a third set of civil liberties considerations emerged, and significantly, they surrounded the process of enforcing the prohibition laws. Chief Justice Taft had, somewhat ironically, opposed adoption of the prohibition amendment not only because he preferred local option but also because he disliked any changes in the Constitution and felt national prohibition would be unenforceable.[16] Once the Eighteenth Amendment was ratified, however, he accepted it completely and became one of its strongest advocates. From 1921 to 1930 he sought to have the prohibition laws strictly enforced and took upon himself the writing of a number of prohibition-related decisions.

However, changing public opinion undermined Taft's rigidity, especially as prohibition began to become unpopular and people perceived the methods of its enforcement as a threat to certain of their rights and liberties. Supreme Court rulings in this area turned around interpretation of the Fourth Amendment and went through three distinct phases, reflecting the initial enthusiasm for enforcement, growing doubts about the methods being used, and eventually the beginnings of pressure for its repeal.[17]

In the early period to 1927, the Court had little trouble circumscribing the Fourth Amendment's reach by distinguishing lawful observations of enforcement authorities from search and by excluding "open fields" surrounding a house from the amendment's protection. Holmes in a 1924 decision distinguished searches covered by the amendment from permissible police surveillance. Even if agents did commit a trespass, he concluded, their testimony was admissible since it was not obtained by an illegal search or seizure. The violator's actions (leaving a house with suspicious materials), which they had observed from a distance, had only led officers to examine the contents of bottles he was moving. These had, indeed, contained whiskey. The unanimous opinion clearly conformed to the early public approval of prohibition. By accepting surreptitious trespass on the property of private citizens as a natural incident of the effective enforcement of the Eighteenth Amendment, the court indicated that it—like the general public—had not yet developed serious reservations about techniques of prohibition enforcement.[18]

But such reservations did begin to develop. A well-recognized exception to the requirement that officials obtain a warrant before conducting a search allowed police officers to search persons they had arrested and to use incriminating material in court. This "incident-to-arrest" exception had been generally upheld by the courts in the early years of the decade, especially in a 1926 case involving the seizure of a motorboat containing seventy-one cases of grain alcohol at a point twenty-four miles off Gloucester, Massachusetts, in a region commonly spoken of as Rum Row. The principal issue concerned the authority of customs officials to search American vessels beyond the twelve-mile boundary. Justice Brandeis here offered the "incident-to-arrest" exception as an alternate justification for the search, implicitly treating the motorboat as the "premises" on which the search continued.[19] However, in *U.S. v. Marron,* decided the following year, the

Court's approach in this area began to shift, with the justices beginning to perceive the dangers in prohibition enforcement although still unwilling to let serious offenders go free.[20] By the early 1930s, in *Go-Bart v. U.S.*[21] and *U.S. v. Lefkowitz*,[22] the Court moved to a strict rendering of the Fourth Amendment, striking hard at the "incident-to-arrest" exceptions even when that construction resulted in freeing some relatively serious offenders. Again the ruling displayed the Court's increased concern about abusive enforcement techniques and reflected quite accurately public attitudes in this area.

In connection with automobile searches, the justices had ruled in 1925 in *Carroll v. U.S.* that a prohibition agent who searched a car without warrant was not engaging in an unreasonable search.[23] But again the Court backed away. In *Husty v. U.S.* in 1931, it used this *Carroll* rule to uphold an arrest but refused to approve the rather harsh sentence that the trial court had imposed and remanded the case to the district court for resentencing.[24] And in *Taylor v. U.S.* in 1932, the Court found invalid a search without warrant of a garage. It conceded that agents had sufficient evidence to obtain a search warrant. Nonetheless, it emphasized, the availability of such evidence did not allow officers to search a building without obtaining such a warrant.[25] Thus the automobile cases, like the prohibition cases generally, reflected the Court's tendency to mirror public opinion.

A similar pattern involved the initial judicial condoning of the use of nonfederal investigators in prohibition enforcement, a common practice in many states and cities. But in the 1927 *Byars*[26] and *Gambino*[27] cases, clear doubts as to the legitimacy of this practice were raised. The justices expressed increasing concern over the methods of prohibition enforcement, particularly when questionable agents and their testimony were utilized.

On the Fourth Amendment's requirement that search warrants be issued only upon probable cause, the Court again moved toward strictness, especially when reviewing search warrant cases. The best example of this strict review is *Grau v. U.S.* in 1932, in which the Court found the facts presented to the magistrate insufficient to establish probable cause. Justice Roberts declared that the Grau warrant should be judged by the reasonableness standard, concluding that "while a dwelling used as a manufactory or headquarters for merchandising may well be and doubtless often is the place of sale, its use for those purposes is not alone probable cause for believing that actual sales are there being made.''[28] The outcome of these stricter standards did not mean that the Court struck down every search. Nonetheless, the cases in which the Court did find adequate showing of probable cause had to be supported by considerable persuasive evidence.

The net result of this reworking and reinterpreting of the Fourth Amendment to meet the challenges of the prohibition situation was to stimulate a greater concern for the individual. The process was slow, however. The Taft Court had split sharply on the privacy issue. Taft had sustained the conviction of a notorious Seattle bootlegger based upon a massive use of wiretap evidence, even though Washington law made wiretapping illegal. In the process he ruled that wiretapping did not constitute unreasonable search and seizure, since nothing was technically searched and nothing was seized. Holmes disagreed sharply, calling wiretapping "dirty business," and Brandeis, who had long advocated the development of a constitutional right of privacy, complained that "if the government becomes a law breaker, it breeds contempt for the law."[29] Subsequently the Court, rather than focusing upon property rights, began to recognize a more generalized (and less absolute) right to privacy as the interest deserving protection. This new approach provided the seed for the modern interpretation of the Fourth Amendment—the ultimate emphasis upon reasonable expectation of privacy—a position eventually embraced in the 1960s.[30] In a more general way, however, this trend reflected a widely expressed concern as to whether prohibition enforcement was not producing more in the way of police-statism and arbitrary government behavior than was desirable in a free society, particularly in a society such as the one of the 1920s whose leaders so frequently paid lip service to laissez-faire and free enterprise.

In this regard, the actions of both Presidents Calvin Coolidge and Herbert Hoover contributed to the freedom-versus-morality debate. Each man in his public statements spoke glowingly of the centrality of the free individual. But Coolidge, as a result of the persuasion of General Lincoln C. Andrews of the Prohibition Bureau, was talked into issuing an executive order in 1926 deputizing state, country, and municipal officers as agents of the Treasury Department for prohibition purposes.[31] Subsequently he authorized and supported a move to strengthen the Volstead Act, urging the passage in March 1929 of the Jones Act, substantially increasing the amount of the fines and imprisonment which could be imposed.[32] And although it eventually backfired, Hoover's

Wickersham Commission was set up to find more effective ways to enforce the prohibition laws.[33] Both Coolidge and Hoover seemed generally oblivious to the fact that imposing a single federal standard of conduct upon the whole people of the United States, without regard to local sentiment, values, and habits, constituted central statism in the extreme. Thus, when the chips were down in the 1920s, the record seems rather clear that the opponents of prohibition, who eventually brought it down, did not do so on civil liberties grounds but through a body of argumentation which focused upon the excessive power of the state.

The advent of the 1930s produced changes which could not fail to impact upon the prohibition situation. The Supreme Court changed, especially with a new chief justice, Charles Evans Hughes, and the appointment of Benjamin Cardozo. That Court moved rather quickly to embrace assumptions maintained by Holmes and Brandeis during the previous decade. The federal government's responsibility, various of the justices argued in cases in 1931 and 1932, was to protect the rights of free individuals.[34] And to the extent that uniform national standards were to be enforced by the courts, they should be standards which protected the individual from local and private coercion which operationally more often threatened his freedom than did action at the federal level. This did not represent a departure from federal police power or positive government. It did make clear that the federal government had responsibilities toward utilizing its power to protect individual freedom rather than to coerce.

Similarly, congressional attitudes changed in those depression years. In March 1933 Congress passed the Beer-Wine Revenue Act, aimed at securing additional monies by amending the Volstead Act to legalize wine, beer, lager beer, ale, and porter of 3.2 percent maximum alcoholic content by weight. The act left to the states all regulatory control measures, especially those relating to sale and distribution, and incorporated safeguards for states whose prohibition laws stipulated a lesser alcoholic content.[35]

But above all, and in ironic kinds of ways, the election of Franklin Roosevelt changed national leadership's attitudes on the prohibition question. Roosevelt was certainly no doctrinaire enemy of positive government, and the New Deal's expansion of federal functions and the federal role was startling. But Roosevelt was apprehensive about using federal power to legislate morality. He was prepared to support and work for repeal not only as a desirable social change but, above all, as an important recasting of the law's function and limitations. Thus on December 5, 1933, a thirsty nation rejoiced and the "noble experiment" was over.[36]

One cannot resist speculating on whether it could happen again. One's instinctive reaction is that this is highly unlikely. But the use of the law for allegedly moral ends has had its supporters from that time to the present day. The "Moral Majority" is not at all reluctant to use the same kind of arguments regarding federal imposition of proper standards which the early prohibitionists used—that massive federal authority is necessary to intervene in people's moral behavior, both for their own good and to save them from themselves; and that, there being no such thing as a victimless crime, individual sin hurts the community and produces disruption and immorality. Thus, it is claimed, we need anti-abortion laws, federal informers on teenage contraceptive use, required prayer in the schools, censorship of books, movies, and textbooks, laws punishing homosexuality, and certainly public proscription on the home-threatening immoral equal rights amendment.

What I think will ultimately preclude and forestall the success of such movements is a whole attitudinal shift which took place especially in the late 1950s and 1960s regarding the importance of individual rights transcending community standards which, in their operation, deny people their rights. The majority of Americans came in those years to accept the idea that people do have rights against the state. And we have begun, in Ronald Dworkin's phrase, to take rights seriously.[37] In fact, we have taken them so seriously, or at least the Warren Court took them so seriously, that now rather than censor books and movies, we rule censorship statutes unconstitutional as an infringement on the individual's freedom; rather than arrest the agitator, we protect his soapbox; rather than punish homosexuals, we guarantee them equality of access; rather than segregate schools to prevent immoral black-white cohabitation from starting, we order them integrated; rather than extorting confessions, we require the police to read people the Miranda rule.

But the pressures back toward societal morality are strong and currently enjoy White House support.[38] Time will tell whether those leading the charge are sufficiently skillful to muster the kind of support necessary to achieve their ends.

NOTES

1. David H. Flaherty, "Law and the Enforcement of Morals in Early America," in *Law In American History*, ed. Donald Fleming and Bernard Bailyn (Boston: Little, Brown, 1971), pp. 203–53.

2. *Charles River Bridge v. Warren Bridge,* 11 Peters 420, 458 (1837).

3. On Pound, *see* David Wigdor, *Roscoe Pound* (Westport, Conn.: Greenwood, 1974), p. 183 ff.

4. Patrick Lord Devlin, *The Enforcement of Morals* (London: Oxford, 1965). Devlin was responding to the famous 1957 Wolfenden Report, which, following a study of homosexual offenses and prostitution in Great Britain, took the position that "it is not, in our view, the function of the law to intervene in the private lives of citizens, or to seek to enforce any particular pattern of behavior." *The Wolfenden Report: Report of the Committee on Homosexual Offenses and Prostitution* (New York: Stein and Day, 1963), paragraph 13.

5. Paul L. Murphy, *World War I and the Origin of Civil Liberties in the United States* (New York: Norton, 1979).

6. *Moyer v. Peabody,* 212 U.S. 78, 86 (1909).

7. *Jacobson v. Massachusetts,* 197 U.S. 11, 26 (1905).

8. *Patterson v. Colorado,* 204 U.S. 454, 462 (1907).

9. John Stuart Mill, *On Liberty* (London: Oxford, 1966), p. 15.

10. Paul L. Murphy, *The Meaning of Freedom of Speech: First Amendment Freedoms from Wilson to F.D.R.* (Westport, Conn.: Greenwood, 1972), p. 86 ff.

11. David E. Kyvig, *Repealing National Prohibition* (Chicago: University of Chicago Press, 1979), pp. 1–2.

12. Ibid., p. 141.

13. Ibid., p. 42.

14. Ibid., p. 77.

15. A revealing case was *Buck v. Bell,* 274 U.S. 200 (1927), in which Holmes for the Court sustained a Virginia statute permitting sterilization of inmates in institutions for the feebleminded. The welfare of the state here transcended any individual right to be free from such legal coercion.

16. On Taft, *see* Alpheus T. Mason, *William Howard Taft: Chief Justice* (New York: Simon and Schuster, 1964), p. 224.

17. There were misgivings on other constitutional grounds, especially regarding the rigidity of the rule in *U.S. v. Lanza,* (260 U.S. 377 [1922]). There the Court had unanimously upheld a federal prosecution case in which the defendant had already been convicted by the state. By denying that this was double jeopardy, the Court had created a legal situation in which prohibition violators could be indicted and punished twice for almost every offense.

18. *Hester v. U.S.,* 265 U.S. 57 (1924).

19. *U.S. v. Lee,* 274 U.S. 559 (1927).
20. 275 U.S. 192 (1927).
21. 282 U.S. 344 (1931).
22. 285 U.S. 452 (1932).
23. 267 U.S. 132 (1925).
24. 282 U.S. 692 (1931).
25. 286 U.S. 1 (1932).
26. *Byars v. U.S.,* 273 U.S. 28 (1927).
27. *Gambino v. U.S.,* 275 U.S. 310 (1927).
28. 287 U.S. 127 (1932).
29. *Olmstead v. U.S.,* 277 U.S. 438, 470, 485 (1928). For a detailed assessment of the general topic, *see* Kenneth M. Murchison, "Prohibition and the Fourth Amendment: A New Look at Some Old Cases," *Journal of Criminal Law and Criminology* 73 (Summer 1982): 471–532.
30. *Katz v. U.S.,* 389 U.S. 347 (1967). The decision specifically overruled *Olmstead.*
31. William Swindler, *Court and Constitution in the 20th Century: The Old Legality, 1889–1932* (Indianapolis: Bobbs-Merrill, 1979), pp. 264–65.
32. 45 *Stat.* 1446 (1929).
33. On the Wickersham Commission, *see* Murphy, *Meaning of Freedom of Speech*, pp. 159, 236, 265; and Kyvig, *Repealing National Prohibition,* pp. 111–15.
34. *Stromberg v. California,* 283 U.S. 359 (1931); *Near v. Minnesota,* 283 U.S. 697 (1931); *Powell v. Alabama,* 287 U.S. 45 (1932).
35. 48 *Stat.* 16 (1933).
36. The measure was proposed on February 20, 1933, and ratified by the necessary number of states less than nine months later.
37. Ronald Dworkin, *Taking Rights Seriously* (Cambridge: Harvard University Press, 1977).
38. "Reverend Reagan," *New Republic* 188 (April 4, 1983): 7.

Regulating the Regulators: Prohibition Enforcement in the Seventh Circuit

The papers in this volume are abundant evidence of the fact that national prohibition is a much-studied topic. Historians, lawyers, public health policymakers, and criminologists have all turned their attention to the passage, implementation, and repeal of the Eighteenth Amendment to the United States Constitution. Their studies have deepened our understanding of prohibition, and, as well, their own disciplines. Legal historians have thus far added to these studies primarily by focusing their attention on the Supreme Court's development of legal doctrines that grew out of America's great social experiment. This chapter will shift that focus from the highest court to an intermediate federal appellate court. Specifically, I will examine the prohibition issues presented to the U.S. Court of Appeals for the Seventh Circuit. In looking at the cases brought to the court, not only can one see the range of legal issues raised by prohibition and understand the role the appeals court played in enforcement, but one can also examine the effects of the prohibition cases on the court. For it is in this last respect that national prohibition left a legacy for the courts of appeals. The prohibition cases were the first sizable group of appeals to present the Seventh Circuit with the issues involved in exercising its new role as supervisor of the federal bureaucracy. Studying how the court performed this role reveals the judges' concerns with constraining perceived lawless conduct by federal agents.

I would like to thank Carol Avins, Al Alschuler, Robert Nelson, Jamil Zainaldin, and Frank Zimring for their helpful comments and suggestions. I also wish to thank Jack Heinz and the American Bar Foundation for supporting this work.

Before turning to these issues, a brief description of the organization of the Seventh Circuit is necessary. The Seventh Circuit was one of the ten regional federal courts of appeals established in 1891 to hear appeals from the federal district courts, thus providing relief for an overburdened U.S. Supreme Court. A major goal of the Evarts Act, which set up the courts, was to reduce the number of appeals which the Supreme Court had a statutory obligation to accept. By enlarging the Supreme Court's discretionary jurisdiction and giving all litigants a right of appeal to the circuit courts, Congress sought to make the latter the primary forum for correction of trial court errors. The Supreme Court, having been freed of this task, could concentrate on major policy issues arising from the state and federal courts. Examination of the prohibition cases will demonstrate how the courts of appeals performed their role.[1]

The Seventh Circuit's jurisdiction covered the states of Illinois, Indiana, and Wisconsin. During the prohibition era, 1919–33, the court was alloted four judgeships. Although mandated by custom, not statute, one circuit judge resided in Wisconsin, one in Indiana, and two in Illinois (one from Chicago and one from downstate) throughout this period. This distribution reflected not only the fact that Illinois had the largest population but also that about 50 percent of the Seventh Circuit's docket consisted of appeals from the U.S. District Court for the Northern District of Illinois. A three-judge panel heard each appeal.[2]

The Seventh Circuit's personnel remained largely unchanged during prohibition. Two of the judges served throughout the period; only two judges occupied the downstate Illinois position; three men from Indiana served on the court. Republicans held the Indiana position, while Democrats occupied the other three seats. Judges Samuel Alschuler of Chicago and Evan Evans of Wisconsin both received appointment from Woodrow Wilson and served until after 1935. George Page, another Wilsonian appointee, served as an active judge from 1918 until he took senior status in 1930, though he continued to hear cases until his death in 1941. He was replaced on the court by the promotion of a Democrat, U.S. District Judge Louis FitzHenry of the U.S. District Court for the Southern District of Illinois. The three Indiana Republicans were Judge Francis Baker (1902–24), Judge Albert Anderson (1924–28), and Judge Will M. Sparks (1928–48).[3]

The Justice Department had screened the three Wilsonian appointees before their appointment to determine that they generally supported

Wilson's programs to expand economic and social regulation through the creation of federal agencies. The Republicans, on the other hand, had been selected primarily because of their relationship with the Indiana senators. An additional factor in Hoover's appointment of Sparks was the latter's professional reputation as the leading state trial court judge.[4]

Only one member of this bench—Judge Louis FitzHenry—was strongly identified with prohibition issues, and his involvement was as a trial judge. FitzHenry gained a reputation in downstate Illinois as a tough sentencer whose court, the local newspaper claimed, set a record for the number of convictions and the size of fines in Volstead Act cases. FitzHenry constantly received commendation from temperance groups in addition to their support in his efforts to be promoted from the district court to the Seventh Circuit. The judge's temperance law efforts extended beyond the courtroom, as he informed the prohibition agents of the names of local restaurants which he suspected served liquor.[5]

Because the Seventh Circuit's jurisdiction extended from the German breweries of Wisconsin through the speakeasy districts of Chicago to the bootlegging regions of southern Indiana and Illinois, the Volstead Act provided the court a major portion of its work from the law's enactment until its repeal. To understand the dimensions of this involvement, it is necessary to look briefly at the Seventh Circuit's case load. From its beginnings in 1891 until the New Deal era, the Seventh Circuit adjudicated mainly disputes between private litigants. The appeals coming to the court were tort and contract suits between citizens of different states (diversity jurisdiction issues), bankruptcy petitions, and patent claims. In its first year, 1892, the court wrote sixteen opinions: seven were diversity, six patent, and one admirality. In two cases the U.S. government was plaintiff, but in both the government sued to recover debts on bonds. Ten years later, despite the increase in the number of opinions written by the Court (eighty-two), the overwhelming number were still diversity (fifty-four), patent (thirteen), admiralty (six), and bankruptcy (six). Over the next twenty years, the number of opinions written annually fluctuated between sixty and ninety-five, with the average about sixty-nine per year. The percentage of these opinions which involved suits by or against the federal government increased over that of the first decade, but still averaged only about 13 percent. These cases were divided about equally between federal criminal prosecutions and civil suits by or against the government. During the 1920s and 1930s, both the number of opinions written and the percentage of government litigation increased tremendously. By 1932 the average number of opinions had reached one hundred, and by 1941 it had doubled to two hundred per year. The percentage of government litigation averaged 36 percent during the 1920s and 49 percent during the 1930s. The impact of prohibition on the court can be seen in this increase. In the 1920s about half of the federal government cases were criminal prosecutions. Of this number, half were Volstead Act prosecutions. Put another way, the 110 Volstead Act cases were the largest single source of federal governmental appeals during the 1920s and accounted for about 8 percent of all of the opinions written by the Seventh Circuit during prohibition.[6]

What can be observed in these 110 cases? First, we can see examples of the various patterns of federal enforcement of prohibition. Government agent infiltration of large bootleg organizations led to several of the appeals. In *Allen v. U.S.* seventy-five downstate Illinois defendants were convicted of conspiracy to manufacture, transport, and sell alcohol.[7] In this case, as in *O'Brien v. U.S.*[8] and *Collenger v. U.S.*,[9] the targets of the government investigations were public officials. In all three cases police, mayors, justices of the peace, and other government officials were prosecuted. A second pattern was the prosecution of the owners of "place(s) where liquor was kept."[10] One common form was for either state or federal officials to obtain an injunction in federal court forbidding the owner of the premises to sell liquor. If evidence appeared that the owner violated the injunction, the federal judge could find the defendant in criminal contempt of court and sentence him to jail without a jury trial. The Seventh Circuit upheld this procedure in a series of cases in 1921–22.[11] Although technically it does not concern Volstead Act violations, a third type of prosecution should also be noted here: income tax trials of bootleggers. The most famous of these was the appeal of Al Capone, whose conviction the Seventh Circuit affirmed in 1932.[12] Although there are a range of other types of defendants in the Seventh Circuit's cases, they need not all be detailed here. For although these appeals reflect to some degree patterns in prohibition enforcement, they should not be taken as a representative sample. Because plea bargains, decisions by prosecutors not to prosecute, dismissals by trial courts, and decisions by defendants not to appeal kept the overwhelming majority of cases from ever reaching the appellate court,[13] representative samples of enforcement policy can be found only by turning to district court, prosecutorial, and Bureau of Prohibition records.

What can be identified in the prohibition appeals, however, are the legal issues raised by prohibition and the role the court of appeals played in prohibition enforcement. To examine these questions, the 110 appeals have been read and divided into three categories on the basis of the issues presented in them. First, there are issues of the correctness of the trial process and the sufficiency of evidence. Second are questions of statutory construction of the Volstead Act. Third are questions dealing with the propriety of the conduct of the government's agents. The first category is by far the largest. Eighty-two of the 110 cases involved challenges either to the sufficiency of the evidence or to the correctness of the trial judge's rulings regarding the trial process. The latter ranged from claims of errors in the indictment to evidentiary rulings and instructions to the jury. The former were claims by defendants that the government had not met its burden of proof; i.e., the government had not offered enough relevant and competent evidence to establish guilt beyond a reasonable doubt.

Three legal rules controlled the disposition of most of these trial process and evidence appeals: the substantial evidence rule, the harmless error rule, and deference to the discretion of the trial judge. The substantial evidence rule is designed to limit the scope of the appellate court's review of factual questions. The court is to affirm the district court's factual findings if there is *any* evidence in the record to support them. Thus, the three court of appeals judges do not weigh the conflicting claims, but look at the record for some evidence to support the judgment of the district court. When defendants claim that their conviction must be reversed because it was based on insufficient evidence, the substantial evidence rule limits the court of appeals inquiry. The harmless error rule limits reversals of district court judgments to cases where the appellate court finds the error was sufficiently prejudicial that it may have influenced the verdict. Even though a trial judge may have erred in making an evidentiary ruling or in giving an instruction to a jury, reversal will not be required if the evidence of guilt is overwhelming or if the mistake was so trivial as not to prejudice the judge or jury's determination of guilt or innocence. The rule requiring the appellate court to defer to the discretion of the trial court judge attempts to prevent the appellate court from substituting its judgment for the trial judge's in certain procedural rulings unless the appellate court finds that the district judge abused his discretion. Because the trial judge is a firsthand observer of the trial, while an appellate court has only a cold record describing events, deference is given to the district judge in determining questions such as whether the jury should be removed during a discussion of an objection to the admission of a piece of evidence or whether a juror should be dismissed for some cause once a trial has begun. The purpose of all of these doctrines is to limit the intervention of the appellate court to cases where the trial court's decisions substantially prejudiced the fairness of the defendant's trial or placed substantial burdens on the defendant's ability to defend himself. The rules favor finality of decision over perfection in the trial process and attempt to limit the opportunities for the appellate court to substitute its judgment for that of the jury or trial judge.[14]

As might be expected, reversal rates were low, with the Seventh Circuit overturning less than 15 percent of the convictions in this category. Examples of reversals are *Verna v. U.S.*, *McFadden v. U.S.*, and *Echikovitz v. U.S.* In *Verna* two defendants were charged with conspiracy to manufacture alcohol. The only evidence linking Verna to the conspiracy was that he owned the farmland where the still was located. Verna argued in his appeal that there was insufficient evidence to convict him. The Seventh Circuit agreed, as it held that mere absentee ownership did not prove that he knowingly participated in the conspiracy.[15] In *McFadden* the Seventh Circuit reversed a conviction following a bench trial in which, the transcript revealed, the district judge had predetermined the defendant's guilt. The court found that the district judge had abused his discretion in not granting the defendant's motion that the judge recuse himself from the trial and allow another judge to try the case.[16] In *Echikovitz* the court reversed because hearsay testimony had been improperly admitted. Since the improper evidence was all that linked the defendant to the manufacture of moonshine, the court found that the trial judge's error was so prejudicial as not to be harmless and granted the defendant a new trial.[17]

The cases in this category demonstrate the Seventh Circuit fulfilling its error-correction role. As indicated earlier, the courts of appeals were established in large part to free the U.S. Supreme Court from supervising the individual fairness of the trial process in each case and instead to leave that court free to concentrate on major policy issues. The fact that in 82 percent of all Seventh Circuit prohibition cases, certiorari to the Supreme Court was not sought, and that the Supreme Court only granted review in one of the 110 prohibition appeals, evidences the success of the Seventh Circuit in performing its error-correction function. The appeals in this, the largest category (82 of 110 cases), reveal that the Seventh Circuit was not involved with major policy issues of prohibition enforcement but rather with supervising the fairness of the trial process itself.

The second category of appeals presented questions of statutory construction of the Volstead Act. In six of the seven cases, the court read the language of the statute literally, even when, as in one case, the court admitted that to do so produced a ridiculous result. In *Henry v. U.S.* the appellant sought to recover a $100 bond he had posted for an accused bootlegger. When the bootlegger fled, the bond was forfeited. Henry successfully tracked the man down and returned him for trial. The court, however, refused to return the bond money as it stated that the statute does not allow return when there had been a "willful default of the party." Despite the fact that Henry had not "willfully defaulted," the court held that "the party" meant the criminal, not the bondsman. Thus, Henry's attempt to receive a refund failed. The court commented that it is for the legislature to remedy the problem as the court was bound by the statutory language.[18]

A representative example of the type of statutory question presented to the court (and the only one which led to a reversal) was *Cassville Beverage Co. v. U.S.* In that case the company was convicted of manufacturing illegal beer. The statute forbade the sale of beer that was above the .5 percent limit of alcohol content. The beer was below the limit when the company sold it, but when stored, it continued to ferment until it exceeded the .5 percent level. The Seventh Circuit held that the statute defined the legal limit of alcoholic content at the time of the sale and that the conviction could not stand unless the evidence showed the beer exceeded the limit at the time of sale.[19] Again, Congress had spoken and the court must follow its words.

The one case in which the literal language of the statute was not conclusive provoked one of the rare dissents. The question involved whether a club which allowed patrons to bring their own liquor could be closed as a public nuisance because it was a place where liquor was "kept." This was the statutory term. The majority affirmed the district court's injunction, finding that "kept" did not imply any period of duration and that Congress intended to outlaw a "public restaurant where persons were continually permitted to congregate and consume . . . their own liquor." The majority found this intent in the Volstead Act's section which declared "all the provisions of this act shall be liberally construed to the end that the use of intoxicating liquor as a beverage may be prevented." In dissent, Judge Samuel Alschuler relied on U.S. Supreme Court and federal appellate court interpretations of the word "kept," all of which required a nexus between the possession and a sale or commercial transaction. He then argued that the club could not be enjoined as it did not keep any liquor for sale. He acknowledged that such a reading created a loophole but added it is not "for the courts to supply inadvertent legislative omissions."[20]

The discussion of these cases reveals the great deference the court paid to the legislative branch. The Seventh Circuit answered statutory questions by traditional means of statutory construction: reliance on literal language and discerning legislative intent from the statute itself. These statutory cases, unlike the cases in the first category, do involve the court in questions of enforcement policies. However, that involvement remained narrowly limited by the court's jurisprudential approach combined with the small number of appeals.

The third category consists of twenty-one appeals which raised questions of the lawfulness of the conduct of governmental agents. They arose in the context of claims that government agents' searches and seizures violated the Fourth Amendment to the Constitution and, in two cases, that agents had entrapped defendants into illegal action. In deciding these appeals, the court exercised a supervisory role over the prohibition agency and its agents. The tone of the opinions reveals the hostility the court displayed to agent misconduct. In a 1923 appeal, *Miucki v. U.S.*, the defendants, a husband and wife who operated a "soft-drink parlor," claimed their convictions were based on evidence obtained following a federal agent's illegal search of their business. They cited the Fourth Amendment: "The right of the people to be secure in their persons, houses, papers, and effects, against unreasonable searches and seizures, shall not be violated, and no warrants shall issue, but upon probable cause. . . . " Since the agent entered their business without a warrrant, they maintained the search was unreasonable and thus the evidence must be suppressed. The agents had seized from the defendants' cash drawer two marked one-dollar bills given by an informant to the defendants to purchase liquor. The government argued that no warrant was needed for the search of the cash drawer or seizure of the bills because the two defendants had given their consent to have the drawer searched. The validity of the search was never decided by the trial court, as the Seventh Circuit pointed out, because defendants' counsel was incompetent and failed to give the proper reason for objecting to introduction of the evidence. After establishing a rule that trial courts in the future were to hear motions to suppress evidence in the absence of the jury, the Seventh Circuit reversed the defendants' conviction and ordered a new trial. Judge Evans expressed grave doubts that consent to the warrantless search of the cash drawer was voluntary. Not only did the defendants testify that the agent obtained the consent while holding a gun on them, but the judge noted that the record showed the accused to be ''very ignorant'' and thus likely to be intimidated by the agent, whom he termed ''an officious government official.''[21]

Fowler v. U.S., a 1932 appeal, questioned the ''silver platter'' rule. Under that rule, ''evidence obtained improperly by state officials could nevertheless be used by federal prosecutors, on the reasoning that no federal official had participated in the underlying violation of the defendant's rights.'' This rule allowed state officials to hand over ''on a silver platter'' evidence illegally obtained.[22] The arrangement followed the Supreme Court's 1914 holding in *Weeks v. United States* that ''evidence obtained pursuant to a violation of the Fourth Amendment's prohibition against unreasonable searches and seizures could not be admitted in federal criminal trials.''[23] The *Fowler* appeal showed that Indianapolis federal and state prohibition agents had cooperated in investigations for a number of years on the understanding that if the operation uncovered major violations of the Volstead Act, the state would turn over its evidence to the federal agents, who would prosecute in federal court. The state agents, under an invalid warrant, seized a large quantity of liquor from Fowler and then turned the case over to the federal agents. The Seventh Circuit held that through this long-term agreement between state and federal authorities, the federal agents had ratified the state's illegal action. The court reversed the conviction and ordered that defendant's motion to supress the evidence be granted. Judge Alschuler wrote, ''It would be hardly consistent with a proper regard for the protection accorded by the Fourth Amendment to permit any department of the federal government in this manner to set the Amendment at defiance.''[24] He then quoted at length the Supreme Court's language in *Byars v. U.S.,* which stated that ''the court must be vigilant to scrutinize the attendant facts with an eye to detect and a hand to prevent violations of the Constitution by circuitous and indirect methods.''[25]

In a 1931 appeal, *O'Brien v. U.S.*, five Indianapolis policemen sought reversal of their conviction of conspiracy to violate the Volstead Act on the grounds that they had been entrapped by the federal agents. An entrapment defense asserts that a defendant cannot be punished if he is "not previously disposed to commit a crime" but "is induced to commit it by a government agent.''[26] The evidence revealed that federal prohibition agents had set up a pool hall-saloon and hired an informant to run it. The object was to sell liquor to policemen, who would then be indicted for participating in the conspiracy by sanctioning the illegal activity. In a strongly worded opinion, the Seventh Circuit reversed and ordered the district court to enter a directed verdict for the defendants. Judge Evans found that the government had "induced" the defendants into committing the offense and was thus stopped from prosecuting them. The judge's dislike of the agents' tactics was clear. He wrote:

In approaching this question, it is assumed that there are instances in criminal law, as well as civil actions, where the end, though laudable enough, does not justify the means. . . . We see no reason why the government should not be subjected to the same rule of conduct. Although it be sovereign, it should not be permitted to adopt means which are condemned by the courts when practiced by its citizens. . . . If the conduct of one be unconscionable, if it be intentionally deceptive and designed to induce, and does induce another to do something *which he would not otherwise have done,* the wrongdoer is not and should not be permitted to profit thereby. . . . Similiar questions are arising with ever increasing frequency in criminal cases involving prosecutions under the National Prohibition Act.[27]

These three cases along with four similar cases comprised a group of seven reversals in the twenty-one cases in this category. That reversal rate is over twice that of the cases in the first category, which raised issues of the trial process. This rate of intervention by the court is even more significant when two points are made. The first is that three of the fourteen affirmances of agents' conduct were frivolous appeals which came within a year after the court had reversed two convictions because unreasonable warrantless searches had occurred. In the three appeals there appeared to be no possible valid claim that the searches were illegal, but defendants' attorneys made the arguments. In the third opinion, where the agents not only had a valid warrant but there was evidence of consent, Judge Evans threatened to drop attorneys from the roll of attorneys who could practice before the court if there continued to be such frivolous appeals, which he believed were only brought to delay the imposition of sentence.[28]

It must also be pointed out that the Seventh Circuit's perception of the propriety of government conduct was, in part, determined by the pronouncements of the U.S. Supreme Court. After *U.S. v. Carroll* convictions were perfunctorily affirmed in four cases in which the illegality of a warrantless stop and search of their automobiles was claimed.[29] For in *Carroll* the Supreme Court held that federal prohibition agents could stop and search an automobile observed on a highway as long as the agents had probable cause to believe that the automobile contained contraband. The agents in *Carroll* recognized the drivers as having offered to make liquor sales in the past, knew that they traveled frequently on the road, and knew that liquor traffic was prevalent in the area.[30] Similarly, after *Olmstead* the court affirmed the one appeal which raised the question of the validity of a wiretap. *Olmstead* "held that the placing of a tap on telephone wires and thereby eavesdropping upon defendant's telephone conversations 'did not amount to a search . . . within the meaning of the Fourth Amendment.' " Since the federal agents in *Olmstead* had not physically intruded on the defendant's home, no warrant was necessary.[31] Not only did the court behave differently in this category of cases when measured quantitatively, but in these cases the court was more likely not to defer to the district court nor to invoke the substantial evidence rule. For example, in *Miucki* the court found the failure to excuse the jury during counsels' argument over the motion to suppress to be an abuse of discretion.[32] The court in *O'Brien* found, contrary to the district court, that there was no evidence that the defendants intended to conspire to violate the prohibition statutes until the police induced them.[33]

There could be several explanations for why these cases involving the conduct of the agents were more frequently reversed. First, it could be argued that since these cases raised prohibition enforcement policy issues, not issues of the trial process as did cases in the largest category, the judges' votes reflected their personal views about prohibition. That this is an overly simplistic explanation can be seen in the fact that, allowing for the cases controlled by the Supreme Court, the same group of judges affirmed convictions about as often as they reversed them in this category of cases: of twenty-one appeals, five decisions were dictated by Supreme Court precedent, seven were reversed, and nine were affirmed. A second explanation for the court's handling of these cases might be that these cases reflect the judges' attempts to protect civil liberties. Again, if the judges' concerns were individual rights, it is difficult to square this with the almost equal number of affirmances and reversals. More importantly, formulating the issue in that way obscures the point that the essence of Fourth Amendment jurisprudence is drawing the line between the citizen's right of privacy and the government's ability to intrude on that zone of privacy. Thus, the act of protecting the civil liberties of the defendant necessitates establishing the reasonableness of the conduct of government agents. The question then becomes why the judges distinguished the protection of the obviously guilty defendants' civil liberties in *Miucki* from those of the other four cases in which a search could only be justified if the defendant had consented to it. For in each of the four the Seventh Circuit without much discussion or expression of doubt affirmed the finding of the district court that the consent had been voluntarily given by the defendant.[34] Only in *Miucki*, where there was some evidence that the agent had drawn his gun, did the court look behind the district court's finding and reverse the verdict. It was thus the unjustified use of force which the judges refused to sanction.

In order to understand why these judges reversed convictions and strongly condemned the perceived misconduct of the prohibition agents, it is necessary first to understand prohibition in its historical context. As historians such as David E. Kyvig and James Timberlake have argued, prohibition was a part of the Progressive era's regulatory agenda.[35] The Eighteenth Amendment passed with support from many of the same reform groups which formed other coalitions to secure passage of economic and political reform. These Progressives sought to expand the federal government's role in regulating American society. In addition to securing passage of the Eighteenth Amendment, they passed the Sixteenth Amendment authorizing an income tax, created the Federal Trade Commission and the Federal Reserve Board, and strengthened antitrust laws.

However, it is not solely the expanded scope of federal regulation that is significant; the form Congress chose is crucial. The reforms of the New Nationalism, New Freedom, and New Deal created executive agencies whose employees were responsible for investigation, adjudication, and rule making. Effective social and economic regulation depended on the proper working of Federal Trade Commission administrators and Internal Revenue Service agents. Robert Wiebe and others have shown that the creation of this government by bureaucratic agency was at the heart of Progressive reform.[36] Progressives thought that it was only through these bureaucratic structures, administered by men and women trained in the social and physical sciences, that efficiency could be achieved, suffering of the needy eliminated, and corruption removed from politics. The enactment and enforcement of prohibition followed this same pattern. Victory in securing enactment of the Eighteenth Amendment led to the creation of an agency that was under the direction of the commissioner of prohibition and within the Treasury Department. Each state had a federal prohibition director who was to recruit, train, and supervise federal enforcement agents within the state. Agents numbered 1,500 in the initial years and had doubled by 1930. This represented the largest nonmilitary federal law enforcement force, far exceeding the number of agents in the scandal-ridden but reorganized Federal Bureau of Investigation. Throughout the years of prohibition, congressional committees continually complained that agents were corrupt and inefficient and that enforcement was inadequate. Despite administrative and legislative efforts to reorganize the force, the public perception of the agents and their ineffectiveness was not altered.[37]

Congress placed the responsibility of overseeing the work of the newly created federal agencies in the lower federal courts. The federal judiciary was to decide the multitude of questions raised by interpretation of the new regulatory legislation and to hear challenges to and petitions for enforcement of administrative orders. The three categories of prohibition cases examined here represented the first large-scale group of these regulatory cases to come before the Seventh Circuit.

The importance of the agent misconduct cases derives from the fact that this category raised for the court the issues of its new responsibility and role. Questions involving statutory interpretation and the fairness of the trial process were standard issues for the court, whether the cases concerned bankruptcy, patent, or railroad accident cases. But supervising the conduct of government agents was a new responsibility. The lawlessness and irresponsibility of these prohibition agents challenged the integrity of the regulatory process itself, and the judges intervened and refused to sanction it. The opinions condemning the agent's behavior were all written by Judges Alschuler and Evans, who, as indicated earlier, had been Justice Department—not senatorial—selections and had been chosen for the bench because they shared the Wilsonian belief in agency regulation of a larger sphere of economic and social life. Essential to that regulatory process were trained agents in a well-ordered agency. Convictions based on improper agent conduct must be reversed.

Prohibition appeals first brought federal regulatory activity to the Seventh Circuit. These cases involved the court in supervising the work of the bureaucratic agency and its agents, who were charged with enforcing the Eighteenth Amendment. This supervisory role was new, and the court sought to exercise its responsibility by striking out at perceived cases of lawlessness by the federal agents. Although the Eighteenth Amendment was repealed by the Twenty-first Amendment in 1933 and the court ceased to receive prohibition appeals, its role as supervisor of the bureaucracy continued to expand. The federal regulatory bureaucracy expanded tremendously during the 1930s and 1940s as the myriad New Deal alphabet agencies were organized. In the 1960s and 1970s Congress again established federal agencies, such as the Occupational Health and Safety Administration and the Equal Employment Opportunity Commission. The constitutional developments following *Brown v. Board of Education* further increased this role of the courts of appeals as they became responsible for supervising state educational systems and, later, prisons, mental hospitals, and welfare bureaucracies. In superivsing regulatory agencies over the subsequent fifty years, the basic focus of the courts has continued to be controlling bureaucratic abuse. As U.S. Supreme Court interpretations brought questions of state, as well as federal, law enforcement before the lower federal courts, they had to decide issues involving the range of permissible police action in conducting searches, making arrests, interrogating suspects, extracting confessions, and conducting lineups. When welfare recipients or state prisoners challenged the practices of state agencies, they called upon the federal courts to restrain the ability of bureaucrats to act arbitrarily. Those subject to the actions of the agencies demanded rights to notice, a hearing, and adversarial safeguards, in order to limit claimed bureaucratic abuse. How the courts balanced the operational needs of agencies against the rights of citizens to be free of arbitrary government power is far too complex a story to be summarized here. The 110 Volstead Act appeals which the Seventh

Circuit decided between 1918 and 1933 formed an integral part of the first chapter of that story and foreshadowed the expanding role of those courts as major influences on public policy formulation in American society.

NOTES

1. Felix Frankfurter and James M. Landis, *The Business of the Supreme Court* (New York: Macmillan, 1928), pp. 56–192.

2. Information on the organization of the Seventh Circuit can be found in Rayman L. Solomon, *History of the Seventh Circuit: 1891–1941* (Chicago: Seventh Circuit, 1981), pp. 23–44, 137–54.

3. Ibid., pp. 45–70, 81–136.

4. Rayman L. Solomon, "The Politics of Appointment and the Federal Courts' Role in Regulating America: U.S. Courts of Appeals Judgeships from T.R. to F.D.R.," *American Bar Foundation Research Journal*, Spring 1984, pp. 285–343.

5. Solomon, *History of the Seventh Circuit*, pp. 118–19.

6. These statistics are taken from a workload study of the Seventh Circuit prepared for Solomon, *History of the Seventh Circuit*. The jurisdictional source was examined for all reported appeals decided between 1891 and 1945.

7. 4 F. 2d 688 (7th Cir.), *cert. denied* 267 U.S. 597 (1925).

8. 51 F. 2d 674 (7th Cir., 1934).

9. 50 F. 2d 345 (7th Cir.), *cert. denied* 284 U.S. 654 (1931).

10. *Fritzel v. U.S.*, 17 F. 2d 965, 966 (7th Cir., 1927).

11. *Lewinsohn v. U.S.*, 278 F. 421 (7th Cir., 1921), *cert. denied* 258 U.S. 630 (1922); *U.S. v. Pino*, 278 F. 479 (7th Cir., 1921); *McGovern v. U.S.*, 280 F. 73 (7th Cir.), *cert. denied* 259 U.S. 580 (1922); *Galligan v. U.S.*, 282 F. 606 (7th Cir., 1922).

12. *Capone v. U.S.*, 56 F. 2d 927 (7th Cir.), *cert. denied* 286 U.S. 553 (1932).

13. U.S., National Commission on Law Observance and Enforcement, *Progress Report on the Study of the Federal Courts* (Washington, D.C.: GPO, 1931), pp. 20–27.

14. For an excellent discussion of these rules, *see* Thomas Y. Davies, "Affirmed: A Study of Criminal Appeals and Decision-Making Norms in a California Court of Appeal," *American Bar Foundation Research Journal*, Summer 1982, pp. 591–606.

15. 54 F. 2d 919 (7th Cir., 1931).

16. 63 F. 2d 111 (7th Cir., 1933).

17. 25 F. 2d 865 (7th Cir., 1928).

18. 288 F. 843 (7th Cir., 1923).

19. 1 F. 2d 925 (7th Cir., 1924).

20. *Fritzel v. U.S.*, 17 F. 2d 965–68, (7th Cir., 1927).

21. 289 F. 47 (7th Cir., 1923).

22. See *Elkins v. U.S.*, 364 U.S. 206 (1960), which overturned the "silver platter" doctrine and held that illegally gathered evidence could not be used by federal authorities, even absent collusion with the state authorities. Yale Kamisar, "The Warren Court (Was It Really So Defense-Minded?), the Burger Court (Is It Really So Prosecution-Oriented?) and Police Investigatory Practices," in *The Burger Court: The Counter Revolution That Wasn't*, ed. Vincent Blasi (New Haven: Yale University Press, 1983), pp. 62–91, and n. 66, p. 277. Justice Frankfurter had used the "silver platter" imagery first in *Lustig v. U.S.*, 338 U.S. 74 (1949).

23. 232 U.S. 383 (1941); Wayne R. LaFave, *Search and Seizure: A Treatise on the Fourth Amendment* (St. Paul: West, 1978), 1: 7–9.

24. 62 F. 2d 656, 657 (7th Circ., 1932).

25. 273 U.S. 28 (1927).

26. The complexities and philosophical confusions of the entrapment defense are set forth in Louis M. Seidman, "The Supreme Court, Entrapment, and Our Criminal Justice Dilemma," *Supreme Court Review*, 1981, pp. 111–55.

27. *O'Brien v. U.S.*, 51 F. 2d 674, 677–78 (7th Cir., 1931).

28. *Pauik v. U.S.*, 4 F. 2d 250 (7th Cir., 1924).

29. *See*, for example, *Delahunt v. U.S.*, 5 F. 2d 1014 (7th Cir., 1925).

30. 267 U.S. 132 (1925); LaFave, *Search and Seizure*, 2: 509–15.

31. *Olmstead v. U.S.*, 227 U.S. 438 (1928); LaFave, *Search and Seizure*, 2: 223–24.

32. 289 F. 47 (7th Cir., 1923).

33. 51 F. 2d 674 (7th Cir., 1931).

34. *Wurm v. U.S.* 3 F. 2d 143 (7th Cir., 1924); *Flynn v. U.S.*, 50 F. 2d 1021 (7th Cir., 1931); *Hartzell v. U.S.*, 50 F. 2d 1021 (7th Cir., 1931); *Milyonico v. U.S.*, 53 F. 2d 937 (7th Cir., 1931), *cert. denied* 286 U.S. 551 (1932).

35. David E. Kyvig, *Repealing National Prohibition* (Chicago: University of Chicago Press, 1979), pp. 1–13; James H. Timberlake, *Prohibition and the Progressive Movement, 1900–1920* (Cambridge: Harvard University Press, 1963), pp. 152–84.

36. Robert H. Wiebe, *The Search for Order, 1877–1920* (New York: Hill and Wang, 1967), pp. 164–95.

37. U.S., National Commission on Law Observance and Enforcement, *Report on the Enforcement of the Prohibition Laws of the United States* (Washington: GPO, 1931), pp. 44–60.

7   CLEMENT E. VOSE

Repeal as a Political Achievement

The repeal of national prohibition in 1933 is a memorable political accomplishment when compared to other major amendment efforts that have had strong public backing but that, nevertheless, failed. The equal rights amendment fell short of ratification by three states in 1983, although the Gallup Poll reported 61 percent of the nation favored its adoption.[1] In March 1984 a constitutional amendment to permit prayer in public schools failed to receive the needed two-thirds vote in the U.S. Senate, although 73 percent of the public were said to favor it.[2] A constitutional amendment to balance the federal budget has been considered for years, but despite 75 percent public support, Congress has yet to propose it.[3] These three examples illustrate the difficulty of obtaining any amendment and underline the political competence of wets in repealing constitutionally imposed prohibition fifty years ago.

Repeal is an achievement that still awaits adequate political explanation. Studies of the Twenty-first Amendment inevitably focus on the constitutional amendment institution process set forth in Article V. Though recent failed amendment efforts abound, a group of little-known congressmen, law writers, and leaders of voluntary associations did succeed in adding the Twenty-first Amendment to the Constitution. The 1930s produced two explanations for this success: one insidious, the other benign. In one view, organized pressure groups expressing the self-interest of wealthy liquor merchants bought off the press and the politicians. In the other view, basic social changes occurring in the 1920s made the repeal of prohibition inevitable.[4] As late as 1965 these conflicting and evasive claims led Joseph Gusfield, a leading sociologist of the temperance movement, to state that "the repeal of the Eighteenth Amendment has never been subject to a scholarly analysis."[5]

Shortly after Gusfield wrote those words, I learned about the Voluntary Committee of Lawyers, Inc. (VCL), and its leaders, Joseph H. Choate, Jr., and Harrison Tweed. After talking with Tweed and acquiring and studying VCL papers, I ultimately concluded that this organization, by handling many of the tactical details in the ratification campaign and with due attention to the electorate, almost single-handedly won repeal.[6] In contrast to this heroic interpretation, political scientist Alan P. Grimes in 1978 searched out the key economic and political determinants behind repeal and identified as leading "objective factors" the Reapportionment Act of 1929, which would reduce rural power in the House of Representatives following the 1930 census; the advent of the Great Depression; and the shifts in public opinion expressed in the 1932 elections. Grimes focuses on roll-call votes and congressional leadership, neglecting the battle for ratification in the states.[7] These two studies were balanced and corrected in 1979 by historian David E. Kyvig's accomplished book *Repealing National Prohibition*. He shows that the repeal campaign was broad-based, led by the energetic Association Against the Prohibition Amendment, a bipartisan group of business and political figures. This group worked particularly within the Democratic party to influence public opinion and within Congress to convert this reservoir into effective legislative action. Kyvig sees convention ratification as a practical outflanking of the continuing rural prohibitionist power in state legislatures. He credits the Voluntary Committee of Lawyers and other organizations for a resourceful effort in gaining repeal. My own earlier study—together with those of Grimes and Kyvig, complete as they are when taken together—does not explore sufficiently the role of convention ratification in the condemnation of prohibition and adoption of the Twenty-first Amendment.

THE PROBLEM: NATIONAL PROHIBITION BY AMENDMENT

National prohibition of the manufacture, sale, transportation, and importation of intoxicating liquors did not come about through ordinary legislation, an executive order, or a ruling of the Supreme Court. On January 16, 1919, this policy became a part of the United States

Constitution and was to become effective one year later. The Eighteenth Amendment was proposed by Congress on December 18, 1917, passing the Senate by the required two-thirds vote by a margin of forty-seven to eight (85.45 percent) and having passed the House on December 17 by a vote of 282 to 128 (68.78 percent).[8] Ratification came on January 16, 1919, when the thirty-sixth of the forty-eight state legislatures approved the amendment. Ten additional states ratified the amendment early in 1919; New Jersey followed in 1922; only Rhode Island refused to ratify. Congress then confirmed the public's approval of temperance in voting for the Volstead Act over President Wilson's veto. Charges that the Eighteenth Amendment and the Volstead Act were unconstitutional were answered when the Supreme Court unanimously approved both in June 1920.[10] David Kyvig aptly expressed the hopelessness of the minority opposed to national prohibition when he wrote:

The Eighteenth Amendment appeared as impregnable as a medieval stone fortress to a band of ill-equipped foot soldiers, and complaining about its constitutional deficiencies seemed about as effective as kicking the base of the fortress wall. Initial efforts to breach the walls or circumvent the fortress proved equally futile. After a half dozen years of siege, the fortress remained unshaken, while the attackers found themselves limp from exertion, disheartened by their lack of progress, and searching for new tactics.[11]

Miraculously, the foundations of this fortress appeared to move enough so that as the 1930s began, there was reason to believe that a substantial majority of the American public favored repeal.[12] How could opponents of prohibition, even in a favorable context, achieve change through the constitutional amendment institution?

Although still in its infancy during prohibition, public opinion polling predicted and helped pave the way for repeal. Wet lawyers, regarding themselves as opinion leaders, took straw polls in New York, Boston, Chicago, and Philadelphia, among other cities, to advertise their view that national prohibition—as sumptuary legislation—had no place in the United States Constitution.[13] At the same time, samplings of a broader public showed marked growth of antiprohibition sentiment from 1922 to 1930 and 1932.[14] A coalition of business and professional leaders was joining with the new generation of ethnics to provide the political basis for repeal.[15]

Measuring public opinion is one skill; mobilizing it is another; managing the constitutional amendment institution is yet another.[16]This political task occurred as an interlocking set of events bringing the Twenty-first Amendment to fruition. These events were controlled not by a single mind but by wet leaders playing different roles—groping at times, planning precisely at others—for the repeal of national prohibition.

THE SOLUTION: MOLDING AN OVERLOOKED MODE OF AMENDMENT

Opponents of national prohibition complained that legislative ratification of the Eighteenth Amendment was illegitimate. Most legislatures acting on prohibition were elected in 1916, prior to its proposal to the states. Voters thus had not had this issue before them because local issues and personalities had dominated those elections. Pointing to this, critics of the Eighteenth Amendment argued that such ratification of sumptuary legislation was inherently unconstitutional. An incipient notion in 1919, the moral superiority of convention ratification gradually took hold during the next decade. Proponents of conventions then relied on Article V, the amending clause of the Constitution, to argue the appropriateness of Congress's choosing this mode of ratification when ready to propose the abandonment of prohibition. These advocates pointed to the text of Article V:

The Congress, whenever two thirds of both Houses shall deem it necessary, shall propose Amendments to this Constitution or, on the Application of the Legislatures of two thirds of the several States, shall call a Convention for proposing Amendments, which, in either Case, shall be valid to all Intents and Purposes, as part of this Constitution, when ratified by the Legislatures of three fourths of the several States, or by Conventions in three fourths thereof, as the one or the other Mode of Ratification may be proposed by the Congress. . . .
[17]

Article V affords Congress a choice between legislative and convention ratification but provides no guidance, let alone criteria, for choosing one mode over the other. Angered by prohibition, in 1919 some lawyers attacked legislative ratification for misrepresenting ''the people.'' Their critique established a presumption against legislative ratification for repeal. State convention delegates, if elected directly on a statewide ballot, would offset the rural bias of prohibition inherent in the election of legislators from localities. Debate between wets and drys became a dispute over electorial systems, wets favoring statewide balloting for delegates as against drys, who continued to champion legislative ratification of constitutional amendments. Who "the people" are and how their opinion is expressed becomes part of the constitutional and political debate.

The concept that a repeal amendment should be ratified by state conventions rather than by legislatures arose not only from those who objected to prohibition but also for those who opposed suffrage for blacks and women as well as the income tax. The arguments, which began over policy and then moved to procedures, stemmed from a special view of the nature of constitutional government. In 1919 a leading conservative, states-rights Democrat William L. Marbury of Baltimore, wrote in the *Harvard Law Review* that both the prohibition and women's suffrage amendments, by being ratified by legislatures, violated the people's right to rule.

If the framers of the Constitution had been told that the time would ever come in the United States when a comparatively small but highly organized and determined minority could cause the legislatures of numbers of states to ratify amendments to the Constitution of the United States contrary to the well-known sentiments and wishes of a vast majority of the people of those states, recently manifested at the polls, the suggestion would probably have been received with absolute incredulity; and if the further suggestion had been made that the ratification of amendments could be secured in that the way, which would strip the people of the states of an important part of their legislative powers, such as the right to determine who should be qualified to vote for state officers, or the right to regulate their own habits in regard to eating and drinking, that incredulity would have been still greater. Nevertheless, the American people are now witnessing exactly such a spectacle.[18]

In a statewide referendum, Massachusetts voters had recently opposed women's suffrage, yet their legislature ratified the federal women's suffrage amendment. To Marbury, the legislators thereby voted "contrary to the wishes of their constituents." He believed legislative ratification of an amendment was questionable and asked, "Is there any limit to the right of power to amend the Constitution, which was conferred upon the legislatures of three-fourths of the states, by the people of the United States in Article Five of the Constitution?"[19]

Often, to raise a question is to answer it. In his article Marbury controlled his rage at the income tax, prohibition, and women's suffrage amendments, urging his readers merely to consider the possibility of an amendment's being unconstitutional. He pointed to Chief Justice Marshall's distinction between the "people" of a state and the "government" of a state, quoting this passage from *McCulloch v. Maryland* on the formation of the Constitution:

The Convention which framed the Constitution was indeed elected by the State legislatures. But the instrument, when it came from their hands, was a mere proposal, without obligation, or pretensions to it. It was reported to the then existing Congress of the United States, with a request that it might "be submitted to a Convention of Delegates, chosen in each State by the people thereof, under the recommendation of its Legislature, for their assent and ratification." This mode of proceeding was adopted; and by the Convention, by Congress, and by the State Legislatures, the instrument was submitted to the *people*. They acted upon it in the only manner in which they can act safely, effectively, and wisely, on such a subject, by assembling in Convention.[20]

To summarize, Marbury believed the Constitution of 1787 is legitimate because its ratification by state conventions expressed the true views of "the people." Further, the nature of the Constitution implies it cannot be amended to regulate individual habits, as this is within the police power of each state and cannot lodge with the national government. It follows that fundamental changes in the Constitution cannot be made by amendments ratified by state legislatures as these institutions do not express the will of "the people." Legislative ratification is appropriate only for amendments dealing with government structure and procedure. For a substantive policy amendment such as prohibition, ratification by state conventions is needed.

Marbury's views were not his alone. They had been published in a variety of law review articles, pamphlets, and books by a host of lawyers who questioned the constitutionality of several amendments in the first third of the century. Other conservatives questioned the validity of the Fifteenth; later, the Nineteenth Amendment was opposed not merely on political or policy grounds but on grounds of unconstitutionality.[21] Similar attacks on the Eighteenth Amendment appeared soon after the adoption of prohibition, reaching a high point in March 1930 in the writings of Selden Bacon, who expressed the views of a study committee of the New York County Lawyers Association. While his style differed from Marbury's, he argued unequivocally that where individual rights were concerned, as they were in the Eighteenth Amendment, both the Ninth and the Tenth Amendments limited the power to amend as expressed in Article V. Even though the limiting language of Amendments Nine and Ten is quite general, Bacon insisted that in light of them, a policy amendment required state convention ratification.[22]

The cohort of lawyers opposed to Amendments Fifteen through Nineteen tried to convince the Supreme Court that their views were correct. Although they failed, the string of cases questioning the validity of amendments is as long as it is little known. In 1915 Marbury and associates from Baltimore asserted in *Myers v. Anderson* that a Maryland "grandfather clause" was valid because the Fifteenth Amendment protecting the vote from state denial "on account of race, color, or previous condition of servitude" was invalid.[23] In 1920, in a set of seven cases grouped together in argument and decision as the *National Prohibition Cases*, such lawyers as William D. Guthrie, William Marshall Bullitt, Herbert A. Rice, and Levy Mayer presented briefs against the validity of the Eighteenth Amendment.[24] While Marbury declined to participate in the *Prohibition Cases*, he did pursue in the Supreme Court, with Thomas F. Cadwalader, also a Baltimore attorney, argument against the constitutionality of the Nineteenth Amendment in the case of *Leser v. Garnett*. In February 1922 the Supreme Court decided against them.[25]

Finally in 1930, in response to a brief by Selden Bacon, Daniel F. Cohalon, and Julius Henry Cohen connected with the case of *Sprague v. United States*, U.S. District Judge William Clark, sitting in Newark, New Jersey, ruled that the Eighteenth Amendment was unconstitutional.[26] News of this remarkable decision appeared as a four-column headline on page one of the *New York Times* on December 17, 1930: "FEDERAL JUDGE HOLDS PROHIBITION VOID, FINDS METHOD OF ITS ADOPTION ILLEGAL: RULING IN NEW JERSEY STIRS WASHINGTON."[27] Treating this as a lead story, the *Times* printed Judge Clark's entire opinion. This opinion reciting the history of the Eighteenth Amendment, takes up twenty pages in the *Federal Reporter* and is a veritable book of quotations of the writings of political theorists. Clark, echoing Marbury, fulminated against the evils of legislative ratification. This is all wonderfully simplified by the squib written by the clerk at the beginning of the opinion, as follows: "Eighteenth Amendment *held* invalid because of adoption by means of ratification by state legislatures rather than constitutional conventions.''[28] The Department of Justice immediately appealed Judge Clark's order, which quashed a federal indictment for bootlegging. *United States v. Sprague* was argued in Washington on January 21, 1930. There were four *amici curiae* briefs supporting Selden Bacon and Julius Henry Cohen, attorneys for Sprague. The lawyers on these briefs included Eliot Tuckerman, Jeremiah M. Evarts, Henry W. Jessup, and Austen G. Fox, prominent opponents of the prohibition amendment. Their briefs insisted that under the American theory of government, only the people, acting through state conventions, could endorse the kind of power attempted to be delegated in the Eighteenth Amendment. They based their case on the Tenth Amendment's provision that ''the powers not delegated to the national government are reserved to the states or to the people.'' They argued that the Eighteenth Amendment assigned those powers to the national government and that, accordingly, the Eighteenth Amendment was null and void.[29]

The Supreme Court reversed Judge Clark in the *Sprague* case. Justice Owen J. Roberts's opinion for the Court excoriated Judge Clark for departing from sound constitutional analysis and ''resorting to 'political science,' and 'political thought' of the times, and a 'scientific approach to the problem of government.' ''[30] Quoting Article V, Roberts repeated its simple words that a constitutional amendment may be referred either to state legislatures or state conventions ''as one or the other mode of ratification may be proposed by the Congress.'' The two modes were equally valid. The Court announced its decision in *United States v. Sprague* on February 24, 1931. Justice Roberts clearly rejected the claim that legislative ratification was tainted. The litigation was over. However, other thoughts and actions kept the idea of convention ratification alive.

The so-called back-to-the-people amendment, introduced in Congress in early 1921, emerged from a conviction that convention rather than legislative ratification was more appropriate to the nature of the American constitutional system. Senator James W. Wadsworth, Jr., Republican of New York, and Representative Finis J. Garrett, Democrat of Tennessee, sponsored the amendment. Thomas F. Cadwalader credited conservatives Charles S. Fairchild, Waldo G. Morse, and Everett Wheeler with inspiring the amendment, while the *Woman Patriot*, a publication of opponents to the Nineteenth Amendment, praised it for abolishing ''the power of minority lobbies to amend the supreme law of the land.''[31]

The Wadsworth-Garrett back-to-the-people plan proposed three changes in Article V with respect to legislative ratification. First, members of at least one house of each legislature acting on a proposed amendment would be required to have been elected after its proposal. Second, any state could require legislative ratification to be confirmed by a referendum. Third, any state voting to ratify an amendment could subsequently reject it up to the point where three-fourths of the states had ratified it. Thus, the Wadsworth-Garrett idea structured legislative ratification to lend influence to an election, a referendum, or a change of heart among legislators to give greater voice to "the people." It retained the option of ratification by state conventions, underlining a preference for this method by providing that the Wadsworth-Garrett amendment itself be referred to "conventions of delegates in each state chosen by the people thereof." [32]

A symbol of the interest in state convention ratification, the back-to-the-people amendment quietly expired. A Senate judiciary subcommittee reported on it favorably in 1924, but neither the whole committee nor its counterpart in the House held hearings. [33] Failures both, the Wadsworth-Garrett amendment in Congress and Judge Clark's *Sprague* opinion in the courts lent credence to arguments for the superiority of convention over legislative ratification of constitutional amendments.

In 1932 political scientist William B. Munro noted that direct legislation, while a progressive invention in the United States, had been widely exploited by American conservatives so that referenda in the form of the election of ratifying convention delegates was neither new nor unique. Munro's words on the subject are an unintended description of how advocates of repeal acted:

The adoption of the initiative and referendum was urged a quarter of a century ago by the progressive elements, who took for granted that if the people were allowed to legislate directly they would give their assent to progressive measures. On this basis the conservatives fought the movement at its early stages. . . . But direct legislation has not proved to be revolutionary; on the contrary, it has been at least of equal value as a bulwark of conservatism. [34]

As practical conservatives, wet activists were opportunists, not ideologues, in choosing electoral modes to gain repeal. A wet businessman such as Pierre S. du Pont, a wet politician such as Wadsworth, a wet lawyer such as Choate, and even a wet judge such as Clark gladly embraced direct legislation to achieve their ends, thereby illustrating Munro's point. Congress had proposed all amendments since 1789 to legislatures for ratification. For repeal, this pattern was broken. I once believed that voluntary associations—specially the Association Against the Prohibition Amendment, which dated from 1918, and the Voluntary Committee of Lawyers, Inc., formed in late 1928— had seized upon the unused convention mode and had passed it along to friendly members of Congress. Recent reexamination of the papers of these organizations, and those of Pierre S. du Pont and John J. Raskob of the AAPA, however, does not support this assumption.[35] A straight chronology of the convention ratification idea of repeal reveals something of a muddle, with the AAPA and VCL joining wholeheartedly to support this approach only when the bandwagon was well underway.

On June 30, 1926, U.S. Senator Edward I. Edwards, serving as a one-term Democrat from New Jersey, introduced a joint resolution providing that repeal of the Eighteenth Amendment would become valid "when ratified by conventions in three-fourths of the several states."[36] John J. Cochran, a Democratic representative from Missouri, did the same in the House. The joint resolutions were referred to Senate and House judiciary committees, which failed to act.[37] Thus, Edwards and Cochran have the distinction of first introducing in Congress the idea of repeal by convention ratification. Nearly every Congress thereafter had similar measures introduced, but the earliest hearings came in February 1930 before the House Committee on the Juciciary.[38]

The *New York Times* for these years contains a small number of references to repeal among hosts of items about prohibition generally. There is a slight increase in 1930 and 1931, but the preponderance of entries are contradictory, in that individuals variously "advocated," "demanded," "favored," "opposed," "predicted," "held inevitable," or "forecast" that there would never be repeal of prohibition. However, in 1930 Clarence Darrow predicted repeal within four years, while Henry Curran of the Assoication Against the Prohibition Amendment said it would take five.[39]

In his 1979 book, *Repealing National Prohibition*, David Kyvig sees the movement for repeal quickening in favor of convention ratification after Judge Clark's ruling in *Sprague*. Judge Clark had written of his hope that his opinion "will at least have the effect of focusing the country's thought upon the neglected method of considering constitutional amendments in conventions."[40] Two weeks after Clark ruled in

1930, Selden Bacon wrote the AAPA leader William Stayton that Clark "has so widely advertised the subject that almost any lawyer now who can get a copy of it will really study our brief."[41]

On January 30, 1931, the Wickersham National Commission on Law Observance and Enforcement, appointed by President Herbert Hoover, filed a final report which included criticism of legislative ratification of the Eighteenth Amendment as part of the problem of enforcement on grounds that it was not "truly representative of all elements of the community."[42] Three members of the commission, including Chairman George Wickersham, went from criticism to remedy, recommending that a repeal amendment be submitted by Congress to popularly elected state conventions. The report itself did not oppose prohibition altogether, but there were sufficient questions raised about the difficulties of its enforcement to permit champions of repeal to call the commission an ally.

Nearly everything positive for repeal came together in 1932, when a constellation of wet organizations joined forces in the United Repeal Council, with Pierre S. du Pont at its head. AAPA continued as the single most important organization in a coalition that included the Women's Organization for National Prohibition Reform, the Voluntary Committee of Lawyers, and the Crusaders. Each of these organizations, as well as smaller ones, included both Republicans and Democrats so that each could appeal to the national party conventions in June 1932 to endorse their position. In a fascinating political exercise, the leaders in the repeal movement argued that by submitting an amendment to conventions, Congress would remove the subject from "politics." W. W. Atterbury, president of the Pennsylvania Railroad, stated this in a January 1932 letter to du Pont:

I still believe that the immediate solution of this question is to get both parties to adopt a plank which will submit the entire matter to a series of conventions by the individual states. This would get the question out of politics and the people would be given an opportunity to decide for themselves what they want.[43]

What a splendid way to avoid politics!

On June 16, 1932, the Republican National Convention approved a perfectly compromised platform plank by opposing repeal while endorsing conventions as the ratifying mode should an amendment be proposed. While not deserting the drys, Republicans made hard-core wets jubilant. Each side wanted more, of course, but wet tacticians like William Stayton of the Association Against the Prohibition Amendment and Joseph H. Choate of the Voluntary Committee of Lawyers gained what they wanted most. The wording came verbatim from Judge Clark's opinion in the *Sprague* case, which stated that conventions in each state should be called to ratify a repeal amendment and that these conventions should be "truly representative." Meanwhile, rural members of Congress were outvoted on the Reapportionment Act of 1929.[44] Now, after each decennial census, the president would submit to Congress a plan prepared by the Bureau of the Census, to become law in fifteen days. The phrase "truly representative" sprang, it should be remembered, from wets who believed the Eighteenth Amendment's ratification by legislatures to have been illegitimate. Mere conventions were not enough compared to the Republican performance. It was heartening, but not striking, news that on July 1, 1933, the Democratic National Convention, which nominated Franklin D. Roosevelt, backed repeal and also intoned the words "truly representative conventions."[45]

In Kyvig's analysis the November 1932 election demonstrated dramatically that public opinion had become markedly wet. Referenda results in eleven states favored easing prohibition by margins of 60, 70, and even 80 percent. Election of the Seventy-third Congress saw many drys defeated, including such leaders as Senator Reed Smoot of Utah. Though not all Democrats were wet, more were than not, and Democrats held majorities of 310 to 117 (72.59 percent) in the House and 60 to 35 (63.15 percent) in the Senate. The wet-dry lineup looked to be 343 to 84 (80.32 percent) in the House, 61 to 35 (63.45 percent) in the Senate. "Whatever part advocacy of repeal actually contributed to the Democratic landslide," Kyvig observes, "politicians and other contemporary observers gave it major credit for the outcome."[46]

Because the Twentieth Amendment, which modernized terms of Congress, was not yet in effect, those elected in 1932 would not meet for thirteen months, unless called into special session. However, public opinion, as revealed by the November elections, showed its force at the opening of the December 1932 meeting of the old Seventy-second Congress, when a constitutional amendment offered by Representatives Henry T. Rainey and John Nance Garner narrowly missed adoption.[47] The signals (in Janury 1932, from the Wickersham Commission; in June, from the party conventions; in November, from the general election; and in December, from the lame-duck Congress) encouraged the repeal pressure groups and their lawyers to intensify efforts as legislatures in forty states convened in January 1933.

To be ready should Congress propose a repeal amendment to conventions in the states, and, in fact, to insist that Congress do so, Choate and others in the Voluntary Committee of Lawyers raced to set up convention machinery as early in 1933 as possible. When the Maryland legislature met on January 4, for example, Arthur W. Machen, Jr., and William L. Marbury had a bill ready to provide "for the calling of a convention by the Governor of Maryland for the purpose of acting upon any proposed amendment to the Constitution which might be proposed by Congress."[48] When a Milwaukee attorney urged prompt action in every state, but in Wisconsin favored "one delegate from every assembly district,"[49] Choate was wary. He felt that the first bills to be enacted "will doubtless be taken as a model by other legislatures." Choate continued in this vein:

It is therefore highly important that this first bill be such as will produce a real expression of public opinion in doubtful states. For that reason, we rather fear the suggestion in your letter that the convention for Wisconsin be chosen by districts like the legislatures. This will be perfectly safe in a state certain to be wet, but would be exceedingly dangerous in some of the states which still have dry legislatures. We therefore suggest that the bill adopt the analogy of the presidential electors and provide for the election of delegates-at-large in the same manner as the electors from the state are chosen. This, like your proposition, adopts a normal state method and should therefore not excite much opposition.[50]

Discussion continued over whether Congress should adopt legislation setting up ratifying conventions in each state, as A. Mitchell Palmer urged, or whether it lacked the constitutional authority to do so, as James A. Beck argued in opposition.[51] Continually sounding out other opinions, Choate sent copies of both views to 150 VCL members and, by the end of January, had fifty replies which he found "pretty unsatisfactory." The vote stood at thirty for Palmer and twenty for Beck, which meant, in Choate's opinion, "that forty percent of our membership is incapable of letting new ideas overcome an original preconception."[52] If Congress wouldn't prescribe how conventions should be elected, then the Voluntary Committee of Lawyers would do so. If their own members believed Congress lacked power to dictate how conventions should work, then Choate would see that the VCL itself would at least prescribe guidelines. Choate conferred with his colleagues and acted quickly.

On January 30 Choate telegraphed and wrote to a VCL member in each of the states in which the legislature was then meeting to urge prompt action. He warned that if Congress left arrangements to the states, no convention in any state could come into existence without the action of its legislature.[53] The VCL executive committee recommended that each legislature include an escape clause in case of a subsequent enactment by Congress. The telegram asked, "Won't you initiate such enactment in your state?" adding by letter what was becoming a standard line about the method of election:

We think that in order to insure a real expression of public opinion the conventions wherever possible should be elected not by districts but at-large. The bills might adopt the analogy of the College of Electors and provide that the members of the State's convention be chosen in the same manner as the State's Presidential Electors.[54]

Professor Noel T. Dowling of Columbia Law School led a committee in drafting a model bill, which the VCL executive committee endorsed and sent on to the states. On January 31 Dowling first sent Choate a bill "drawn specifically to fit in with the New Jersey law."[55] A colleague, Joseph P. Chamberlain, joined with Dowling in the Columbia Legislative Drafting Fund. In addition, for the New Jersey bill at least, two others engaged in the drafting: State Senator Emerson L. Richards and Federal Judge William Clark. Nothing was said of Clark's conflict of interest as a federal judge drafting legislation. Another provocative aspect of drafting the model occurs in Dowling's published report of the timing:

There has been a striking illustration of how legislative development of the law may be advanced by private organizations. Shortly after Congress proposed the amendment, draft bills to provide for conventions were submitted for legislative consideration by the Voluntary Committee of Lawyers, chiefly through the efforts of Joseph H. Choate, Jr. These bills had an immediate and substantial effect upon a large part of the legislation that followed.[56]

But evidence abounds that Dowling is incorrect; Congress did not propose and thus provoke state action. The truth is the opposite. First came bills in the Maryland and Wisconsin legislatures, inducing panic among repeal advocates to get control. Then came the New Jersey repeal bill drafted by Dowling, Chamberlain, Richards, and Clark. Activity in numerous states followed, with the debate coming back to Choate and Dowling to influence the shape of more polished model bills. Again, Dowling is clearly wrong in reporting that all this activity, which he calls "a veritable 'race to ratify,' " was set off "by the sudden and unexpected action of Congress in adopting the resolution."[57] If anything, the stampede for repeal was from the states to Congress, not the other way around.

To know how legislation unfolds, as against an overly neat portrayal by an actor in the process, such as Dowling, is to begin to penetrate the mystery of the truth as against the mystification of the fanciful. Evidence contradicting Dowling's account is most cogently displayed in a report on the VCL Executive Committee, prepared by Choate:

Before the middle of February and more than a week before the action of Congress, the Committee's draft bills, together with a printed memorandum explaining the difficulties likely to be met and the reasons for the several provisions of the bills, were in the hands of the Committee's State representatives. With the assistance of the Association Against the Prohibition Amendment, the Crusaders, and the American Hotel Association, they were also placed before those interested in a position to be influential, in most of the states. Before February 20th, 1933, when Congress unexpectedly submitted the repealing Amendment, one State had completed convention legislation and twenty-eight had statutes pending or in preparation.[58]

The behavior of many politicians and the public in the debates and votes on repeal showed gradations in sentiment likely to be concealed by labeling positions as dry or wet. Some abstainers did not believe their preference should be inflicted upon others. As the prospect of repeal came closer to realization, wets moderated their opposition to prohibition by working to establish government regulation of alcoholic beverages. The idea of submitting repeal to the people appealed particularly to the uncommitted lawmakers who preferred a popular election on an issue so that they could avoid having to vote in Congress on its merits. Members of Congress performed the same favor for state legislators as well, by allowing them to set up conventions and at the same time relieving them of having to vote on the merits. Even a prominent dry could be righteous over voting in Congress to propose repeal to the voting public for the election of convention delegates. They were saying, in effect, that they didn't care how the issue was settled as long as *they* did not have to settle it. Thus, in the U.S. Senate, thirteen members who voted in 1918 to propose prohibition to legislatures voted in 1933 to propose repeal to conventions.[59] The important role of drys and moderates is exemplified by Senate majority leader Joseph T. Robinson of Arkansas, who personally was dry but was active in bringing the repeal amendment to a vote in the Senate. Hardcore wets and drys made this middle-of-the-road position difficult, but the advocates of convention ratification had made it easier for them both, by making the action a vote in favor of letting the people speak and by working toward a licensing system and local option that would bring back alcohol in moderate doses.

Repeal leaders in the voluntary organizations and in Congress kept resisting the submission of an amendment to legislatures, while pushing for submission to conventions. Their breakthrough came on February 16, 1933, when they halted an amendment introduced by Senator John J. Blaine of Wisconsin that provided for legislative ratification. Senator Robinson led the Senate in amending the Blaine resolution, 45 to 15 (75.00 percent), to substitute convention ratification. The new resolution then was adopted by a vote of 63 to 23 (73.26 percent), easily passing the two-thirds hurdle. The House battle was much longer and more public. The first roll-call vote on repeal by legislative ratification had come in March 1932 on a discharge petition of the Beck-Linthicum resolution, which gained 227, with 187 against (54.83 percent). Then, the House voted on December 5, 1932, in favor of the Rainey-Garner resolution, 272 to 144 (65.38 percent). On February 20, 1933, following the action of the Senate, the House approved of submitting repeal to state conventions by a vote of 289 to 121 (70.49 percent).[60]

The reason Congress did not act on Fiorello H. LaGuardia's bill to provide for state conventions was because by February 20 twenty-nine states already were in the process of legislating to establish conventions. A dozen more were doing so by the end of the month.[61] This development eclipsed a need for congressional action. Typically enough, some members of Congress argued it would be unconstitutional for them

to act, while others disagreed. A debate of sorts also showed a division over whether enactment of the LaGuardia bill would irritate the states and make them oppose repeal on the principled, if peevish, ground that Congress could not tell the states what to do. The upshot remains that either the legislatures or Congress can specify the structure of conventions to act on ratifying amendments to the federal Constitution.[62] Circumstances in 1933 saw the initiative taken in a sufficient number of states.

Joseph H. Choate, Jr., and his Voluntary Committee of Lawyers carried the day, preempting any need for congressional action, by first placing a model bill for at-large elections in the hands of every governor and then coming up with a ''modified'' model bill showing how this could be softened by having some delegates elected by districts. Forty-three states eventually legislated on conventions, thirty-nine within four months of the submission of the repeal amendment. Kyvig provides us with a dependable summary of Choate's importance:

Twelve states followed the model bill exactly, at least eight others used it with minor modifications, several more adapted portions, and many of the rest incorporated its ideas. Twenty-five states chose their convention delegates at large, fourteen selected them by district, and four combined the methods. In the absence of congressional direction, the VCL measure provided guidelines for states, although practically every convention had its own peculiar feature.[63]

Contemporary commentaries on referendums depict more clearly the various traits of state elections of ratifying convention delegates. Beginning in April 1933, these elections came up nearly every week. Conventions followed elections by one to four months. The general ticket system binding delegates meant that these elections precisely forecast later convention action. By November, when thirty-seven states had elected delegates, the aggregate vote cast stood at 21 million, with 15 million favoring repeal, a vote in favor of 72.9 percent.[64] This outcome testifies to the accuracy of the straw polls of the previous year.

Traits of the state elections of ratifying convention delegates are best seen in terms of contemporary depictions of referendums, one of the expressions of the Progressive movement. Between 1898 and 1932 twenty-three states provided for the enactment of ordinary legislation by referenda. Professor William B. Munro, a contemporary student of referenda, concluded that direct legislation has proved to be lawmaking by a minority. On the average, not more than 80 percent of those registered vote on election day, and the proportion is usually much smaller. . . . Hence, measures are sometimes adopted or defeated at the polls by only 25 or 30 percent of the whole electorate.[65]

His observation proved consistent with elections for the state conventions on repeal. Total turnout in Delaware, for instance, in the presidential election of 1932 reached 101,000, but in the convention delegate election on May 27, 1933, only 58,000 cast ballots, with 45,000 for the repeal amendment. But minorities settle most American elections. Turnout in modern congressional elections, for example, has been about 35 percent. Voting in other states conformed to this pattern. While repeal won overwhelmingly in all but one state that voted, there was only one state to spare above the necessary thirty-six.

The repeal amendment gained its thirty-sixth state convention vote on December 5, 1933, with Acting Secretary of State William Phillips certifying ratification of the new Twenty-first Amendment at 5:32 P.M., eastern standard time. As a token measure, President Franklin D. Roosevelt proclaimed repeal the same day.[66] The conventions themselves had been *pro forma* but the notion of direct legislation that lay behind them explains their success.

A SUCCESSFUL AMENDMENT MODEL

Was convention ratification crucial to the repeal amendment? Would legislatures also have voted to ratify had Congress entrusted them with the choice? Answering these questions calls first for a summary of how close the results were: thirty-six states were needed and only thirty-eight convened conventions. In 1933 thirty-seven states—only one more than the required thirty-six—ratified the Twenty-first Amendment. The state of Maine's convention was just one day late, coming on December 6, 1933. Montana added to this total with a convention the following summer, on August 6, 1934. Among these thirty-eight, only Tennessee had a close election, with barely 51 percent favoring repeal. Alabama and Arkansas each voted 59 percent wet, all other states were above 60, and some were higher than 70 percent. Stumbling in two states would have held up repeal until August 1934, though no longer, because Nebraska, Oklahoma, and South Dakota judged that authorizing conventions would be redundant and so called no elections.

Repeal was blocked flatly in seven states. The legislatures of Georgia, Kansas, Louisiana, Mississippi, and North Dakota refused to enact a convention law, so none could be held. North Carolina also declined through a statewide referendum to establish a convention. South Carolina's dry candidates won in that state's election for delegates to a convention. Antipathy to repeal matches the continuation of state prohibition. As of 1936, eight states were virtually dry: Alabama, Georgia, Kansas, Mississippi, North Carolina, North Dakota, Oklahoma, and Tennessee. Only three, Kansas, Mississippi, and Oklahoma, remained dry in 1940. Thus, it seems certain that repeal would have come in the 1930s if left to legislative ratification, but not nearly as soon.

Convention ratification, then, made a difference for it speeded the repeal of prohibition and also legitimated it. But the choice of this mode of ratification was not a simple, cynical, short-range tactic, as I once thought. The choice cannot be understood in terms of the year 1933 alone because the seeds of this choice were sown in 1918 and 1919 by referral to, and adoption in, the 1919 legislatures of the Eighteenth Amendment. Prohibition's critics, through books, articles, and briefs in court cases, condemned legislative ratification of constitutional amendments as unconnected with people's sentiments on the issue. Constitutional change is special, and advocates of repeal invoked the norm of electoral responsiveness in order to legitimate that change. This position had been thoroughly aired through the 1920s in the writings of Marbury, Jessup, Bacon, and others, by the oratory of Senator Wadsworth and his back-to-the-people amendment idea, and by Judge Clark's opinion in the *Sprague* case. Moreover, from 1926 onward, bills to repeal the Eighteenth commonly specified that the amendment be ratified by conventions, not legislatures. The pressure groups and politicians ran with this idea and put it across. The code words "truly representative conventions" turned into a bipartisan chorus that led inexorably to referendum-like elections on repeal. Finally, when Congress officially proposed a repeal amendment in February 1933 and required convention approval, its accomplishment seemed relatively natural and swift. It could not have happened without the intellectual cushion of more than a decade of touting convention ratification as a fitting and proper means of amending the Constitution. Thus, it was not a quick fix, although formal ratification of the Twenty-first Amendment was uncommonly swift.

Somewhat incongruously, the conservative champions spoke in the idiom of the Progressives who, in 1913, gained the Seventeenth Amendment requiring election of U.S. senators by direct popular vote rather than by state legislatures. There is no evidence of cynicism among these conservatives. They appear merely to have been resourceful in their earnest pleas for convention ratification. They argued that the referendum—a centerpiece of direct democracy—should be linked to conventions to repeal prohibition. Ironically, Progressives generally had favored national prohibition.[67] Thus, in gaining repeal through ratifying conventions, conservatives, wets, and legal experts advocated a procedure originally fashioned by their opponents. The politicians in 1933 could not have accomplished repeal if thinking lawyers had not already built up convention ratification as an appealing mode of constitutional change.

These leaders found in Article V an overlooked mode of amendment and defined convention ratification in terms favorable to their cause. The Twenty-first Amendment is an instance of political achievement, a rare exception in a broader pattern of failed constitutional amendment efforts. Advocates of amendments today might learn much from how wets, against inseparable odds, repealed prohibition.

NOTES

Following the Eleutherian Mills symposium of April 1983, I embarked on further research on convention ratification of the amendment repealing national prohibition, including an examination of the papers of Pierre du Pont in the Eleutherian Mills Historical Library. My ideas and drafts have gained much from discussion with and/or critiques from Richard W. Boyd, John G. Grumm, Gertrude Reif Hughes, Russell D. Murphy, and Hubert J. O'Gorman.

1. *Gallup Report* 206 (November 1982): 3. For fuller discussion, *see* Janet K. Boles, *The Politics of The Equal Rights Amendment: Conflict and the Decision Process* (New York: Longman, 1979).

2. On the Senate vote, *see New York Times*, March 21, 1984, p. 1, which states that "polls showed that 80 percent of the American people supported the measure." The lower figure is in *Gallup Report* 206 (November 1982): 14. Differences on such questions are explained in John M. Benson, "The Polls: A Rebirth of Religion?" *Public Opinion Quarterly* 45 (Winter 1981): 576–85.

3. *Gallup Report* 206 (November 1982): 1.

4. David E. Kyvig discusses early accounts in his *Repealing National Prohibition* (Chicago: University of Chicago Press, 1979), xiii–iv. Two books established the malignant-forces theory: Fletcher Dobyns, *The Amazing Story*

of Repeal: An Exposé of the Power of Propaganda (Chicago: Willett, Clark, 1940), and Ernest R. Gordon, *The Wrecking of the Eighteenth Amendment* (Francestown, N.H.: Alcohol Information Press, 1943). Kyvig found the more benign view best expressed in Richard Hofstadter, *The Age of Reform: From Bryan to F.D.R.* (New York: Knopf, 1955), pp. 289–90, and Norman H. Clark, *Deliver Us from Evil: An Interpretation of American Prohibition* (New York: W. W. Norton, 1976).

5. Joseph R. Gusfield, *Symbolic Crusade: Status Politics and the American Temperance Movement* (Urbana: University of Illinois Press, 1963), p. 126.

6. Clement E. Vose, *Constitutional Change: Amendment Politics and Supreme Court Litigation since 1900* (Lexington, Mass.: Lexington Books, 1972) pp. 101–37. For an account of other quixotic amendment forays, *see* Vose, "Conservatism by Amendment," *Yale Review*, Winter 1957, pp. 176–90.

7. Alan P. Grimes, *Democracy and the Amendments to the Constitution* (Lexington, Mass.: Lexington Books, 1978), pp. 109–12.

8. In a test case over the validity of the Eighteenth Amendment, the Supreme Court ruled that "the two thirds vote in each House which is required in proposing an amendment is a vote of two thirds of the members present,— assuming the presence of a quorum,—and not a vote of two thirds of the entire membership, present and absent." *National Prohibition Cases,* 253 U.S. 350, 386 (1920).

9. *National Prohibition Act,* ch. 85, 41 *Stat.* 305 (1919) (repealed 1933).

10. *National Prohibition Cases,* 253 U.S. 350 (1920).

11. Kyvig, *Repealing National Prohibition,* p. 53.

12. For a careful examination of the *Literary Digest* and other polls and writings of the day on prohibition, *see* Claude E. Robinson, *Straw Votes: A Study of Political Prediction* (New York: Columbia University Press, 1932), especially at pp. 145–71.

13. Details about these straw votes by city bar associations are in the Voluntary Committee of Lawyers, Inc., Papers (hereafter cited as VCL Papers), Collection on Legal Change, Wesleyan University, Middletown, Conn. Straw polls continue to be a political tactic and can be exploited effectively as they were by Walter Mondale in the presidential nomination contest of 1983–84, explained by Elizabeth Drew, "A Political Journal," *New Yorker,* November 1983, pp. 169, 179.

14. Robinson, *Straw Votes,* diagrams at pp. 166, 168.

15. This argument is delineated in Paul Kleppner, "Critical Realignments and Electoral Systems," in Kleppner et al., *The Evolution of American Electoral Systems* (Westport, Conn.: Greenwood, 1981), pp. 3–32.

16. For an elaboration, *see* Clement E. Vose, "When District of Columbia Representation Collides with the Constitutional Amendment Institution," *Publius* 10 (Winter 1979): 105–25. The Twenty-third Amendment, providing Dis-

trict of Columbia votes in the electoral college, is treated as a model of ratification politics at pp. 114–20.

17. United States Constitution, Article V. For the best brief introduction to the intent of the framers, the meaning of the text, and cases interpreting points of contention, *see The Constitution of the United States: Analysis and Interpretation,* 92rd Cong., 2nd sess. (1973), S. Doc. 92–82, pp. 855–61.

18. William L. Marbury, "The Limitations upon the Amending Power," *Harvard Law Review* 33 (1919): 223, 225–26.

19. Ibid., pp. 224–25.

20. Ibid., pp. 231–32, quoting *McCulloch v. Maryland,* 4 Wheat. (U.S.) 316, 401 (1819).

21. Arthur W. Machen, Jr., "Is the Fifteenth Amendment Void?" *Harvard Law Review* 23 (1910): 169; Henry St. George Tucker, *Woman Suffrage by Constitutional Amendment* (New Haven: Yale University Press, 1916).

22. I first learned of Bacon's writings in Kyvig, *Repealing National Prohibition,* pp. 138–40, 231. I have since examined Bacon's publications in the Eleutherian Mills Historical Library. The citation is Selden Bacon, *The Tenth Amendment* (New York, 1930), Eleutherian Mills Historical Library pamphlet collection. A similar and more conveniently found article is Selden Bacon, "How the Tenth Amendment Affected the Fifth Article of the Constitution," *Virginia Law Review* 16 (1930): 771–91.

23. *Myers v. Anderson,* 328 U.S. 368 (1915).

24. *National Prohibition Cases,* 253 U.S. 350 (1920).

25. Leser v. Garnett, 258 U.S. 130 (1922).

26. *United States v. Sprague,* 44 F. 2d. 967 (1930).

27. *New York Times,* December 17, 1930, p. 1.

28. *United States v. Sprague,* 44 F. 2d. 967 (1930).

29. *United States v. Sprague,* 282 U.S. 716, 75 L. Ed. 641–43 (1931).

30. *United States v. Sprague,* 282 U.S. 716, 730 (1931).

31. *Woman Patriot* 8 (March 1, 1924): 5. Quoted in Vose, *Constitutional Change,* p. 246. My belief that the Wadsworth-Garrett amendment had wide support among conservative critics of the Progressive prohibition, women's suffrage, and child labor amendments is supported by the extensive writings over a decade about this data, of which the following are representative: Walter Clark, "Back to the Constitution," *Virginia Law Review* 3 (1915): 214; Alton B. Parker, "Back to the Constitution," *American Law Review* 56 (1922): 149; George Stewart Brown, "The 'New Bill of Rights' Amendment," *Virginia Law Review* 9 (1922): 14. Books containing similar arguments include William MacDonald, *A New Constitution for a New America* (New York: B. W. Heubsch, 1921), pp. 202–31, arguing for a new national convention to adequately represent the people; and Henry Wynans Jessup, *The Bill of Rights and Its Destruction by Alleged Due Process of Law* (Chicago: Callaghan and

Company, 1927), p. 86. Against legislative ratification of amendments, and judicial usurpation, wrote Jessup, a "Constitutional convention of delegates elected by the people of the United States" is paramount.

32. S.J. Res. 21, H.J. Res. 69, *Congressional Record*, 67th Cong., 1st sess., 1921, pp. 188, 575. An earlier, lesser known example occurred when Senator Joseph S. Frelinghuysen (R., N.J.) urged changing Article V to enable popular voting to ratify future constitutional amendments. S.J. Res. 126, *Congressional Record*, 66th Cong., 1st sess., 1919, p. 8412.

33. The connection between Senator Wadsworth's opposition to the prohibition and women's suffrage amendments and his advocacy of the back-to-the-people amendment is well explained in Martin L. Fausold, *James W. Wadsworth, Jr.: The Gentleman from New York* (Syracuse, N.Y.: Syracuse University Press, 1974), pp. 139–43. It is thought that Wadsworth lost his seat in the U.S. Senate in 1926 on account of his opposition to prohibition, women's suffrage, and the child labor amendment.

34. William B. Munro, "Initiative and Referendum," in *Encyclopedia of the Social Sciences* (New York: Macmillan, 1932), 8: 50–52.

35. The Pierre S. du Pont and John J. Raskob papers are in the Eleutherian Mills Historical Library, Wilmington, Delaware.

36. S.J. Res. 122, *Congressional Record*, 69th Cong., 1st sess., 1926, p. 12310. This joint resolution provided that such state conventions "shall be held prior to the day in 1928 designated for choosing electors" for president of the United States and "shall be composed of delegates elected thereto by a majority of the fully qualified voters in each of the several States." Also, *see New York Times*, July 1, 1926, p. 2.

37. H.J. Res. 320, *Congressional Record*, 69th Cong., 2nd sess., 1927, p. 1105.

38. U.S. House of Representatives, Committee on the Judiciary, *The Prohibition Amendment: Hearings*, 71st Cong., 2nd sess. (Washington, D.C.: GPO, 1929).

39. *New York Times*, April 3, 1930, p. 18; April 17, 1930, p. 1.

40. *United States v. Sprague*, 44 F. 2d 967.

41. Bacon to Stayton, December 29, 1930, Pierre S. du Pont Papers.

42. National Commission on Law Observance and Enforcement, *Report on the Enforcement of the Prohibition Laws of the United States*. 71st Cong., 3rd sess., House Doc. 722 (Washington, D.C.: GPO, 1931).

43. Atterbury to P. S. du Pont, January 13, 1923, Pierre S. du Pont Papers.

44. An Act to provide for the fifteenth and subsequence decennial censuses and to provide for apportionment of Representatives in Congress, Act of June 18, 1929, c. 28, 43 *Stat.* 21 (1929).

45. The 1932 Republican party platform reads: "Such an amendment should be promptly submitted to the States by Congress, to be acted upon by state

conventions called for that sole purpose . . . and adequately safeguarded so as to be truly representative." The 1932 Democratic party platform states: "We advocate the repeal of the Eighteenth Amendment. To effect such repeal we demand that Congress immediately propose a constitutional amendment to truly representative conventions in the states called to act solely on the subject." Donald Bruce Johnson, comp., *National Party Platforms*, Vol. 2, *1840–1956* (Urbana: University of Illinois Press, 1978), pp. 332, 349.

46. Kyvig, *Repealing National Prohibition*, p. 168.

47. Ibid., p. 169. The House vote on the Garner-Rainey resolution was 272 in favor, 144 opposed. Only six more favorable votes were needed to achieve the necessary two-thirds. The roll call vote may be found in *Congressional Record*, 72nd Cong., 2nd sess, 1932, pp. 6–13.

48. Machen to Choate, January 30, 1933, VCL Papers.

49. Arthur K. Stebbins to Choate, January 26, 1933, VCL Papers.

50. Choate to Stebbins, January 28, 1933, VCL Papers.

51. Vose, *Constitutional Change*, pp. 112–15.

52. Choate telegram for Executive Committee to VCL State Representatives, January 30, 1933, VCL Papers.

53. Ibid.

54. Choate to VCL state representatives, January 30, 1933, VCL Papers.

55. Dowling to Choate, January 31, 1933, VCL Papers.

56. Noel T. Dowling, "A New Experiment in Ratification," *American Bar Association Journal* 19 (June 1933): 383–87.

57. Ibid.

58. Voluntary Committee of Lawyers, Inc., [6th] Report, February 25, 1933, VCL Papers.

59. Kyvig, *Repealing National Prohibition*, p. 173.

60. Ibid.

61. The earliest state legislative approval of ratifying conventions were: Wyoming, February 18, the only state to complete adoption prior to congressional proposal of the repeal amendment; Wisconsin, March 6; Indiana and South Dakota, March 8; West Virginia, March 10; Michigan, March 11; Idaho and New Mexico, March 13; Oregon, March 15; Montana, March 17; Arizona, March 18; Washington, March 20; Utah, March 22; New Jersey and Ohio, March 23; Arkansas and Nevada, March 25; Alabama, March 28; Maine and Tennessee, March 31. Dowling, "A New Experiment," p. 386; E. S. Brown, *Ratification of the Twenty-first Amendment to the Constitution: State Convention Records and Laws* (Ann Arbor: University of Michigan Press, 1938).

62. *See* Abraham C. Weinfield, "Power to Congress over State Ratifying Conventions," *Harvard Law Review* 51 (1938): 473. After the equal rights amendment in 1982 failed of ratification by three-fourths of the state legislatures, Professor Walter Dellinger of the Duke University Law School sug-

gested that Congress, next time, propose ERA to state conventions. Dellinger, "Another Route to the ERA," *Newsweek,* August 2, 1982, p. 8.

63. Kyvig, *Repealing National Prohibition,* p. 174.

64. For a table of the popular vote in the states on ratification of the Twenty-first Amendment, *see* Leonard V. Harrison and Elizabeth Laine, *After Repeal: A Study of Liquor Control Administration* (New York: Harper & Brothers, 1936), p. 230.

65. Munro, "Initiative and Referendum," n. 34, p. 52.

66. Certification is reported officially at 48 *Stat.* 1749. The president's announcement had no legal force. Proclamation No. 2065 (December 5, 1933), "The President Proclaims the Repeal of the Eighteenth Amendment," *The Public Papers and Addresses of Franklin D. Roosevelt,* comp. Samuel I. Rosenman (New York: Random House, 1938), 2 (1933): 510–12.

67. James H. Timberlake, *Prohibition and the Progressive Movement: 1900–1920* (Cambridge: Harvard University Press, 1963).

8   HUMBERT S. NELLI

American Syndicate Crime: A Legacy of Prohibition

It is appropriate in a volume devoted to an examination of the impact of prohibition to focus attention on one of the most durable monuments of the era of the "noble experiment." That monument is, of course, syndicate (or entrepreneurial) crime. Prohibition was most assuredly a major landmark in the history of American syndicate crime.

Criminal syndicates are illicit business organizations established to further underworld interests in such economic endeavors as bootlegging, gambling, loan sharking, narcotics, and business and labor racketeering. Henry Barrett Chamberlain, operating director of the Chicago Crime Commission, recognized as early as 1919 that "modern crime, like modern business is tending toward centralization, organization, and commercialization. Ours is a business nation. Our criminals apply business methods. . . . The men and women of evil have formed trusts."[1] Although offering illegal commodities, the businesses satisfy the needs or interests of a segment of the general public, which thus views the syndicates as benefactors providing a public service. This, in turn, has made it possible for criminal syndicates to obtain the protection from politicians, police, and, on occasion, even the courts which has enabled them to continue in existence for so many decades in Chicago, New York, and numerous other cities across the nation. (The term "organized crime" has been used in so many different contexts and to describe such a wide variety of illegal activities, from relatively unstructured to highly centralized, that it no longer has a precise meaning. Therefore it will not be used in this study.)

The origins of organized illegal enterprise can be traced back at least to the 1860s and 1870s to the gambling syndicates formed in New York, Chicago, New Orleans, and other cities. The syndicates emerged in response to a threat posed to the livelihood of professional gamblers by the emergence of political reform groups. For example, in 1867 the Anti-Gambling Society of New York staged successful raids on several of the city's major gambling houses. John ("Old Smoke") Morrissey led the counterattack of the gambling forces. The city's gamblers contributed money, and Morrissey doled it out to both reformers and police with the result that, in the words of Henry Chafetz, "for some years there were no further raids." By 1870 Morrissey and his fellow gamblers had emerged as a major force in New York City machine politics.[2]

By 1870 a formal system also existed in New Orleans whereby the gambling interests pooled their resources to satisfy police officers at all levels from commissioners down to patrolmen. The New Orleans *Times* on June 9, 1870, noted that "this is the day set aside every month by the Metropolitan Board of Police for collection of its $1400 blackmail, in return for which it grants immunity and support to gamblers." The spirit of cooperation apparently extended to politicians as well, as the paper ruefully noted: "As not the least notice has been taken of the expose made recently, it is now taken for granted that both the State and city administration endorse the outrage as regular."

A similar system evolved at about the same time in Chicago. In the aftermath of the Great Fire, reform forces organized under the leadership of Mayor Joseph Medill to drive the criminal elements out of the city. The gamblers responded by winning the next election for a mayoral candidate sympathetic to their needs and interests. In the following years a pattern emerged: a strong criminal organization exerting great influence over politicians, political processes, and the police. The extent of corruption in terms of both money and influence was still relatively limited.[3]

Gambling was the original impetus for the formation of criminal syndicates and remained the principal source of income for the organizations during the half century prior to prohibition.

When the Eighteenth Amendment and the Prohibition Enforcement Act (or Volstead Act) went into effect on January 16, 1920, the American public and its elected officials had no conception of the violence, corruption, and disrespect for the law that the so-called noble experiment would cause or encourage. In fact, national prohibition was ushered in with a great deal of optimism and hope. In a statement released to the press on January 15, the Anti-Saloon League of New York observed that "at one minute past midnight tomorrow a new nation will be born." It predicted that "tonight John Barleycorn makes his last will and testament. Now for an era of clean thinking and clean living!"[4] This optimistic outlook died almost immediately. Within hours after John Barleycorn was supposedly put to rest, Volstead Act violations were reported in various cities, large and small, across the nation. Within days, police departments were carrying out raids in an effort to end the growing and highly profitable traffic in illicit alcohol. Dry laws or not, Americans wanted their drinks and were ready to do business with anyone who could supply them.

The early 1920s were a period of intense competition among criminal entrepreneurs attracted by prohibition's economic opportunities. The small capital outlay required to enter the business, and the potential for high financial returns, convinced formerly law-abiding citizens as well as small-time criminals to try their luck in a highly competitive but—at least in the early years after the passage of the Volstead Act—wide-open field of enterprise.[5]

Bootlegging was especially attractive to already existing criminal syndicates. The network of contacts with police, politicians, and members of the legal system developed during decades of illegal gambling activities, prostitution, and labor racketeering were readily adapted to the new situation. For all involved, violation of the liquor laws was more acceptable to the public than were the other forms of criminal enterprise. Even the murder and maiming of rival gang members in the scramble to expand markets and increase profits stirred remarkably little anger or dismay. To many Americans, the shootings resembled a modern version of the Old West shoot-out. Only when innocent bystanders, and especially children, were hurt or killed did public opinion demand action against the gangsters. The underworld recognized the importance of public relations and the need to limit violence to insiders. Those who violated the rule to "only kill each other" were dealt with severely.[6]

The bootlegging business, it must be emphasized, was a violent and vicious line of activity. Markets were expanded and mergers were formed or partnerships ended generally either at the point of a gun or with the implied threat of violence. Competitors and even unwanted or unneeded partners or associates were eliminated in a direct and permanent manner. The method generally employed was, of course, the "one-way ride." Literally hundreds of criminals were murdered in Chicago, New York, and other cities. Gang warfare over the vast profits to be obtained from the illicit sale of alcohol was fierce.[7]

Although intense competition existed and a great deal of blood was shed, the general tendency during the prohibition era was toward co-operation and consolidation. In the early days of prohibition, there existed an open market situation with unrestrained competition and uncertainty of supply and distribution. While shootings, murders, and hijackings generally did not provoke public outrage or force effective action on the part of police or courts, criminals came to realize that such behavior was undesirable from a very pragmatic business standpoint. The reason, very simply, was the element of uncertainty injected into operations. As a result, although considerable violence—by the standards of a normal business—continued to characterize bootlegging, certain individuals or groups emerged as dominant forces by the end of prohibition. From New York to Kansas City and Chicago to San Francisco, these men established their ascendancy because they encouraged, or even demanded, cooperation rather than competition.

Although Italians were to be found in criminal syndicates in all the major cities across the country, they did not constitute the only criminal force during prohibition. Thus the so-called Capone syndicate that established its hegemony over Chicago's gangland by the beginning of the 1930s contained large numbers of Italians, but was not limited in membership to any one ethnic group. Among the non-Italians in the organization's hierarchy were Jack Guzik, who was widely regarded as the "brains" of the gang, Murray Humphreys, Sam Hunt, Dennis Cooney, Hymie Levin, and Edward Vogel.[8]

In Boston, syndicate crime was headed by Jewish criminals, first by Charles ("King") Solomon and after his murder in 1933 by Hyman Abrams. In Philadelphia in the late 1920s, the most powerful bootlegging gang was headed by a former Jewish prizefight promoter named Max ("Boo Boo") Hoff. Other syndicates, composed of Italians, Poles, Irish, and other ethnics, also operated in the City of Brotherly Love during this period. Jewish criminals, led by Moe Dalitz, Sam Tucker, Morris Kleinman, and Louis Rathkopf, made a fortune importing liquor from Canada across Lake Erie by boat and plane to their home base of Cleveland. From there they distributed high-quality Canadian liquor throughout Ohio and Pennsylvania and even New York.[9]

Jewish criminals in Detroit, the so-called Purple Gang, prospered for several years as suppliers of Canadian whisky for the Capone organization in Chicago. By 1931, however, the Purple Gang as well as other bootlegging groups in Detroit had been elbowed aside by Joseph Zerilli, Pete Licavoli, Angelo Meli, and other Italian gangsters. Italians played a prominent role in booze wars carried on in the 1920s in Kansas City, Denver, and Los Angeles and emerged in a dominant position by the end of the decade. In contrast, no individual or group was able to win undisputed control in either New Orleans or San Francisco. In the Louisiana metropolis, state and local politicians held a tight rein over the local groups, while in San Francisco police officers determined which illegal activities would be permitted as well as which criminals would be allowed to operate. Thus, a grand jury report released on March 16, 1937, disclosed that each of San Francisco's four police captains had for years controlled and regulated gambling, prostitution, and other illegal activities in his own district.[10]

The situation was far more vicious and complex in New York than in any other American city. With its numerous gangs and an enormous population providing the nation's largest and richest market for illicit alcohol, New York during the 1920s featured a bewildering maze of shifting rivalries, controversies, and alliances. During the bootleg wars of the 1920s, more than one thousand gangsters were killed in New York. By the early 1930s Italians had established a position of primacy, but not of dominance, in the New York area.[11]

Although bootleggers engaged in an illegal enterprise, it was of a nature which millions of otherwise honest and law-abiding citizens fully supported—in fact, it was a service they demanded. The consuming public, in effect, became willing, and even eager, accomplices in the widespread violation of the Constitution. Thus, paradoxically, bootleggers were, in the popular mind, glamorous and mysterious benefactors, and not corruptors of public and private morals.

The hypocrisy of prohibition was a corrosive agent. It permitted Al Capone and other underworld figures to self-righteously maintain that their function was deliberately misunderstood or misrepresented by law enforcement authorities and the media. As Capone piously claimed, ''I make my money by supplying a public need. If I break the law, my customers, who number hundreds of the best people in Chicago, are as guilty as I am. The only difference between us is that I sell and they buy.''[12] If, as Calvin Coolidge claimed, ''the business of America is business,'' then Capone and his peers were in tune with the spirit of the age because, in a very real sense, they were businessmen. Very successful businessmen, in fact. However, the price which the nation, and its citizens, paid for the goods and services offered was far greater than the millions of dollars reaped by syndicate criminals between 1920 and 1933.

Prohibition overburdened the criminal justice system and undermined respect for the nation's law. Until the administration of Herbert Hoover, no serious effort was made to enforce what had become a very unpopular law. The morale and sense of self-worth of law enforcement agents were severely eroded during the 1920s.

The lesson that the young are traditionally supposed to be taught—that is, that crime does not pay—was clearly proven to be false. Crime paid very well, and everyone knew it. Not only did profits obtained from illegal liquor sales enrich criminals almost beyond belief but they provided the capital to expand syndicate activities into new fields of enterprise, as well as to make possible the purchase of political protection, and even to buy a certain degree of respectability. The open flaunting of wealth and influence by syndicate members, combined with the apparent inability of enforcement agencies and the courts to ''bring the wrongdoers to justice,'' created a pervasive disregard for the law.

The groundwork for the criminal syndicates of the post-World War II era was laid during prohibition. Many of what we now regard as traditional areas of illegal enterprise gained a powerful impetus during the 1920s and early 1930s. The most obvious was, of course, bootlegging. During the era of the ''noble experiment,'' the manufacture and sale of alcoholic beverages became the underworld's biggest moneymaker, supplanting gambling, which had held this position since at least the 1870s. Bootlegging is still a money-making activity for criminal syndicates, but a variety of other items, including furs, cigarettes, and electrical appliances, have supplanted alcohol. In fact, any scarce or heavily taxed item holds potential for illegal profit, but bootlegging has, since World War II, played a relatively minor role in the overall operations of criminal syndicates. Other ventures which were overshadowed during the 1920s and early 1930s have, however, more than made up for the decline of bootlegging. These include labor and business racketeering, loan sharking, and the traffic in narcotics. Even the long-established business of gambling gained new importance with the discovery of the profits to be made from the so-called numbers racket, while the much-discussed and much-lamented movement into legitimate business began during prohibition.

Labor and business racketeering, which made its appearance in the midst of the bootlegging era of the 1920s, was by the following decade a major source of syndicate income, as well as a means to enter legitimate business and organized labor. As it developed in the 1920s and 1930s, it was "a system whereby, through the creation of a so-called trade association, by the connivance, cooperation or control of a labor union and the use of a strongarm squad, a process of shaking down merchants or other industrialists was smoothed out to machine efficiency."[13]

In the following years racketeering grew to such proportions that the Senate Permanent Subcommittee on Investigations, under the chairmanship of Senator John McClellan, conducted a three-year inquiry into corrupt practices in labor-management relations. Conditions were regarded to be so serious that in 1959 Congress passed the Landrum-Griffin Act, which assigned the Department of Labor a big role in removing the influence of organized crime in labor unions. In 1978 the permanent subcommittee ruefully admitted that "it is now all too apparent that labor-management racketeering has not disappeared in the 20 years since those hearings." It can safely be stated that as of this date it has still not disappeared.[14]

Loan sharking was another enterprise that benefited from prohibition. The huge amounts of money bootlegging generated were available to be loaned, at outrageously high interest rates, to gamblers and others who were in need—often desperate need—of money but who were prevented for various reasons from turning to banks or other legal lending institutions. Loan sharking has been a consistent moneymaker for the underworld since at least the 1930s. Simply stated, loan sharking involves lending money at a higher rate of interest than that charged by legal lending institutions or permitted by state usury laws. Interest rates charged vary according to the size of the loan, the potential for repayment, the intended use of the money, and the relationship between borrower and lender. Customers are willing to pay exorbitant interest rates because they are considered to be poor credit risks by banks and savings and loan institutions. Customers include gamblers and bookmakers who borrow money to pay gambling losses, small businessmen with cash flow problems, and narcotics users who borrow to buy heroin. A study conducted by the Russell Sage Foundation in the mid–1930s found that the gross annual income from loan sharking in New York City was in excess of $10 million. By the 1960s the President's Commission on Law Enforcement judged the loan sharking business to be "in the multi-billion dollar range" and noted that the profit margins it provides are higher than those obtained from gambling operations.[15]

Gambling, which had been syndicate crime's greatest source of income in the period before prohibition, returned to its dominant position after repeal. By the early 1950s gambling brought an estimated $20 million a year, with annual net profits of approximately $7 million. Although most of the money came from such illegal operations as slot machines, bookmaking, and policy, illicit entrepreneurs also discovered the opportunities offered by legal gambling in Nevada.[16]

At the time it opened in December 1946, Benjamin ("Bugsy") Siegel's creation, the "fabulous Flamingo Hotel," appeared to be a six-million-dollar miscalculation. As events soon proved, of course, it was a stroke of genius. Unfortunately for him, Siegel did not live to enjoy the benefits of his vision. On June 20, 1947, Siegel was murdered in Los Angeles, apparently on order from East Coast and Middle West syndicate leaders who believed he had wasted or misused their money. Meyer Lansky and Frank Costello of New York; Cleveland leaders Moe Dalitz, Sam Tucker, Thomas J. McGinty, and Morris Kleinman; Hyman Abrams of Boston; New Jersey's Joseph ("Doc") Stacher; Pete Licavoli of Detroit; Miami's Edward Levinson; Isadore ("Kid Cann") Blumenfeld of Minneapolis; Chicago's Tony Accardo; as well as numerous other syndicate leaders and hangers-on quickly recognized the opportunities in Las Vegas and invested (either openly or through fronts) in the casino-hotels that sprang up during the 1950s. In the process, they turned Las Vegas into "the most lucrative gambling spa in the world."[17]

By 1967, when the President's Commission on Law Enforcement and Administration of Justice presented its findings on the extent of organized crime in the United States, profits from illegal wagering on horse races, lotteries, and sporting events reached a minimum of at least $20 billion a year, of which criminal syndicates received perhaps $6 or $7 billion. This income remained the major source of underworld revenue. In 1978 New York City police estimated that just one syndicate in the city, the Vito Genovese family, netted more than $100 million annually just from bets on professional football's Super Bowl in the New York–New Jersey area.[18]

In the years since repeal, the crime syndicates have also tapped new sources of revenue. These include arson for hire, credit card and real estate frauds, the pornography business, as well as the theft and sale of securities. During World War II criminal entrepreneurs catered to public demands for a wide range of illegal services or commodities in short supply. Such items as gasoline, meat, automobiles, tin and rubber were provided to customers, for a price. In addition to black market operations, the war proved to be a boon to underworld gambling operations. People played the numbers and flocked to horse and dog tracks, gambling casinos, and bookmakers. Black market and gambling operations continued into the postwar era, and underworld syndicates maintained a tight grasp on both.

During the 1960s stolen securities became a new and lucrative source of revenue. Federal investigators found that although Italian syndicates played a prominent role, "a number of other groups, syndicates and combinations of criminals in a loosely organized confederation" participated extensively in the crimes. Securities were generally obtained in one of two ways: either through inside operators in banks or stockbrokerage houses, or by theft of registered mail at airports. In 1971 a congressional committee investigating the involvement of syndicate crime in the stolen securities business found that the securities were disposed of "through confidence men, stockbrokers and attorneys of shady reputation, fences, and other persons who have the ability, technical knowledge, skill, and contacts to sell the securities or to place them advantageously as collateral in financial transactions." The National Crime Information Center estimated the value of government and private securities stolen in 1970 to be at least $227 million, a figure other authorities considered to be short of the mark.[19]

In recent decades criminal entrepreneurs have devoted increasingly more attention to legitimate business. There is some disagreement among authorities as to whether this focus represents an effort to use profits obtained from illegal activities as a means to infiltrate and corrupt legitimate enterprises, or an attempt on the part of upwardly mobile entrepreneurs to leave a sordid life and gain respectability. The Kefauver committee, which subscribed to the former theory, noted the presence of syndicate figures in approximately fifty areas of business enterprise.

The desire to "go legitimate" has continued to the present. A congressional investigation in 1980 found that profits obtained from illicit enterprises are invested "over time" in legitimate businesses which cover "the whole gamut of our private enterprise system." Businesses infiltrated through the use of "laundered" profits cover some seventy areas of economic activity and "include liquor, transportation, entertainment, sports, hotels and motels, brokerage houses, labor unions, insurance companies, construction firms, vending machines, the food industry, trade associations, trucking, waste collection, parking lots, garment manufacturing, resorts and casinos, holding and finance companies, and real estate development." An estimated 85 percent of the syndicate criminals in America have invested at least a part of their ill-gotten gain in legitimate business ventures.[20]

A significant portion of the enormous profits accruing to criminal organizations has in recent years come from the traffic in illegal narcotics. Contrary to popular belief, this is not a recent phenomenon, but rather, as an organized enterprise, dates from at least the 1920s and 1930s. Nevertheless, the illegal narcotics business has taken on a significantly greater importance in the years since World War II.

In 1973 *Newsday*, a Long Island daily, printed a thirty-two-part report that traced the flow of narcotics from the poppy fields of Turkey to the streets of New York. The Pulitzer Prize–winning investigative study noted that New York is the center of America's heroin industry, with more than half of the industry's customers believed to be living in the five boroughs along with many of the suppliers, wholesalers, retailers, and street peddlers. "In dollar terms, it may be one of the city's biggest industries, with annual sales of $1 billion or more." Control of the business had shifted over the decades from Jewish criminals in the 1930s to Italians in the next two decades. In the late 1950s, however, a new federal conspiracy law went into effect which permitted prosecution of bosses who never actually handled the drugs. "Shortly afterward, around 1960, the five New York crime families prohibited their members from dealing in narcotics." The decision was apparently based in large part on the fear that those given long prison terms would turn informer to lighten their sentences. Although not all Italians moved out of the business, enough did to create the opportunity for Cuban groups to move in. The Cubans, unlike their black competitors, "had connections throughout Latin America and Europe, the sources of the drugs."[21]

Rapid changes took place throughout the 1970s in the nature of drug trafficking. Strong action by American authorities disrupted the traffic in heroin from Turkey as well as trade routes that had been formed during the Vietnam War to Thailand, Laos, and Cambodia. To fill the void created by these law enforcement activities, heroin production increased in Mexico, and Colombia became a major source of marijuana and cocaine. A new element emerged to tap the lushly profitable Colombian connection. Doctors, lawyers, businessmen, and other ostensibly honest and respectable professionals provided financial backing for individual entrepreneurs (most of them white, middle-class young men) to purchase and transport the drugs by sea or air to the United States. Profits are so enormous that those at the lower end of the drug smuggling ladder pick up for a single venture what ordinary citizens would consider to be substantial profits. Off-loaders receive $10,000 to $15,000 for one night's work in unloading a boatload of marijuana, while airplane pilots are paid $50,000 to $100,000 for a round trip to Colombia to transport a planeload of marijuana.[22]

In recent years other groups have entered the scramble for narcotics dollars. Colombians have expanded roles developed during the 1960s and early 1970s as producers and couriers for other distribution networks to the actual trafficking and distribution of the Colombian-produced marijuana and cocaine in the United States. Although until 1979 outlaw motorcycle gangs such as the Hell's Angels, Bandidos, and Outlaws were viewed by authorities mostly as "local nuisances," they now are considered to display "all the characteristics of the more traditional organized crime groups. They also have a formal, recognized rank structure that delineates authority and privilege." In addition to drug trafficking, the motorcycle gangs are involved in welfare frauds, auto and motorcycle theft, and murder.[23]

While the outlaw bikers have been compared by the press to the Italian criminal syndicates, or Mafia, a confederation of drug smugglers, pimps, pornography peddlers, burglars, car thieves, and killers-for-hire operating in Florida, Georgia, Alabama, Virginia, Tennessee, Kentucky, and other southern states has been named the Dixie Mafia by law enforcement authorities.[24]

The complicated nature of the organized crime situation, especially with regard to the illicit traffic in narcotis, led a Senate subcommittee investigating the current state of the underworld to conclude in 1980 that "there is no one specific ethnic stereotype that is synonymous with 'organized crime.' The composition of organized crime syndicates varies from place to place, from year to year, and from drug to drug."[25] It must be emphasized that the Italian syndicate leaders are not encouraging the changes that are taking place in the world of organized crime, nor are they pleased with these changes. Rather, they have made prodigious efforts to maintain the status quo, but as the most highly publicized and visible element in the underworld, they have found this to be a difficult task.

Pressures from law enforcement agencies, the advancing age of syndicate leaders, and an inability to attract new local talent, combined with increasing competition from blacks, Hispanics, and others, may signify the beginning of the decline of Italian American syndicates in the highly competitive New York area as well as in the narcotics business. Increasingly, criminal syndicates have found it extremely difficult to attract able, intelligent, ambitious Italian Americans of the younger generation. As a result, they have found it necessary to import ambitious young toughs from Sicily to provide needed manpower in the scramble for narcotics dollars.[26]

Although the Italian syndicates are not as powerful as they once were, the organizations are far from dead. They and their new competitors will continue to prosper by supplying and exploiting the seemingly endless need of the American public for illegal products and services—a process that received powerful impetus from the prohibition experience. If the noble experiment can teach a lesson, it is that human nature cannot be altered simply by passing laws.

Despite the obviously undesirable effects on values and morals, it is clear that a sizable element of the American public needs or desires the various syndicate-controlled products and services. It may be illegal, but people willingly buy sexual favors, frequent bookie establishments, and smoke marijuana or snort cocaine. Remember that money received from the sale of these and other products and enterprises comprises the syndicate's lifeblood. Thus, if syndicate crime is a serious problem in contemporary society, and I believe it is, we have these alternatives in dealing with it: to fully and equitably enforce the laws, to legalize (or decriminalize) certain forms of illegal enterprise, or to just close our eyes to the situation and muddle along.

Each of the alternatives is prickly with problems. The last alternative, to do nothing, is simply intolerable. We are still suffering from the legacy of prohibition. Corrosive damage has been done to the system of criminal justice, to the morale of law enforcement agencies, and to the nation's morals by the open and cynical high-stakes corruption which has typified the business of syndicate crime since the 1920s.

A declaration of war on the syndicates, which is what full enforcement of the laws would constitute, has a powerful appeal for law enforcement agencies. It would, however, be extremely expensive, and whether the taxpaying public could be convinced of the need for huge expenditures to fight a domestic enemy that so many Americans doubt even exists is questionable. There is also no more assurance that a war on the syndicates would be any more successful than that in Vietnam in the 1960s and 1970s. In fact, the early results of the Reagan administration's "war on drugs" launched in the winter of 1982 raise serious doubts about the effectiveness of such campaigns. Reporting in February 1983 on the progress made during the previous year, officials of the Drug Enforcement Administration (DEA) were forced to admit that even an optimistic reading of the evidence demonstrated that there was "no appreciable decline in the availability or use of illegal drugs during 1982." Instead, government statistics showed that "heroin and cocaine are slightly more plentiful, cheaper and purer, and that marijuana prices have remained stable." In a statement reminiscent of the "light at the end of the tunnel" pronouncements made during the Vietnam War, Gary Liming, the DEA's assistant administrator for intelligence, observed, "Drug traffickers paid a higher price to operate in 1982, but we haven't hurt them bad enough for them to make major changes. They've just made adjustments so far—but that day will come." [27] It is sincerely to be hoped that the day will indeed come, but previous unsuccessful campaigns against the illegal traffic in drugs raise serious doubts.

If an all-out war on crime is in fact not feasible, then the most workable alternative is to decriminalize (or legalize) some currently illegal enterprises while intensively enforcing laws dealing with more socially destructive syndicate activites. Thus, like the production and sale of alcoholic beverages, off-track betting and wagering on athletic events should produce revenue for the citizens of our states and our nation rather than for underworld organizations. Also, prostitution should probably be decriminalized, as should the use of marijuana.

In addition to generating tax revenue, decriminalization could bring some degree of governmental control of product quality. There is another important potential benefit: manpower, money, and other law enforcement resources could be freed to combat more serious syndicate activities. These include white-collar crime and the trade in heroin and cocaine. There is no guarantee, of course, that this course of action will eliminate the scourge of syndicate crime, but it would be an improvement over past, and current, policy.

NOTES

1. Chicago Crime Commission, *Bulletin,* no. 6 (October 1, 1919), p. 1.

2. Henry Chafetz, *Play the Devil: A History of Gambling in the United States from 1492 to 1955* (New York: Bonanza Books, 1960), pp. 290–91.

3. Virgil W. Peterson, *Barbarians in Our Midst: A History of Chicago Crime and Politics* (Boston: Little, Brown, 1952), pp. 84–91; John Landesco, *Organized Crime in Chicago* (Chicago: University of Chicago Press, 1968), chap. 3.

4. *New York Herald,* January 15, 1920.

5. Edward Dean Sullivan, *Chicago Surrenders* (New York: Vanguard, 1930), p. 205.

6. Craig Thompson and Allen Raymond, *Gang Rule in New York: The Story of a Lawless Era* (New York: Dial, 1940), pp. 314–18.

7. Walter Noble Burns, *The One-Way Ride* (Garden City, N.Y.: Doubleday, Doran, 1931).

8. Files of the Chicago Crime Commission at the offices of the commission.

9. Hank Messick, *The Silent Syndicate* (New York: Macmillan, 1967).

10. U.S. Senate, Special Committee to Investigate Organized Crime in Interstate Commerce, *Hearings,* 81st Cong., 2nd sess. (Washington, D.C.: GPO, 1951), p. 9 ff.

11. Thompson and Raymond, *Gang Rule in New York,* p. 100.

12. Andrew Sinclair, *Era of Excess: A Social History of the Prohibition Movement* (New York: Harper and Row, 1964), p. 220.

13. Thompson and Raymond, *Gang Rule in New York,* p. 219.

14. U.S. Senate, Committee on Government Operations, Permanent Subcommittee on Investigations, *Hearings on Labor Management Racketeering,* 95th Cong., 2nd sess. (Washington, D.C.: GPO, 1978), p. 6.

15. *New York Times,* December 4, 1935; President's Commission on Law Enforcement and Administration of Justice, *The Challenge of Crime in a Free Society* (Washington, D.C.: GPO, 1967), p. 189.

16. U.S. Senate, Special Committee to Investigate Organized Crime in Interstate Commerce, *Second Interim Report,* 82nd Cong., 1st sess. (Washington, D.C.: GPO, 1951), pp. 13–14.

17. Frank Browning and John Gerassi, *The American Way of Crime* (New York: G. P. Putnam's Sons, 1980), p. 441.

18. President's Commission on Law Enforcement, *Challenge of Crime,* p. 189; *Washington Post,* January 16, 1978.

19. U.S. Senate, Committee on Government Operations, Permanent Subcommittee on Investigations, *Hearings on Organized Crime—Stolen Securities,* 92nd Cong., 1st sess. (Washington, D.C.: GPO, 1971), pp. 2–5.

20. U.S. Senate, Committee on Government Operations, Permanent Sub-

committee on Investigations, *Hearings on Organized Crime and Use of Violence*, 96th Cong., 2nd sess. (Washington, D.C.: GPO, 1980) p. 13; Jeff Gerth, "Nixon and the Mafia," *Sundance* 1 (July 1972): 30.

21. The Staff and Editors of *Newsday*, *The Heroin Trail*, (New York: New American Library, 1974), pp. 198–200.

22. U.S. Senate, Committee on Government Operations, Permanent Subcommittee on Investigations, *Hearings on Illegal Narcotics Profits*, 96th Cong., 2nd sess. (Washington, D.C.: GPO, 1980),p. 18.

23. *Washington Post*, September 2, 1981; U.S. Senate, *Organized Crime and Use of Violence*, p. 61.

24. *Louisville Courier-Journal*, December 19, 1982.

25. U.S. Senate, *Organized Crime and Use of Violence*, p. 61.

26. Nicholas Pileggi, "Anatomy of the Drug War," *New York Magazine* 6 (January 8, 1973): 36; Staff and Editors of *Newsday*, *The Heroin Trail*, pp. 207–9.

27. *Louisville Courier-Journal*, February 22, 1983.

Bootleggers as Businessmen: From City Slums to City Builders

Shortly after World War II, a group of entrepreneurs began construction of a large hotel-casino in the desert several miles outside the moribund town of Las Vegas, Nevada. Improbably, they named their gaudy structure the Flamingo. When the Flamingo succeeded, the same entrepreneurs and their associates built other huge structures in the desert, thereby initiating the transformation of Las Vegas into a national center of entertainment as well as the most rapidly growing city in the United States. Modern Las Vegas might not have been possible without the vision and resources of men who, forty years earlier, had been raised in the ethnic slums of American cities and then struggled to success as bootleggers during the prohibition era of the 1920s. Las Vegas, then, can be seen as their crowning achievement. And by exploring their careers from slum youths to city builders, we can learn much about the business of bootlegging and the impact of bootleggers upon American life after prohibition.

   If ex-bootleggers were improbable agents for transforming a dying desert town into a booming city, it was equally improbable that the same men would rise to dominate bootlegging in the 1920s. Their backgrounds provided little that marked them for future business success. When national prohibition began in 1920, most of those who became leading bootleggers in the major cities were still young men, often in their teens or early twenties. Their formative years were spent in the ethnic slums of the cities. About half were of Eastern European Jewish background, a quarter were Italian, and the final quarter were largely Irish and Polish. Typically, they had left school by age fourteen and then had spent time on the streets—as newsboys, gang members, petty crooks. With the coming of prohibition, they found, like many Americans, that they could hustle some money by small-time bootlegging. With luck, skill, and (sometimes) violence, successful bootleggers rapidly expanded into extensive importing, manufacturing, or wholesaling activities. When prohibition ended in 1933, they were relatively young, generally in their early to mid thirties. Their adult careers still lay ahead of them.[1]

Newspapers of the day—as well as subsequent histories—have stressed the violence that often accompanied the rise of bootlegging. Indeed, Chicago (and Al Capone) gained worldwide notoriety because of the hundreds of deaths in that city in the 1920s. At sea and on land, bootleggers had to protect their booze from hijackers, so that successful bootleggers were often those most able to use gunmen to safeguard their shipments and warehouses. The gunmen, initially used to protect against hijacking, were sometimes then employed in competition with rival entrepreneurs. In all probability, the young men from the slums rose to prominence as bootleggers precisely because they were willing to operate in the sometimes violent world of bootlegging.

The emphasis on gang rivalries, however important, has nevertheless obscured what was far more significant about the structure of bootlegging: the systematic and ongoing cooperation among bootleggers that was necessary to supply alcohol to major metropolitan markets. In a metropolitan market, diverse tastes required a broad range of alcoholic beverages. The beverages derived from importation, diversion of industrial alcohol, large but clandestine distilleries, beer breweries, and many other sources. The alcohol often needed processing (caramel, creosote, and prune juice could be added, for instance, to give the taste and color of scotch). Once processed, the beverages were bottled and labeled. Only then would wholesalers truck the booze to warehouses and deliver it to retail outlets. (See Figure 9.1.)[2]

Leading bootleggers and their partners, then, tended to specialize either in importation, in various forms of manufacture, or in wholesaling. By the late 1920s a wholesaling group in Chicago, such as that associated with Al Capone and Jack Guzik, might have ongoing arrangements with importers in Detroit, New York, New Orleans, and Florida; with brewers in Joliet, Illinois, and Racine, Wisconsin; with Philadelphia entrepreneurs who diverted industrial alcohol; and with illegal distillers throughout the Midwest. Similarly, successful importers or manufac-

Figure 9.1
Structure of Metropolitan Bootlegging Markets

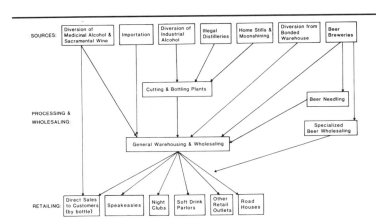

turers cut deals with a variety of wholesalers to ensure a market for their often fluctuating businesses.

For the young men from the slums who climbed to success in the 1920s, coordination of bootlegging activities was a crash course in a number of business skills. Partly because of the brief thirteen years that prohibition lasted, few if any became managers of large-scale bureaucratic structures. To the extent that they needed ships' captains, warehouse foremen, distillers, or brewers to manage enterprises, bootleggers normally secured their cooperation by offering them a piece of the profits or a set amount for completing a project. As compared to the so-called Whiskey Trust of earlier years or the giant distributors who rose after repeal, bootleggers were relatively small-time operators. Leading bootleggers had interests in varied short-term and long-term operations of limited scale; they were primarily hustlers, makers of deals, partners in businesses, coordinators of markets—*not* executives presiding over bureaucratic organizations.

In that capacity, bootleggers confronted a variety of business challenges. (1) They were forced, by the process of building bootlegging operations, to think in terms of regional, national, and even international markets. Importers, in fact, had to plan their activities around

Atlantic or Pacific trade routes and to negotiate deals with foreign manufacturers and shippers. To do this often required meetings of exporters, importers, and shippers: in Nova Scotia in the spring to plan the summer import business on the Atlantic, or in Florida, where many bootleggers wintered by the late 1920s. (2) Bootleggers learned to use partnerships in order to pool resources and share risks in setting up a variety of legal and illegal enterprises. Whether establishing a liquor exporting company in Havana, a brewery in Reading, Pennsylvania, or a bottling plant in New Jersey, they brought together persons with investment capital, managerial skills, political influence, and other needed resources. (3) As illegal entrepreneurs, they also had to learn to use legal institutions to service their illegal enterprises: they had to learn banking to handle money, insurance to protect their ships, and the methods of incorporation to gain control of chemical and cosmetics companies from which they diverted industrial alcohol. They also dealt with varied legitimate companies to purchase trucks, boats, copper tubing, corn sugar, bottles, and labels. (4) Finally, bootleggers early began to diversify their business activities in directions that were predictable given their backgrounds and interests. Importers not only smuggled booze but sometimes smuggled opium, French perfume, or illegal aliens. Because they were often sports fans and high rollers, successful bootleggers invested in gambling houses, numbers syndicates, and slot machine distributorships, as well as race tracks and dog tracks. Many, attracted to the city's nightlife, invested in nightclubs and speakeasies.

By the time of repeal in 1933, then, many leading bootleggers, essentially wheeler-dealers, had nevertheless gained a variety of entrepreneurial skills and business interests. They were still young men. And while some would be killed, jailed, or bankrupted, others found successful business careers in enterprises that reflected the skills and interests they demonstrated in the 1920s. Two of their business activites were of particular importance: first, their role in moving from the illegal to the legal liquor business; and second, their role in promoting regional gambling centers, culminating with the founding of modern Las Vegas.

THE LIQUOR BUSINESS AFTER REPEAL

The history of the liquor business, especially in the years since repeal, has been little explored. On the whole, however, the manufacture of alcoholic beverages appears to have recovered from prohibition without, at first, undergoing major transformation. California wine growers, although they anticipated disaster from prohibition, did quite well in the 1920s by selling wine grapes to those Americans who wished to make home wine. As a result, they kept their vineyards and wineries intact and were ready to return to wine making as repeal approached. The major beer brewers had less success in the 1920s. Although some struggled to stay in business by making near beer, malt syrups, or soft drinks, many turned their breweries into parking lots, warehouses, or factories. But the major brewers, such as Anheuser-Busch, Schlitz, and Pabst, as well as many regional brewers, returned to the brewing of beer in the 1930s. The Kentucky bourbon business, too, rebounded in the 1930s despite a thirteen-year halt in production.[3]

While production of alcoholic beverages emerged reasonably unscathed given the potentially devastating impact of the 1920s, prohibition destroyed the earlier system of national and local distribution. Many bootleggers involved in the export, import, and distribution systems of the 1920s built upon the skills and ties of that period and achieved a central role as distributors after repeal. This was particularly clear among the handful of companies that now dominate national distribution of alcoholic beverages in the United States.[4]

Seagram, now the major national manufacturer and distributor of alcoholic beverages, provides the most obvious example. By the 1890s the Bronfman family, after fleeing the pograms of Russia, operated small hotels in the prairie provinces of Canada. When most of the provinces went dry before World War I, Samuel Bronfman and his brothers started a mail-order business for sale of liquor across provincial borders. When prohibition came to the United States, the Bronfmans quickly became major sellers to American bootleggers who sneaked booze across the border into Montana, North Dakota, and Minnesota. Recognizing that the prairie provinces had no access to the primary U.S. markets, the Bronfmans established headquarters in Nova Scotia in 1924 to participate in the lucrative Atlantic trade. Eventually they joined with other Canadian exporters to set up a shipping company in Vancouver, British Columbia, for smuggling to California ports. Soon they also had outposts in Nassau, Havana, and Belize to coordinate smuggling activities into Florida and Gulf Coast ports. In 1928, as part of their expansion, they purchased the distilling company of Joseph E. Seagram and Sons, Ltd., in Ontario. By this time, the Bronfman interests were the major coordinators of liquor importation into U.S. Pacific, Atlantic, and Gulf Coast cities. After repeal Samuel Bronfman moved Seagram's headquarters to the Chrysler Building in New York. In 1936 Seagram paid the U.S. government $1.5 million in a negotiated settlement of the claims against the company from prohibition violations. Within a few years, Bronfman had purchased major American distilleries and wineries, as well as founding distilleries of his own, so that Seagram became the dominant distributor. By 1980 Seagram sold some 600 brands in 175 countries at a total annual value of nearly $3 billion.

In 1926 Harry C. Hatch purchased Hiram Walker and Sons. This prestigious company, founded by Boston-born Hiram Walker on the Canadian side of the Detroit River in 1858, manufactured the famous Canadian Club brand. Earlier Hatch had purchased Gooderham and Worts, Canada's oldest distillery. In 1928 Hatch and his many Canadian and American associates were indicted by the U.S. government for their extensive smuggling into various American cities through the Detroit and Buffalo areas across Lake Erie. With repeal, Hatch's company built an American distillery in Peoria, Illinois, as well as expanding into European and South American markets. Like Seagram, the company negotiated a settlement of U.S. government claims. Hiram Walker became one of the three biggest American distributors.

By contrast, Schenley's success had American origins. Lewis Rosensteil, whose family had been important in the Cincinnati distilling business, branched out in the 1920s by acquiring distilleries whose warehouses were particularly well stocked. Ostensibly his business was the sale of alcoholic beverages for medicinal purposes. He purchased Schenley Products Company of Schenley, Pennsylvania, about 1924. He also imported liquor from Canada and Bermuda and, in the process, dealt extensively with Samuel Bronfman. By the time of repeal, he and his associates were important owners of American distilleries and had one of the largest stocks of liquor available in the United States. At first Rosensteil and Bronfman planned to jointly develop the American market, but they soon quarreled bitterly. Until 1937 Schenley was the largest legal distributor of alcoholic beverages in the United States, but in that year it was overtaken by Seagram.

The major national distributors of hard liquor, in short, descended directly from companies that first rose to prominence by servicing the American market during prohibition. Because prohibition destroyed the old distribution system, a few of the more capable and ambitious distributors from the 1920s enjoyed crucial advantages in seizing the opportunities opened by repeal. They owned distilleries that had been in active production in the 1920s, they had contacts in major cities through which to distribute their beverages, and, in the depression years of the early 1930s, they had capital to invest in the expansion of their holdings. While bootlegging of the 1920s had been highly competitive and characterized by numerous firms, the legal system was more easily dominated by a handful of national distributors. With the resources that stemmed from national distribution, they purchased American distilleries and wineries, as well as European and Latin American brands, and thus created forms of vertical monopoly.

Not only was national distribution dominated by firms that rose during prohibition, but many bootleggers also became local distributors. Sometimes, no doubt, local distributors continued the ties with suppliers forged during prohibition. Abner (''Longie'') Zwillman, for instance, had been a sixteen-year-old hustler on the streets of Newark, New Jersey, when prohibition began. By the late 1920s he was a partner in the so-called Reinfeld Syndicate, the largerst illegal liquor importers in northern New Jersey. The syndicate's Canadian contacts were with the Bronfman interests. After repeal Zwillman and his partners formed Browne Vintners to distribute liquor in the New York region. In 1940 Zwillman sold the company to Seagram for $7.5 million.[5]

There were many other examples. A 1937 investigation by the Internal Revenue Service uncovered evidence that a New York firm, Alliance Distributors, Inc., with sole rights to sell certain selected Scotch whiskeys in the United States, was apparently backed by Frank Costello, perhaps the most important New York importer during prohibition, and Irving Haim, an ex-bootlegger with interests in New York and Philadelphia. John Torrio put together a bootleg conglomerate in Chicago in the early 1920s but, finding Chicago violence unsettling, departed in 1924, leaving his enterprises to Jack Guzik, Al Capone, and Frank Nitti. In New York, Torrio continued a variety of bootleg activities until repeal. Afterwards, he was the major entrepreneur in establishing Prendergast and Davies, which became an important liquor distributor. In Kansas City, as Humbert Nelli has noted in his book on Italian crime, Midwest Distributing Company was by 1934 the exclusive distributor for Seagram, while Superior Wines and Liquor Company handled Schenley brands. Both had ex-bootleggers as major investors.[6]

In short, the pattern was similar in many cities: ex-bootleggers continued as liquor distributors at the local level. In that business they could use the expertise gained during bootlegging days, as well as their political contacts and their ties with national and foreign distributors. Except for the brewing of beer, the long-range effect of prohibition may have been to reorganize the control of the American liquor business. For many bootleggers, the liquor business was not an interlude of the 1920s but a means by which they gained the resources to control the legal liquor business and thereby achieve success and respectability.

REGIONAL GAMBLING AND THE FOUNDING OF LAS VEGAS

If reshaping the liquor industry was a major accomplishment of ex-bootleggers, a close rival in importance was the creation of Las Vegas as a national entertainment center. Like their impact on the liquor business, Las Vegas represented the ex-bootleggers' ability to think in terms of regional and national markets, to pool resources in joint ventures, and to recruit able managers to run the enterprises for which they provided the entrepreneurial skills. To understand the creation of modern Las Vegas after World War II, one must understand both the special environment of Nevada and the prior experience of ex-bootleggers from many cities in the cooperative formation of regional gambling centers in the fifteen years following repeal. In this brief space it is possible merely to sketch the activities of ex-bootleggers as developers of regional gambling.[7]

Frank Costello, partner in the 1920s in what was probably the largest New York importing syndicate, also became an important figure in the city's nightlife and politics. Even before prohibition ended, he and "Dandy" Phil Kastel established the Tru-Mint Company to install slot machines in the city. When Mayor Fiorello LaGuardia created headlines in 1934 with his campaign against Costello's machines, Costello made arrangements with Senator Huey Long to install the machines in New Orleans. Kastel went there to oversee their joint venture. After World War II, Kastel, with Costello as partner, operated the Beverly Club near New Orleans, the major illegal casino for the city's tourist crowds. By the early 1930s Costello had also become a partner in the extensive bookmaking operations of Frank Erickson—probably the most respected bookmaker for the big bettors of the Big Apple. In the 1940s they also ran sports betting out of Florida hotels. Owney Madden, a

New York beer distributor during prohibition and famous as the owner of the Cotton Club, went to Hot Springs, Arkansas, in the 1930s to revitalize casino gambling in that southern resort city. He was almost certainly backed by Costello, and perhaps by Meyer Lansky as well. In Cleveland, five partners, led by Morris B. ("Moe") Dalitz, engaged in smuggling across Lake Erie into Buffalo, Erie, and Cleveland during the 1920s. Ranging in age from seventeen to twenty-four when prohibition began, they became major investors in a variety of enterprises, legitimate and illegitimate. In addition to investment in various Cleveland gambling enterprises, the partners in 1941 bought into the gambling houses of Newport and Covington, Kentucky, across the Ohio River from Cincinnati. These blue-collar towns had long provided gambling and vice for the big city across the river, but the Cleveland investors made their Beverly Hills Club and Lookout House renowned midwestern centers for gambling. The Cleveland group also invested in a variety of enterprises in Florida and Cuba. Dalitz was second only to Lansky in the importance of his contribution to the development of Las Vegas.

Jack Guzik—a partner with Al Capone, Ralph Capone, and Frank Nitti in Chicago's largest wholesale bootlegging operation—was a key figure afterwards among a number of Chicago gambling entrepreneurs. His chief partner was Nitti until Nitti's suicide in the early 1940s; thereafter, his closest associate, with whom he often filed joint tax returns, was Tony Accardo. In the 1920s Guzik's associates had already made Cicero, a blue-collar suburb west of Chicago, an important gambling center. Guzik by 1930 had his hand in much of the gambling in Chicago's downtown Loop. The Chicago group, often acting through their good friend Johnny Patton (once the teenage mayor of Burnham, Illinois), were eager investors in Florida dog and horse tracks. During World War II, Guzik and his partners established a national race wire, Trans-America Publishing and News Service, in order to bankrupt the dominant Continental Press and give the Chicago group a monopoly in providing sports information to bookmakers, newspapers, and radio news. By the post–World War II period, Guzik and associates had also begun investing in gambling in downstate Illinois.

There were other entrepreneurs as well. In Boston, Hy Abrams and his partners, successful but largely unpublicized bootleggers, invested in a Boston dog track in the 1930s and joined other bootleggers in a variety of ventures. In northern New Jersey, Abner ("Longie") Zwillman, partner in the Reinfeld Syndicate of bootleggers, became a major force in the gambling of Newark and surrounding cities. In the 1930s and 1940s he invested in race tracks in New Jersey, Kentucky, and California. Harry Rosen (*né* Stromberg), born in Russia and raised on the Lower East Side of New York, was a mere seventeen when prohibition began. During the 1920s he became involved in numerous vice and bootlegging activities in the New York–Philadelphia region. After repeal he put together a group of ex-bootleggers to coordinate numbers gambling in Philadelphia. In the mid–1930s he also took over the Maryland Athletic Club, an important gambling house servicing the Washington, D.C., area. By the 1940s Rosen and his associates developed various gambling and other investments in Florida.

The leading figure among those ex-bootleggers involved in gambling was Meyer Lansky. Indeed, he is perhaps the most important gambling entrepreneur in American history. Only eighteen when prohibition began (his partner, Benjamin Siegel, was fourteen), he gradually achieved importance as a New York bootleg importer by the end of the 1920s. Then, in the 1930s, as he pioneered gambling and race track investments in Florida and Cuba, his planning and judgment proved so profitable that he attracted a range of investors eager to have a share in his enterprises. In a move that would be important later in the founding of modern Las Vegas, Siegel went to Los Angeles in the late 1930s, where he became a notorious figure in Hollywood social life while scouting various investment opportunities on the West Coast.

Florida was the crucial arena in which ex-bootleggers developed their cooperative ventures in gambling and entertainment and built the ties that would later be seen in Las Vegas. By the late 1920s, after the Coast Guard effectively reduced smuggling in the North Atlantic, Florida ports were major entry points for imported liquor. East Coast and midwestern bootleggers came to Florida on business, and like other wealthy Americans, many wintered in Florida by the late 1920s and invested in Florida real estate. They were aware, therefore, of Florida's potential as a resort and entertainment center. In 1931, after Florida legalized parimutuel betting at the track, Canadian liquor interests contributed funds to convert Tropical Park near Coral Gables into a horse track and selected Bill Dwyer, Costello's former bootleg partner, as manager. When the track needed additional backing in 1934, Lansky and Erickson purchased the park, while Johnny Patton, probably representing Chicago money, was also involved. Sometimes under Lansky's leadership and sometimes independently, a variety of investors placed money in other Florida tracks, gambling houses, bookmaking operations, hotels, and other ventures. In 1946 Lansky assembled a group of New York, Chicago, and Detroit investors to establish the Colonial Inn near Miami, perhaps the largest illegal casino-nightclub in the United States at that time.

Lansky also provided leadership for the penetration of Cuba. Even in the 1920s, Havana had provided gambling for vacationing Americans and was an important center for smuggling from Europe into the United States. A number of bootleggers, as a result, developed close times with Cuban politicians. By the mid–1930s, through agreements with Fulgencio Batista, Lansky operated a casino in the Hotel Nacional and had an interest in race tracks. After Batista lost power in 1944, American investments declined but made a remarkable recovery after Batista returned to power in 1952. Lansky, Dalitz, Kastel, and others associated with ex-bootleggers turned Havana into an important center of gambling, vice, and entertainment until Fidel Castro drove them out.

By the end of World War II, then, ex-bootleggers were approaching their fifties and the height of their careers. Their youth had been spent in the dangerous but exciting ventures that provided bootleg liquor to a thirsty nation. Since that time, some had engaged in joint investments to develop recreational centers of gambling, racing, and nightlife entertainment. (See Figure 9.2 for a diagram of their relationships.) In this context, they discovered, or created, the opportunities in Las Vegas.

Nevada offered a special environment: a sparsely populated state, still proud of its wide-open frontier ethos and also cynically aware that there was profit to be made by providing services not legally available elsewhere. The Reno divorce, after all, was an important prop for that city's economy. Many wealthy Americans, otherwise unlikely to spend time and money in a desert state, lived in Reno for six weeks to establish residency for divorce purposes. In the late nineteenth and early twentieth centuries, when most states banned or restricted prizefighting, Nevada had no restrictions. Thus, in 1910, when Jim Jeffries, the Great White Hope, emerged from retirement in a vain attempt to wrest the heavyweight title from Jack Johnson, the fight was moved to Reno when the California governor banned it in San Francisco. Crowds of sportsmen and bettors from as far as New York came to see the fight.

Figure 9.2

Ex-Bootleggers and Regional Gambling: 1935–1950

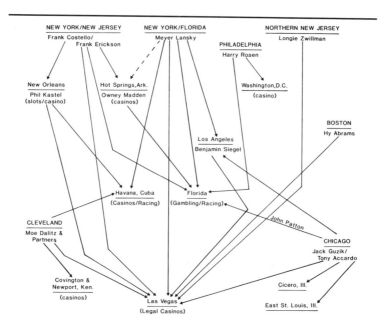

Traditionally a wide-open mining and gambling state, Nevada legally banned gambling in 1909 but established licensed gambling in 1931. In that depression year the state legislature hoped to gain tax revenues and tourist business through a policy of legalization. Reno, by far the largest city in the state, was at first the main beneficiary.

Las Vegas in 1928 was a desert town and county seat with a population of about 5,000. That population swelled slightly in the next few years because of construction of the nearby Hoover Dam. During World War II, when the Army Air Force turned the municipal airport into a training base, the population may have boomed to 20,000, and there was even some new construction of small nightclubs and gambling houses. But with the war over and the dam long since completed, the town faced a bleak future. A desperate chamber of commerce saw but one hope: to attract tourists by advertising the city as a frontier town, including promotion of the downtown main street as a frontier "Glitter Gulch." Las Vegas leaders would welcome investors and not inquire too closely concerning their backgrounds.[8]

Toward the end of the war, Benjamin Siegel (assisted by Mickey Cohen) became the West Coast distributor for the sports information service established in Chicago by the Guzik-Accardo group. Siegel traveled to Las Vegas to peddle his services to the bookmakers operating from the small casinos there. Often, in return for racing information, Siegel expected a partnership interest in the bookmaking operations. On one trip he may have brought Lansky with him. At any rate, Siegel soon believed that he could build a magnificent hotel-casino-nightclub in the desert outside Las Vegas, offering legal gambling for the sporting element of southern California. This was, of course, a wild and unproven scheme for which there could be no adequate sources of legitimate credit.[9]

Siegel estimated the cost of the Flamingo at something over $1 million, but massive overruns sent the cost to at least $6 million. Siegel, Lansky, Hy Abrams, and the other original partners not only invested their own money but eventually may have accepted money from a wide variety of additional investors ranging from Longie Zwillman to Moe Dalitz to Frank Costello. In December 1946, although the hotel was not yet completed, Siegel attempted to open the casino. With Jimmy Durante there to entertain, Xavier Cugat's band to play, and George Raft as host, the casino nevertheless flopped. The Flamingo reopened in March and was soon making a handsome profit. Then, in June, Siegel was shot inside the Beverly Hills mansion of his mistress. He died having proven that his dream was profitable.

Over the next few years, of course, there rose from the desert in quick succession a number of hotel casinos. The Thunderbird, for which Lansky and his associates appear to have been major backers, opened in 1948. Construction began on the Desert Inn in 1947, with Wilbur Clark, who had operated gambling ships off the southern coast of California, as the major sponsor. When his group ran out of funds, Moe Dalitz and his partners purchased a 74 percent interest and thus made possible its opening in 1950. Dalitz moved to Las Vegas and soon was numbered among its most respected citizens. The Sands, completed in 1952, was sponsored chiefly by New Jersey backers such as Longie Zwillman. Frank Sinatra, who was, after all, a Hoboken boy, had a minority interest. The Riviera, opening in 1955, seems to have represented chiefly Chicago investors such as Guzik and Accardo. The Tropicana, ready two years later, had backers such as Costello and Kastel. The Stardust had a somewhat more complex origin. Tony Cornero had been a California bootleg importer in the 1920s. Among his ventures in the next two decades, he occasionally operated a gambling ship in Santa Monica Bay. When the Coast Guard seized his ship, he became a bettor and investor along the Strip. He planned the Stardust but died of a heart attack in 1955. Accardo and other Chicago investors attempted to rescue it but soon sold out to Dalitz and his partners.

The impact of the ex-bootleggers went beyond capital and planning. From their hotels, casinos, and nightclubs in Cleveland, Covington, Miami, Hot Springs, and Havana, they recruited hotel men, casino managers, card dealers, bouncers, and other staff required for the entertainment centers along the Strip. Many men, often with long records of illicit activities, found in Las Vegas an opportunity to use their skills in a new environment.

Without the ex-bootleggers to found and staff the first generation of hotel-casinos, Las Vegas might not have been possible. They were the major entrepreneurs with experience in building entertainment centers based on gambling. For such large-scale yet risky ventures, for which legitimate credit was not available, they had the capital and a long history of pooling resources in order to launch high-risk enterprises. As men accustomed to thinking in terms of regional markets, they could see possibilities where others might not. And with the development of transcontinental air travel, Las Vegas became an entertainment center not simply for the West Coast but for the nation. The dying desert town, chosen as a gamblers' paradise by Siegel in 1945, was a booming growth city of 200,000 twenty years later, and reached a population of 464,000 by the census of 1980.

Despite the crucial role of ex-bootleggers in developing the first generation of hotel-casinos, their impact on the future economic growth of Las Vegas was ambiguous. In 1950–51 the Senate Special Committee to Investigate Organized Crime (known popularly as the Kefauver Committee after its chairman, Senator Estes Kefauver of Tennessee) charged that "organized crime" controlled casino development in the city. Subsequent newspaper exposés not only reinforced the charges of mob control but claimed that profits from casinos were skimmed to evade taxes and finance underworld activities throughout the nation.

By the mid–1950s the entertainment industry in Las Vegas required new capital to expand earlier casinos and construct new ones; but the many charges of underworld control meant that the casinos, although profitable, continued to be viewed as doubtful investments by legitimate credit institutions. Several Las Vegas investors, though, had ties with the Teamsters Union and its Central States Pension Fund. By 1977 the fund had sunk some $240 million into Nevada. Although access to Teamster funds brought needed capital at favorable terms, it did not enhance the respectability of the Nevada gaming industry. On the contrary, numerous congressional investigations and newspaper stories highlighted the corruption and underworld friendships of the Teamster leadership—indeed, the investments in Las Vegas were taken as evidence for such charges.[10]

Then, in 1967, Howard Hughes purchased the Desert Inn from Dalitz and subsequently gained ownership of approximately seventeen casinos in Nevada. For the state's politicians, Hughes, despite his outlandish behavior, was perceived as a saviour who could free the casinos from their reputation as underworld investments. A more important factor in refinancing the casinos, however, was that the Nevada legislature passed laws in 1967 and 1969 permitting publicly held corporations to obtain casino licenses. Soon corporations such as Metro-Goldwyn Mayer, Hyatt Corporation, and Del E. Webb purchased old casinos and built new ones in Las Vegas, Reno, and Lake Tahoe. (In 1971 the Flamingo became a Hilton hotel.) The continued remarkable expansion of Las Vegas in the 1970s was made possible largely by such corporations. By 1980 the twenty largest corporations owned casinos that generated half the gross gambling revenue and provided half the gaming employment in the state. Clearly, the casino industry had been reorganized.

During the fifteen years following the mid–1950s, then, the bootleg generation reached the age when death and retirement caused them to cease active casino development. By that time, in any event, neither their capital nor their skills as casino and entertainment entrepreneurs were necessary for the continued success of Las Vegas. But, for good or ill, they had shaped the growth of a city. And they had attracted to the city ambitious followers and partners. Despite changes in casino ownership, their influence remains. Even as this essay is being written in October 1983, the federal government, after a five-year investigation, has indicted criminal entrepreneurs from Chicago, Milwaukee, and

Kansas City for secret ownership and skimming from two Las Vegas casinos.[11] It has been easier for the casinos to achieve business success than to gain respectability.

IN CONCLUSION

The story told here has implications for understanding the history of what some, rather inaccurately, call organized crime. Remember that in 1950–51, just as Las Vegas was coming to fruition, Senator Kefauver and his Senate committee announced that a mysterious "mafia" controlled "organized crime" in America. Such a view of the coordination of criminal enterprise is historically untenable.[12] Among leading bootleggers, as mentioned earlier, those of Jewish background constituted one-half; they outnumbered Italians two to one. As these same men developed cooperative ventures, criminal and legitimate, in Miami, Hot Springs, Havana, or Las Vegas, the Jewish predominance continued. Furthermore, the brief history provided here gives a clearer model of the structure of cooperation within which these men made their deals and financed their ventures. They were independent businessmen who had learned to pool their resources because this minimized risks and maximized their ability to mobilize capital, influence, and managerial skills. They operated regionally and nationally through a complex set of interlocking partnerships. If men such as Lansky, Dalitz, or Costello sometimes exercised special leadership, it was not because they were crime "bosses" directing hierarchical organizations of master criminals. Rather, they had proven track records as businessmen in legal and illegal enterprises, so that other entrepreneurs competed for the opportunity to participate in their schemes.

Prohibition, by bringing to the fore a group of particularly energetic criminal entrepreneurs, created a general phenomenon in American business history. Approximately twenty years old in 1920, the leading bootleggers gained success during prohibition at an unusually early age. In 1933, still only in their thirties and with careers ahead of them, they put their energies into a variety of business activities. Some restructured the distribution of liquor and achieved both wealth and respectability. The control of the American liquor industry has largely escaped careful scrutiny. Other ex-bootleggers specialized in gambling and entertainment; for them, Las Vegas would finally be their opportunity, also, to hope that they might become legal and therefore respectable. But the many congressional investigations and newspaper exposés have meant that respectability was elusive for those entrepreneurs who made Las Vegas possible.

In 1976, during a deposition in a libel suit that he had brought against *Penthouse* magazine, Dalitz protested his failure to achieve respectability:

For 30 years now I have lived in Nevada. I am considered a good citizen of Nevada. I have done all the things a good citizen should do. I have been charitable. I have been honest. I have raised a family. My life has been just as good as anyone's in this room. . . . I have very candidly told you that I was in the liquor business when it was considered to be illegal. I told you that I was in the casino business. . . . In none of these businesses is moral turpitude involved. These are things that if people didn't patronize a casino we couldn't have one. If people didn't drink liquor it wouldn't have been necessary to bring it over. I did nothing more than the head of Seagram's, than the head of G & W [Gooderham and Worts], the head of Canadian Club. They assembled all this merchandise for runners to bring it across. . . . We didn't regard this as a hideous affair. I don't think you do either in your heart.[13]

Whatever one may think of Dalitz's self-justification, one thing at least is clear: he and other young men who learned business skills as bootleggers had their greatest impact on American society in the years after repeal.

NOTES

1. For a presentation of the evidence about the social backgrounds of bootleggers, *see* Mark H. Haller, "Bootleggers and American Gambling 1920–1950," in Commission on the Review of National Policy toward Gambling, *Gambling in America*, Appendix I (Washington, D.C.: GPO, 1976), especially pp. 109–15.

2. Discussion of the economics of bootlegging here and in subsequent paragraphs is based on a variety of investigative sources: the extensive Coast Guard Intelligence Files, National Archives, Washington, D.C.; the prosecution files involving cases against bootleggers for prohibition violations and income tax evasion, Central Files of the Department of Justice, National Archives; investigative files of the Internal Revenue Service, Treasury Department, Washington, D.C.; and the many drawers of files on Chicago bootlegging in Chicago Crime Commission, Chicago, Illinois. There is some discussion of

bootlegging as a business in Humbert S. Nelli, *The Business of Crime: Italians in American Syndicate Crime* (New York: Oxford, 1976), chap. 6.

3. John R. Meers, "The California Wine and Grape Industry and Prohibition," *California Historical Society Quarterly* 46 (1967): 19–32; Thomas C. Cochran, *The Pabst Brewing Company: The History of an American Business* (New York: New York University Press, 1948); William L. Downard, *The Cincinnati Brewing Industry: A Social and Economic History* (Athens: Ohio University Press, 1973); Robert F. Sexton, "Kentucky Distillers React to Prohibition," paper delivered to American Historical Association, 1974.

4. The basic facts concerning national distributors can be found in William L. Downard, *Dictionary of the History of the American Brewing and Distilling Industries* (Westport, Conn.: Greenwood, 1980); for a popular history of Seagram and the Bronfmans, *see* Peter C. Newman, *King of the Castle, The Making of a Dynasty: Seagram's and the Bronfman Empire* (New York: Atheneum, 1979); also James H. Gray, *Booze: The Impact of Whisky on the Prairie West* (Toronto: Macmillan of Canada, 1972); on bootlegging by Hatch, *see* Coast Guard Intelligence File, Box 56.

5. Hank Messick, *Secret File* (New York: G. P. Putnam's Sons, 1969), chap. 16.

6. Messick, *Secret File*, chap. 14; Jack McPhaul, *Johnny Torrio: First of the Gang Lords* (New Rochelle, N.Y.: Arlington House, 1970), pp. 274 *et. seq.*; Nelli, *Business of Crime*, pp. 220–22.

7. The following discussion of regional gambling is based on a number of sources. The best single source is the nineteen volumes of testimony before the Kefauver Committee in 1950–51; *see* U.S. Senate, Special Committee to Investigate Organized Crime in Interstate Commerce, *Hearings*, 81st and 82nd Cong. (Washington, D.C.: GPO, 1950–51). Much material, particularly on entrepreneurs with Chicago ties, can be found in various files of Chicago Crime Commission. In addition, there are dozens of popular crime histories and biographies with useful, but not always reliable, information: Estes Kefauver, *Crime in America* (New York: Doubleday, 1951); Hank Messick, *Lansky* (New York: G. P. Putnam's Sons, 1971); Messick, *Secret File*; Messick, *The Silent Syndicate* (New York: Macmillan, 1967); Dennis Eisenberg, Uri Dan, and Eli Landau, *Meyer Lansky: Mogul of the Mob* (New York: Paddington Press, 1979); Dean Jennings, *We Only Kill Each Other: The Life and Bad Times of Bugsy Siegel* (Englewood Cliffs, N.J.: Prentice-Hall, 1967); George Wolf with Joseph DiMona, *Frank Costello: Prime Minister of the Underworld* (New York: William Morrow, 1974); Andrew Tully, *Treasury Agent: The Inside Story* (New York: Simon and Schuster, 1958); and Albert Fried, *The Rise and Fall of the Jewish Gangster in America* (New York: Holt, Rinehart and Winston, 1980), chap. 6.

8. For discussion of the background in Nevada and Las Vegas, *see* Donald

Ashbaugh, *Nevada's Turbulent Yesterday* (Las Vegas: Western Lore Press, 1963); Gilman M. Ostrander, *Nevada: The Great Rotten Borough, 1859–1964* (New York: Knopf, 1964); Perry Kaufman, "Public Relations Men, Images, and the Growth of Las Vegas," paper presented at convention of Organization of American Historians, April 1973.

9. This and the next two paragraphs are based on sources in note 7. See also Ed Reid and Ovid Demaris, *The Green Felt Jungle* (New York: Pocket Books, 1964); Wallace Turner, *Gamblers' Money: The New Force in American Life* (Boston: Houghton Mifflin, 1965); and Ralph Pearl, *Las Vegas Is My Beat* (Secaucus, N.J.: Lyle Stuart, 1973). On Tony Cornero's gambling ships, *see* G. Edward White, *Earl Warren: A Public Life* (New York: Oxford, 1982), pp. 50–51.

10. The economic history of the casino industry in this paragraph and the next is based primarily on a series of fine articles by William R. Eadington, including: "The Evolution of Corporate Gambling in Nevada," *Nevada Review of Business & Economics* 6 (Spring 1982): 13–22; "Regulatory Objectives and the Expansion of Casino Gambling," in ibid. 6 (Fall 1982): 4–13. *See also* Howard J. Klein, "The F.B.I. and the Gaming Industry: Annals of Myth and Reality," *Gaming Business Magazine* 3 (1982): 214–24. There are many books on the Teamsters, including Ralph and Estelle James, *Hoffa and the Teamsters: A Study of Union Power* (Princeton, N.J.: D. Van Nostrand Co., 1965), especially part IV and app. II; and Steven Brill, *The Teamsters* (New York: Simon and Schuster, 1978). For an insightful analysis of casinos and their regulation in Nevada, *see* Jerome H. Skolnick, *House of Cards: The Legalization and Control of Casino Gambling* (Boston: Little, Brown, 1978).

11. *New York Times*, October 12, 1983, p. A–1; Philadelphia *Inquirer*, October 16, 1983, p. F–1.

12. For an excellent analysis of the process by which the committee reached conclusions not supported by its evidence, see William Howard Moore, *The Kefauver Committee and the Politics of Crime, 1950–1952* (Columbia: University of Missouri Press, 1974).

13. "Deposition of Morris B. Dalitz," in case of *Rancho LaCosta, Inc., v. Penthouse International, Ltd.*, Superior Court of the State of California for the County of Los Angeles (August 1976), p. 133.

Alcohol Problems and Policies in Historical Perspective

Alcohol was probably discovered by our primitive ancestors by accident. Unguarded fruit left in the sun could have fermented. The effect on the famished hunter-gatherer who first gulped that mess could have been equivocal: happiness followed by hangover. Perhaps that event is symbolized in the biblical narrative of the primal couple who discovered the knowing of good and evil in one fruit. An ancient source identifies that unnamed fruit not as the apple but as the grape. Our clever primitive ancestors soon learned not to rely on accident to provide the magical potion that assuaged hunger and anger, promoted brotherhood as well as violence, prompted passion and stilled it, evoked pain and eased it. They learned to make wine, and beer too.[1]

Early on, our forebears felt a need to develop policies to control the production, the distribution, and the drinking of their wines and beers. Anthropologists have reported such regulations among preliterate peoples throughout the world.[2] The oldest policies suggest two inferences: one, that the beverages were valued; two, that they were troublous. Perhaps those inferences should be ranked in reverse order.

The classical literate peoples left abundant records of legislative treatment of alcoholic beverages. The oldest is the regulation of taverns in the code of Hammurabi, king of Babylon, more than four thousand years ago.[3] Drink was evidently popular and already an important article of commerce. Egyptian records of equal antiquity indicate that there too beer and wine flowed freely and that drunkenness was common, and tolerated. Advice and warning against "drunking" are also recorded, but few could read. It was not until the reign of Hakim the

Wise (A.D. 996) that under Muslim influence the making and import of liquor was prohibited in Egypt. That was a mere thousand years ago and is by no means the oldest prohibition in civil law. A business in bootlegging then developed, and when caught, bootleggers were punished severely.

In the land of Israel, the ancient Hebrews were heavy drinkers. Drunkenness was often reproved by the prophets.[4] But the voluminous record contains no general legislation against drinking. Even the monition of the queen mother in the thirty-first chapter of Proverbs is advice on kingly policy, not a legal interdiction of drinking. The Jews became relatively sober later, in the era of the second temple. The legislation then aimed at integrating wine with religious occasions, and the practice of diluting wine for drinking was incorporated into ritual law. The reform of the drinking ways was gradual, a multigenerational process that involved the reorientation of the whole culture around the Bible.[5]

China provides a rich record. More than two thousand years ago (206 B.C.), in the Han dynasty, social drinking, rather than solitary drinking, was discouraged. Drinking in groups of more than three was punishable by a fine in a specified weight of silver. Clearly, the control was aimed at the party-going rich. Yet the appreciation of drink is evident in a royal decree only a generation later (179 B.C.) that all old men should be provided with grain, meat, and wine. Nevertheless, in the next generation (147 B.C.) the emperor prohibited distillation of fermented beverages. Six centuries later drinking was evidently extremely troublesome and evoked extreme measures, perhaps the oldest recorded total prohibition. In A.D. 459 Emperor Liu Pe'i made drinking as well as selling liquor punishable by beheading. We do not know how many heads were hefted, but it is likely that a lot of payola was passed. More than three centuries later, in 781, Emperor T'ai Tsung introduced one of the modern methods of controlling the consumption of alcohol: he limited the number of liquor shops. Half a millennium later the great Kublai Khan banished all makers of liquor. What effect this measure had on drinking is not known, but no doubt it temporarily relieved some problem of the royal treasury, since the government confiscated the property of the banished.[6]

The ancient Persians adopted a strict policy to control the youth-and-alcohol problem: youngsters were prohibited from even being present when wine was served at festive occasions. To control the drinking by adults, a more moderate rule was ordained: the wine could be served only in cups, not in pitchers. Omar's "loaf of bread, jug of wine, and thou"—with music, yet—is of much later date.[7]

In Greece, the Spartans were sparing in drink as well as food. Yet the classic literature, including the ancient myths and legends, tells that copious drinking was the rule rather than the exception. One legend attributes to Amphictyon of Attica the origination of the policy to dilute wine with water, apparently to avert drunken disputations at the Amphictyonic Council. The most popular god was Dionysus, also known as Bacchus—the wine god.[8]

In ancient Rome too, drink must have been quite troublesome. The Romans tried to cope with the youth-and-alcohol problem by prohibiting men under thirty from drinking wine except at formal ritual occasions. Women were under the same prohibition at all ages. Roman censors were required to punish drunkenness severely. We are comparatively liberal today, allowing mere twenty-one-year-olds to drink. And we do not discriminate against women, although until recently in some jurisdictions women were not permitted to drink standing at the bar, but only seated at a table, perhaps because they were considered the weaker sex. We should note, however, that the law against drinking by women was notoriously ignored in Rome by the second century.[9]

If there is a moral for us in all this old history of alcohol control policy, it is found in the Bible: "There is no new thing under the sun."[10]

In the five or six centuries before and after the beginning of the current era, a fateful mix of three cultures occurred—the Greek, the Hebrew, and the Roman—destined to powerfully influence European culture and its American offspring to this day. Drinking was inherent in the parent cultures and universal among the newly encultured European peoples. The Christian church, torchbearer of the developing European, or Western, culture, had some rules about drinking. Excess in drinking, that is, "drunking," like gluttony, was a punishable sin, but not moderate drinking; for wine, as well as beer, was one of God's goods.[11]

The sin, drunking, came to be commonly indulged. Literary classics from England, France, Germany, Italy, and Russia from the twelfth century on described widespread drunkenness among all classes of the Christianized populations.[12] Not that the people were irreligious, but alcohol was irresistible.

The ecclesiastical rules against drunkenness were incorporated into English civil law under James I and were thus brought over to America. Being drunk was a punishable offense in New England as in old England. The records of the Massachusetts colony tell of people who got drunk repeatedly and were repeatedly fined or punished physically, and who nevertheless repeated getting drunk. A perceptive judge remarked in one case that evidently drunkenness in the accused was "a sinn rooted in him."[13] We must suspect, with that colonial judge, that this sinner was disabled from choosing not to get drunk—an alcoholic.

This brief adumbration of history suggests that from the beginning alcohol was a double-dealer with humankind. And yet, it has ever been irresistible. Seductive yet treacherous, rewarding yet punitive, alcohol is the Delilah of drugs.

America had a spirited affair with alcohol in the eighteenth century, and in the nineteenth. Drinking was the popular diversion. Indulgent imbibing was customary on important occasions. Drunking was not uncommon. On the expanding frontier, heavy drinking was practically the sign of belonging. You had to be a "man's man" to survive, so you had to "drink like a man."[14]

In cities and towns, the reputable colonial tavern, the meeting place of the folk, was displaced by the disreputable saloon, headquarters of gambling, prostitution, crime, corruption, and hard drinking. With that development, alcohol made a lot of enemies. In the nineteenth century, a time of growing materialism, people tended increasingly to focus on things rather than on people. The religious people, the church folk, did not entirely escape the influence of overwhelming materialism. I suspect it was in the spirit of the times that their attention came to be focused on the thing, alcohol, rather than on the people who used or abused it.[15] So alcohol the thing was seen as the enemy. "A good familiar creature," Shakespeare's Iago called it.[16] "Good creature of God," the pious pilgrims called it.[17] And it was metamorphosed as the Demon Rum. The original temperance movement had defined "temperance" etymologically as moderation in drinking. It was overwhelmed and taken over by the teetotalists of abstinence. "Temperance movement" came to mean anti-alcohol movement.

By the twentieth century the anti-alcohol movement was riding high in the political saddle. Its leadership had discovered single-issue manipulation of politicians. With some help from the circumstances of World War I, the American classical temperance movement achieved by 1919 teetotal success: national constitutional prohibition of the manufacture, import, transport, or sale of alcoholic beverages.[18]

Prohibition manifested immediate benefits. Those wicked saloons closed. A lot of drinkers were caught short, or their supply was exhausted before long. The total of alcohol consumed was reduced drastically.[19] The effect was seen in diminished rates of arrests for drunkenness and of alcohol-related admissions to hospitals. An interesting phenomenon was the closing of hospitals that had specialized in treating alcoholics. They apparently believed that as alcohol was outlawed, there would soon be no more alcoholics.

Before long the needy ones found sources of supply. Before long the less needy too were patronizing those sources. By ten years into prohibition, its benefits were invisible. In 1924, in cities, seventeen-year-old kids could buy beer in speakeasies. It was near-beer laced with a shot of alcohol. At fifty cents a stein, it was expensive, but who could afford not to have entrée to a speakeasy? The speakeasies flourished, and the smugglers and the moonshiners and the bootleggers and the gangsters and the grafters flourished. By 1930 a college sophomore had no standing without a flask on his hip. In 1935 I compiled statistics on the alcoholic admissions to one New York hospital. That hospital had more than ten thousand alcoholic admissions a year in the 1930s.[20] Most of them had become alcoholics during prohibition.

When the prohibition amendment was repealed in 1933, alcohol did not automatically become innocent in everybody's eyes. Fear of the return of old evils was widely expressed. Proposals for averting the evils were formulated.[21] Sweden, with its profit-limited monopoly system, personal ration books (but only one to a married couple), and local temperance boards empowered to intervene when anyone was buying too much liquor or getting drunk, was held up as an attractive model. But the Swedes were about to begin looking around for a more attractive side road.

How by happenstance certain new ideas came to predominate is a history too complex to be recited here in more than the barest outline.[22] A Research Council on Problems of Alcohol was formed in 1937 with the main purpose to promote the funding of scientific research.[23] Solutions to alcohol problems were to be sought from a newly popular respected source—from science. The repeal of the Eighteenth Amendment was seen as a welcome end to a failed experiment. The scientists, scholars, and social do-gooders who were enlisted in the research council were aware of the benefits that had accrued from the curtailment of the supplies of liquor under prohibition. They were more acutely aware of the social damages that had heavily outweighed the benefits. Not convinced that the new legal regulations of alcohol would be more effective than the old in averting or reducing problems, they organized themselves to promote the systematic study of alcohol problems. They anticipated that scientific method would yield a more realistic understanding of the causes of various alcohol-related problems and suggest more effective solutions that society could be persuaded to adopt.

The historically most significant achievement of the council was a grant obtained from the Carnegie Corporation for a review of the biological literature on effects of alcohol, assigned to Karl M. Bowman and Norman Jolliffe at New York University College of Medicine. An executive being needed, Jolliffe persuaded E. M. Jellinek, then at Worcester State Hospital, to abandon schizophrenia research for alcohology. A classicist, polylinguist, biometrician, and much else besides near-genius, Jellinek did not interpret "biological" too strictly and, with eclectic collaborators, produced psychological as well as psychiatric and biological reviews.[24] Out of these reviews came the founding of the *Journal of Studies on Alcohol* at Yale University and the formation there of the Center of Alcohol Studies under the impetus of the famous physiologist-educator Howard W. Haggard and the leadership of the to-be-famous alcohologist-educator Jellinek. Then came the founding of the original Summer School of Alcohol Studies, the first public clinics for the treatment of alcoholics, the formation of a National Committee for Education on Alcoholism, which was to become the National Council on Alcoholism, and the first state commission on alcoholism.[25] These events occurred during the ten years from 1935 on, and they led to the development of what has lately been named the alcoholism movement.

Some recent writings have suggested that the alcoholism movement was the purpose of the original post-prohibition alcohol-related efforts.[26] They have partly mistaken the results for the purpose. This history-oriented symposium is a good occasion to fix on the record some of my remembrances of what was intended and what eventuated.

The Research Council on Problems of Alcohol—and the term is "alcohol," not "alcoholism"—was interested, when founded, in the support of scientific research. The Yale center which effectively carried on the research council's original intentions was called the Center of Alcohol Studies, not the Center of Alcoholism Studies. Its journal, destined to become the foremost scientific voice in its field in the world, was and still is the *Journal of Studies on Alcohol*. Its documentation system covered the alcohol literature, not just alcoholism, and is now formally organized as Alcohol Research Documentation, Inc.[27] Its school was the Summer School of Alcohol Studies, not Alcoholism Studies. An important exception is coming.

The research in the Center of Alcohol Studies by a multidisciplinary staff and the publications that resulted demonstrate that the interest was in alcohol in its multifarious biological and social manifestations and effects, with alcoholism regarded as one of the leading problems. Jellinek analyzed the problems of alcohol.[28] Selden Bacon's brilliant introductory essay was on "foundations for a sociologic study of drinking behavior."[29] He emphasized "the attempt to gain control over problems of alcohol . . . rather than the problem of alcohol" and the need "to recognize the relation of inebriety to all other forms of drinking." Here, for "inebriety" we should read "alcohol misuse" or "drunkenness" or "alcoholism." Even the clinics for the treatment of alcoholism were founded expressly with a research orientation, within which the study and improvement of therapeutics was a main purpose.[30]

The Center of Alcohol Studies announced four programmatic aims: research, education, treatment, prevention. Research was conducted in physiology, biochemistry, psychology, sociology, epidemiology, education, economics, history, law, and documentation. With the opening of the clinics, research was extended to medicine, psychiatry, social work, and therapeutics. Education was conducted by means of technical and nontechnical publication, training of professionals and graduate students, and in the summer school. The laws and the content of alcohol education in the schools were studied, and an association of alcohol and narcotics educators was founded, with an orientation no longer rooted in the temperance–anti-alcohol movement.[31] Treatment of alcoholics and alcoholism was conducted and studied in the clinics. To prevention we paid mainly lip service. We theorized that treatment could have a preventive effect as well. We theorized that education was the ideal means for prevention, and we sought to help fashion it toward that end. We initiated some programs in industry with a preventive as well as remedial aim.[32] But, as I understand it, we knew we could not prevent alcohol; we believed we could not prevent drinking; and we did not know how to prevent the problems. We hoped that our research and experience—social, biological and clinical—would develop useful clues for prevention.

The time was coming when our efforts and aims were to be overwhelmed. Some ten years after the beginning of the science movement at the end of prohibition, a brilliant young woman came to the second session of the summer school. She was Marty Mann, the first woman who achieved sobriety in Bill Wilson's Alcoholics Anonymous group in New York. She suggested to the academicians at the Center of Alcohol Studies that it was not enough to educate the specialists who came to the summer school and the scientists, researchers, and professionals who read the *Journal of Studies on Alcohol*. If the alcoholism problem, the drunkenness problem, the problem of people drinking too much, was to be alleviated, then the wide public must be educated and enlisted.

She was persuasive, and the leading persons in the Center of Alcohol Studies were ready to be persuaded. Scientists may be reformers at heart. Howard W. Haggard, director of the Laboratory of Applied Physiology, had been the first physician-educator to conduct an unsponsored public health program on the radio. E. M. Jellinek, whom Haggard had appointed director of the Center of Alcohol Studies, was by background an educator. (A little-known fact about him is that his only academic degree was in education.) And Selden Bacon, the center's rising young sociologist who was destined to succeed Jellinek as director, was eager to engage in an action aimed at improving the society. So the Center of Alcohol Studies became a center of activism: it sponsored the founding of the National Committee for Education on Alcoholism and for five years housed and supported it.[33]

This was the primary activity that focused on alcoholism especially. This is the important exception that I mentioned previously. As an elucidative aside, I may note that until then we had used chiefly the old-fashioned term "inebriety." It covered our understanding of alcoholism. But it implied also other misuses of alcohol, including plain drunkenness. We limited the meaning of "alcoholism" to a condition which we regarded as a treatable disease, a condition we had already begun treating—and studying—in the Yale Plan clinics. Not that "alcoholism" was a new term. It dates back to the mid-nineteenth century, and we and others had used it all along.[34] But now it was to be popularized. That, in fact, was one of the aims.

The National Committee for Education on Alcoholism took off and soon soared. It had the prestigeful backing of the Yale University Center of Alcohol Studies. It had the skillful leadership of Marty Mann, whose background was in public relations. And it had the useful support of many influential sobered alcoholics and their friends.

Why the scientists in the Center of Alcohol Studies supported this public movement to popularize the cause of alcoholism, to publicize the slogans "alcoholism is a disease," "the alcoholic is sick," "alcoholics can be treated successfully," "alcoholics are worth treatment," is not commonly understood. I was present, a modest assistant to Haggard and Jellinek, when the center staff discussed the question of sponsoring and supporting such a cause. I recall Selden Bacon expressing it well: the problems of alcohol would never be resolved unless the general public could be moved to become concerned. That public could not be interested—we could not involve the public consistently—in the sort of problems that engaged us, the scientific problems which were the subject of most disciplined study. To interest and involve the public, it was necessary to stimulate people with an emotional cause. What was needed was an alcoholism organization similar to those popularizing the causes of poliomyelitis, tuberculosis, heart, mental health, cancer. A large public could be interested in diseases from which many suffered and which could be alleviated by scientific-medical activity. The way to gain public interest and broad support of the study of alcohol problems was to popularize the cause of alcoholism, the disease, and the recovery potential of those suffering humans, the alcoholics.

That was the reasoning of the scientist-academicians in the Center of Alcohol Studies. That was why they "went public," as it were, sponsoring and supporting the National Committee for Education on Alcoholism during its first years (1944–48). Some of them even went out making speeches in the good cause. Some composed pamphlets; our artistically talented colleague, Vera Efron, illustrated the early ones. They supposed that the wider public interest in the disease alcoholism, in helping its victims, and in the prospect of preventing it, would result in the development of a voluntary health organization that would raise money to support scientific research—research not just in alcoholism but in all the problems related to alcohol. In my youthful naiveté, that is what I too imagined.

As it turned out, the alcoholics took over the national committee totally. They succeeded in getting public attention and interest—for alcoholism. Within five years it became evident to the scientists at the Yale center that the people who were working in and for the national committee were interested only in alcoholism and concerned only to help the suffering alcoholic. They were narrowly Alcoholics Anonymous–oriented and could not be interested in other problems of alcohol, not in scientific studies, not even in the prevention of alcoholism. The March of Dimes people understood the importance of scientific research and supported it generously, as did the tuberculosis folk and other health- or disease-oriented organizations. But not the alcoholism folk. True, they never raised a lot of money, perhaps because of their limited interest. The partnership of the national committee and the Center of Alcohol Studies was dissolved as the committee moved out of Yale to headquarters exclusively in New York and became the National Council of Alcoholism.

Eventually, the federal government through the National Institute of Mental Health (NIMH)—stimulated in part by the Center of Alcohol Studies—became a major supporter of research on alcohol problems. There was an "alcohol desk" in the NIMH bureaucracy. That was not enough for the alcoholics. In fact, it was disagreeable to them that alcoholism should be at all connected with NIMH. For didn't that imply that the disease alcoholism was a mental disease, that alcoholics were or had been mentally ill? By the latter 1960s the alcoholics had acquired what I understand is called political clout. They were able to get alcohol moved into a special pigeonhole called an alcohol center. But it was still connected to mental health and was headed by a doctor, Jack H. Mendelson of Harvard, who was interested mainly in research. The alcoholics were, if anything, disappointed. In 1970 they succeeded in getting Congress to establish an independent National Institute on Alcohol Abuse and Alcoholism. An insignificant portion of its rich budget was allocated to the support of research. Actually, its first director, Morris E. Chafetz of Harvard, was a man who understood and valued research. But he also possessed practical political sense. He knew his institute's constituents and how they must be served. The bulk of the budget went to helping alcoholics.

After a few years the pendulum of concern about alcohol began to swing in its reverse direction. Two separate interests were concerned to forward a new, or more accurately, a renewed, perspective on alcohol problems, and their renewed perspectives happened to be similar.

Some of the scientists whose interest was focused on alcohol problems, especially social scientists, began to question the perspective that seemed to have governed the post-prohibition public approaches to those problems.[35] Those approaches had been characterized by the neutrality of the scientists toward alcohol itself, and in the parallel neutrality of the popular movement as represented in the National Council on Alcoholism. The scientists in the original Research Council on Problems of Alcohol, reacting to the exaggerated propaganda of the classical temperance movement and the horrible experience of prohibition, had adopted a carefully neutral policy toward alcohol itself. They saw the problem of alcoholism as one of the alcohol problems, and as inhering essentially in the people, the small minority among drinkers who became alcoholics. While alcohol was essential for alcoholism, the fundamental causes were apprehended in the people who, for internal or circumstantial reasons, or both kinds, drank enough often enough to become addicted. This understanding was well expressed in the book *Alcohol Explored* by Haggard and Jellinek, sponsored by the American Association for the Advancement of Science.[36] The National Committee for Education on Alcoholism was of course heavily influenced at its formation by these very authors and made a point of proclaiming that it was neither for alcohol nor against alcohol, that its concern was for those who suffered from a disease.

In the swing of the pendulum, the scientists and the alcoholism-ists—to name them in parallel—are both now taking a different stand. Up to the 1930s the biological as well as the social literature about alcohol characteristically reported "the evils of alcohol." That also had been the focus of compulsory education in the public schools.[37] Alcohol was blamed for everything from crime and poverty to insanity and tuberculosis. In the post-prohibition recoil of the pendulum, alcohol was absolved. Other causes were recognized, or the role of alcohol was seen as merely auxiliary. In recent years another reversal is evident. Social scientists are again blaming alcohol. Alcohol problems, they say, including alcoholism—which in their view is not a disease—occur simply in direct proportion to the total volume of alcohol consumed by a population. And the solution for the evils of alcohol is to reduce the overall average of alcohol consumed by the entire population.[38] Of course, they do not promote prohibition; that extremity is still remembered with negative affect. But they do recommend a policy of controls, that governments should interfere with the availability of alcohol to the entire population. One critic has called this recommendation neo-prohibition.[39] Perhaps a more just term is "inhibition."

Recent biomedical literature too is again filled with articles that blame alcohol, articles proclaiming that alcohol directly damages the brain, the heart, the stomach, the liver, the pancreas, the muscles, the testicles, the metabolism, and, of course, the fetus.[40] Prospective mothers are being frightened into abstinence.

That is where we stand today. Fifty years after the end of prohibition we are being advised to enact inhibition. Along with the scientists, the alcoholismists—with still mainly alcoholics in their ranks and leadership—are in full cry against alcohol. I have heard the foremost leader among them say, "If it hadn't been for alcohol, I would never have become an alcoholic." What he meant was, alcohol is the cause of alcoholism. And that is what many alcoholics would like to believe: that, of course, there was nothing wrong with them; that they were not primarily weak or defective—especially not mentally weak or deficient; that alcohol just happened to get the best of them. Once they stopped the alcohol, they were all right. So alcohol is the enemy.

In my introduction to volume 1 of the *International Bibliography of Studies on Alcohol*, I needed to justify my inclusion in that work of many articles that had been published in journals sponsored by temperance societies and that appeared to belong to the temperance cause rather than to science. I explained that in the good old days, "the 'fight against alcohol' was hardly differentiated from the 'fight against alcoholism.' "[41] It is fascinating that many of the people in the contemporary alcoholism movement are again abolishing the distinction between the fight against alcoholism and the fight against alcohol.

If after this crude attempt at historiography I may be permitted to indulge in a crude attempt at prophecy, I will predict that the pendulum will swing the other way again. The history of alcohol is marked by pleasure and problems. This history of attempts to cope with the problems is marked by repression and retreat. And the present is the same as the past.

After fifty years in the alcohol field—I began in 1933—I still believe that solutions are more likely to come from science than from legislation, from the evolution of mores rather than from the enactment of laws. But first, the scientists themselves will have to stop believing in legislative solutions. A sweeping view of the history seems to reveal that the peoples who succeeded in substantially reducing their alcohol problems did so through a cultural agency—specifically, religion. Historic examples are the Buddhists, the Rechabites, and the Muslims, who elected for abstinence, and the Jews, who chose moderation. More recent examples are the numerous Christian abstinent groups.[42]

A revolutionary event that would induce the bulk of the pluralistic American population to adopt abstinence seems unlikely. What seems more likely is a gradual adaptation of American culture to what has been aptly called responsible drinking. In that necessarily generations-long process, I believe, as Jolliffe and Haggard and Jellinek and Bacon have believed, that science can be more helpful than legislation.

But most of all I believe in the pendulum. When it has completed its current swing toward legislative repression, it will swing back toward liberal permission. And back again, and again. But as our culture ages, I believe we will achieve the wisdom of a complexity that will include, along with abstinence, enough moderation to reduce the problems enough so that alcohol will be only a moderately distracting Delilah.

NOTES

1. Mark Keller, "Problems with Alcohol: An Historical Perspective," in *Alcohol Problems: New Thinking and New Directions*, ed. William J. Filstead, Jean J. Rossi, and Mark Keller (Cambridge, Mass.: Ballinger, 1976), pp. 5–28.

2. Chandler Washburne, *Primitive Drinking: A Study of the Uses and Functions of Alcohol in Preliterate Societies* (New York: College and Universities Press, 1961).

3. Robert F. Harper, *The Code of Hammurabi, King of Babylon, About 2250 B.C.* (Chicago: University of Chicago Press, 1904), p. 37.

4. Ernest H. Cherrington, ed., *Standard Encyclopedia of the Alcohol Problem* (Westerville, Ohio: American Issue Publishing Co., 1926), 3: 892–97.

5. Mark Keller, "The Great Jewish Drink Mystery," *British Journal of Addiction* 64 (1970): 287–96.

6. Cherrington, *Encyclopedia of Alcohol*, 3: 581–88.

7. Ibid., 5: 2137–40; Robert Graves and Omar Ali-Shah, *The Original Rubayyat of Omar Khayaam* (Garden City, N.Y.: Doubleday, 1968), p. 83.

8. Arthur P. McKinlay, "The Indulgent Dionysius," *Transactions of the American Philological Association* 70 (1939): 51–61; Mark Keller, Mairi

McCormick, and Vera Efron, *A Dictionary of Words about Alcohol* (New Brunswick, N.J.: Rutgers Center of Alcohol Studies, 1982), pp. 97–98; Sabine G. Oswalt, *Concise Encyclopedia of Greek and Roman Mythology* (Glasgow: Collins, 1969), s.v. "Amphitryon"; Paul Francis Foucart, *Le Culte de Dionysos en Attique* (Paris: Imprimerie Nationale, 1904), p. 15.

9. Cherrington, *Encyclopedia of Alcohol*, 5: 2299–301; Arthur P. McKinlay, "The Roman Attitude toward Women's Drinking," *Classical Bulletin* 22 (1945): 14–15.

10. Eccles. 1: 9.

11. Edward G. Baird, "The Alcohol Problem and the Law: I. The Ancient Laws and Customs," *Quarterly Journal of Studies on Alcohol* [hereinafter *QJSA*] 4 (1944): 535–56, and "II. The Common-Law Bases of Modern Liquor Controls," *QJSA* 5 (1944): 126–61.

12. Examples are: Saint Basil the Great, "Slovo Sviatogo Velikogo Vassilija o Tom, Kak Podobaiet Vzderjatsia ot Pianstva" [The Sermon of St. Basil the Great on How it is Seemly to Refrain from Drunkenness], in A. I. Ponomareff, *Pamiatniki Drevne-Russkoi Tzerkovno-Uchitelnoi Literaratury* (St. Petersburg: Strannik, 1897), 3: 102; Der Freudenleere [pseud.], "Der Wiener Merfart," in Hans Lambel, *Erzälungen und Schwänke* (Leipzig, 1872), pp. 216–32; Jean Quentin, "Pèche de glotonie," in *Examen de Conscience pour soy Cognoistre et à Bien se Confesser (Paris, c. 1495); Philippus Beroaldus, Declamatio Lepidissima Ebriosi Scortatoris Aleatoris de Vitiositate Disceptantium* (Bologne, 1499); John Skelton, *Elynor Rummin, The Famous Ale-wife of England* (London, 1525); Sebastian Franck, *Von Dem Grewlichen Laster der Trunckenheyt* (Jestenfelde, 1531?); J. Robins, *Arraigning and Indicting of Sir John Barleycorn and J. Robins the Auther* (London, 1575); Vincentio Obsopœo, *De Arte Bibendi* (Frankfurt am Main, 1582); Thomas Nash, *Pierce Penilesse, His Supplication to the Diuell* (London, 1592).

13. Edward G. Baird, "The Alcohol Problem and the Law: III. The Beginning of the Alcoholic-Beverage Control Laws in America," *QJSA* 6 (1945): 335–83. *See* especially note 22.

14. John A. Krout, *The Origins of Prohibition* (New York: Knopf, 1925); Raymond G. McCarthy and Edgar M. Douglas, *Alcohol and Social Responsibility: A New Educational Approach* (New York: Crowell, 1949), pp. 13–24; Mark E. Lender and James K. Martin, *Drinking in America: A History* (New York: Free Press, 1982), pp. 30–86; Allan M. Winkler, "Drinking on the American Frontier," *QJSA* 29 (1968): 413–25.

15. Mark Keller, *Cultural Aspects of Drinking and Alcoholism* (Toronto: Commission on Temperance Policy and Program, United Chruch of Canada, 1958).

16. *Othello*, act 2, sc. 3.

17. Increase Mather, *Woe to Drunkards* (Cambridge, 1673).

18. Selden D. Bacon, "The Classic Temperance Movement of the U.S.A.: Impact Today on Attitudes, Action and Research," *British Journal of Addiction* 62 (1967): 5–18.

19. Computed as less than one gallon of absolute alcohol per annum per capita of the population aged fifteen years and older. E. M. Jellinek, "Recent Trends in Alcoholism and in Alcohol Consumption," *QJSA* 8 (1947): 1–42.

20. Norman Jolliffe, "Alcoholic Admissions to Bellevue Hospital," *Science* 83 (1936): 306–9.

21. For example, Raymond B. Fosdick and Albert L. Scott, *Toward Liquor Control* (New York: Harper, 1933).

22. For details, *see* Mark Keller, "Alcohol, Science and Society: Hindsight and Forecast," in *Alcohol, Science and Society Revisited*, ed. Edith L. Gombert, Helene R. White, and John A. Carpenter (Ann Arbor: University of Michigan Press, 1982), pp. 1–16. Also "Mark Keller's History of the Alcohol Problems Field," *Drinking and Drug Practices Surveyor*, no. 12 (1979): 1, 22–28.

23. Harry H. Moore, "Activities of the Research Council on Problems of Alcohol," *QJSA* 1 (1940): 104–7. "The main and primary purpose of the Research Council" was stated to be "to ascertain the facts; the secondary objective is to make the facts available. . . . " Among the outstanding scientists in the council were Karl M. Bowman, director of psychiatry, Bellevue Hospital, New York; Walter B. Cannon, professor of physiology, Harvard, author of *The Wisdom of the Body*; Anton J. Carlson, professor of physiology, University of Chicago; Howard W. Haggard, founder of the *QJSA* and the Yale Center of Alcohol Studies; Alexander O. Gettler, professor of chemistry and toxicology, New York University, and chief medical examiner, New York City; Norman Jolliffe, professor of medicine, New York University; Lawrence Kolb, assistant surgeon general, U.S. Public Health Service; F. Roy Moulton, permanent secretary, American Association for the Advancement of Science; A. T. Poffenberger, professor of pyschology, Columbia University; Edward A. Strecker, professor of psychiatry, University of Pennsylvania, president of the American Psychiatric Association, author of *Their Mothers' Sons*; Thorsten Sellin, professor of sociology, University of Pennsylvania; C. H. Watson, medical director, American Telephone and Telegraph; Willis R. Whitney, director of research, General Electric Company; and Clark Wissler, dean of the scientific staff, American Museum of Natural History. The council became an affiliated society of the American Association for the Advancement of Science. It was dissolved in 1949.

24. E. M. Jellinek and Ross A. McFarland, "Analysis of Psychological Experiments on the Effects of Alcohol," *QJSA* 1 (1940): 272–371; E. M. Jellinek, ed., *Alcohol Addiction and Chronic Alcoholism* (New Haven: Yale University Press, 1942).

25. *See* "Current Notes," *QJSA* 3 (1943): 704–9; 4 (1943): 496–508; 5 (1944): 354–58; Selden D. Bacon, "New Legislation for the Control of Alcoholism: The Connecticut Law of 1945," *QJSA* 6 (1945): 188–204.

26. For example, Robin G. W. Room, "Governing Images of Alcohol and Drug Problems: The Structure, Sources and Sequels of Conceptualizations of Intractable Problems," (Ph.D. diss., University of California, Berkeley, 1978); Dan E. Beauchamp, *Beyond Alcoholism: Alcohol and Public Health Policy* (Philadelphia: Temple University Press, 1980).

27. Mark Keller and Vera Efron, "The Classified Abstract Archive of the Alcohol Literature: Part 1: Description of the Archive," *QJSA* 14 (1953): 263–84; Mark Keller, "Documentation of the Alcohol Literature: A Scheme for an Interdisciplinary Field of Study," *QJSA* 25 (1964): 725–41; Mark Keller, "A Documentation Resource for Cross-Cultural Studies on Alcohol," in M. W. Everett, J. O. Waddell, and D. W. Heath, eds., *Cross-Cultural Approaches to the Study of Alcohol: An Interdisciplinary Perspective* (The Hague: Mouton, 1976), pp. 404–10.

28. E. M. Jellinek, "An Outline of Basic Policies for a Research Program on Problems of Alcohol," *QJSA* 3 (1942): 103–24.

29. Selden D. Bacon, "Sociology and the Problems of Alcohol: Foundations for a Sociologic Study of Drinking Behavior," *QJSA* 4 (1943): 402–45.

30. *QJSA* 4 (1943): 496–508.

31. Ann Roe, "Legal Regulation of Alcohol Education," *QJSA* 3 (1942): 433–64; idem., "A Survey of Alcohol Education in the United States," *QJSA* 3 (1943): 574–662; "Current Notes," *QJSA* 12 (1951): 688–89.

32. Ralph M. Henderson and Selden D. Bacon, "Problem Drinking: The Yale Plan for Business and Industry," *QJSA* 14 (1953): 247–62.

33. *QJSA* 5 (1944): 354–58.

34. Magnus Huss, *Alcoholismus Chronicus eller Chronisk Alkoholssjukdom*, (Stockholm, 1849).

35. For example, Kettil Bruun et al., *Alcohol Control Policies in Public Health Perspective* (Helsinki: Finnish Foundation for Alcohol Studies, 1976); Beauchamp, *Beyond Alcoholism*.

36. Howard W. Haggard and E. M. Jellinek, *Alcohol Explored* (Garden City, N.Y.: Doubleday, Doran, 1942).

37. Roe, "Legal Regulation of Alcohol Education," pp. 433–64.

38. Mark Keller, "Perspectives on Medicine and Alcoholism," *Alcoholism: Clinical and Experimental Research* 6 (1982): 327–32; Robin G. W. Room, "Alcohol Control Policies in Public Health Perspective," *Drinking and Drug Practices Surveyor*, no. 11 (1976): 1–2; Bruun, *Alcohol Control Policies*; Beauchamp, *Beyond Alcoholism*; Wolfgang Schmidt and Robert E. Popham, *Alcohol Problems and Their Prevention: A Public Health Perspective* (Toronto: Addiction Research Foundation, 1976).

39. David J. Pittman, *Primary Prevention of Alcohol Abuse and Alcoholism: An Evaluation of the Control of Consumption Policy* (St. Louis: Social Research Institute, Washington University, 1980).

40. Ernest P. Noble, ed., *Third Special Report to the U.S. Congress on Alcohol and Health* (Washington, D.C.: GPO, 1978).

41. Mark Keller, ed., *International Bibliography of Studies on Alcohol* (New Brunswick, N.J.: Rutgers Center on Alcohol Studies, 1966), 1: xxix.

42. Mark Keller, *Encyclopedia Britannica*, 15th ed., s.v. ''Alcohol consumption.''

The Historian and Repeal: A Survey of the Literature and Research Opportunities

On December 5, 1933, at almost exactly 3:32½ P.M., eastern standard time, Utah became the thirty-sixth state to ratify the Twenty-first Amendment to the Constitution. The historic vote brought an end to America's "noble experiment" with national prohibition, and with it much of the acrimony of the wet-dry debate of the previous decade. While a number of raucous celebrations marked the occasion, for the most part Americans took the news calmly. Indeed, President Franklin D. Roosevelt urged just such a response, and the *New York Times* in fact noted that a mood of "quiet restraint" was the most typical reaction to repeal. Pauline Sabin, who had done so much to bring about the wet victory as head of the Women's Organization for National Prohibition Reform, probably summed up popular attitudes as well as anyone: she hoped that "once the custom of drinking" was again open and accepted, "we shall settle down to temperance and moderation."[1] In all of these reactions was the clear message that most Americans wanted to put prohibition behind them, freeing their hands to deal with the crisis of the Great Depression and other issues of the day. Thus, in the public view repeal was an end to a chapter of the past, and to the "liquor question" in particular, not the beginning of something new.

This view of repeal has prevailed since in the work of two generations of scholars. As they dealt with the liquor question, it generally was enough to note that the Twenty-first Amendment closed the book on prohibition and to laud those who carried the wet standard. There were few kind words for the dry crusade, and if historians differed over the roots of prohibition, they almost unanimously denounced it. Repeal emerged in their work as a liberal and beneficial step, or even a sign that after an ill-starred plunge into fanaticism, America had regained its senses.[2]

Yet if they have praised repeal, historians largely have failed to deal with the subject in its own right. Fifty years after the fact, only a handful of studies exist to suggest that the Twenty-first Amendment itself—independent of the Eighteenth—might offer opportunities for productive research. This is somewhat surprising given the usual interest of historians in the constitutional process. Repeal, after all, was the nation's only successful experience with rescinding an amendment to the Constitution. It was also a milestone in America's century-old liquor question, arguably with major implications for attempts to deal with alcohol-related issues even since. Certainly other amendments of less import have received considerably more attention. The apparent neglect of the Twenty-first has been, at least in some respects, a result of historical preoccupation with the national prohibition controversy itself and, one suspects, the continuing American wish to write off that experience as an aberration.[3]

Recently, however, scholarship on the collapse of the "noble experiment" has shown signs, at long last, of coming to life. With the publication of David Kyvig's *Repealing National Prohibition* (1979), a modern study of significant caliber has finally addressed repeal directly. Breaking with older interpretations, he saw nothing inevitable about the fall of prohibition. The temperance movement, Kyvig noted, was losing ground, but the Eighteenth Amendment was still a formidable reality given the difficulties inherent in trying to amend the Constitution. Only the sophisticated political work of the Association Against the Prohibition Amendment and allied groups, Kyvig argued, carried the day for wets. He also dispelled much of the liberal image of repeal, examining its frequently conservative roots and the anti-Progressive and anti-New Deal biases of many prominent wets.[4] Kyvig's book is altogether the best study we have on the politics of repeal; it is also, however, a reflection of a growing interest in the subject in other quarters.

In fact, scholars from a number of disciplines, not just historians, have opened a searching reexamination of the entire American controversy over alcohol use, an effort which has major implications for our understanding of repeal. A number of studies already have demolished the rural-fundamentalist-fanatic stereotype of the dry movement—an image dear to the hearts of repeal leaders (or at least to their public relations personnel). Of equal importance, some of these same works have argued persuasively that if temperance goals and methods were wrong, the motives of the movement as a whole were not ignoble, and that national prohibition briefly conferred some impressive benefits on the nation, especially in reduced rates of drinking-related problems.[5] While it is not the purpose of this essay to offer an exhaustive review of the new literature on prohibition, it is important to note that these revisionist interpretations have rejected any view of the wet-dry struggle as a battle between good and evil. Thus it follows that much of what earlier historians have assumed about repeal is now open to serious question. Additional research, sometimes stemming from a renewed modern interest in alcohol problems, has questioned whether repeal really put a finish to anything other than the Eighteenth Amendment. Suggesting conclusions quite to the contrary, it has pointed to consequences of repeal that may have influenced the ways in which Americans have viewed and dealt with problem drinking ever since. Overlooked for years as a subject for serious research, then, there is now a growing understanding that the repeal experience deserves closer inspection.

This essay will suggest some of the needs and opportunities that scholars might pursue in the further study of repeal. It would be difficult to anticipate the full variety of future research, much less to categorize it at this point. Much of it will cross the lines of traditional political and social history, drawing as well on medicine, the social sciences, and biography. Yet an organizational scheme is necessary, and what follows will deal with potential studies in three separate, although frequently related, areas: the issues and circumstances surrounding the actual process of repeal, its later implications and consequences, and, in a more speculative vein, potential lessons the repeal struggle may hold for the present. Addressing these issues no doubt will send researchers in any number of directions, but the effort should deepen our understanding of the forces that brought down national prohibition. It should also demonstrate that in dealing with the problems inherent in the Eighteenth Amendment, the Twenty-first raised, and left unanswered, some significant questions of its own.

THE PROCESS OF REPEAL: QUESTIONS OF HOW, WHO AND WHY

The initial aims of the Twenty-first Amendment were quite specific: repeal advocates wanted the elimination of the Eighteenth Amendment, an end to its support legislation and bureaucracies, and the return of liquor control policies to the individual states. This is precisely what happened, and with seeming ease the federal government was able to wash its hands of liquor-related issues (except, of course, for the collection of alcohol-related revenues) in the immediate aftermath of repeal. National authorities, openly relieved at the demise of prohibition, hoped that the revival of legal liquor would not produce conditions sparking yet another reform drive; any problems, with luck, would remain at the state level. Speaking for the Roosevelt administration, the first director of the new Federal Alcohol Administration, Joseph H. Choate, Jr., pledged to let the states handle their own affairs in such matters. He also offered the hopeful view that repeal would actually help limit intemperance, that it would lead to people drinking ''less in many cases.''[6] There was a certain irony in all of this: where advocates of national prohibition had sought to eliminate alcohol-related problems through concerted federal action (albeit in cooperation with the states), wets now offered federal inaction—through repeal—as productive of a similar end. In any case, for the first time in years, the focus of liquor legislation had shifted from the national to the state level.

This change, however, welcome as it was to federal authorities, was not a step the nation took lightly. It involved a number of issues that, even if historians have not noted them in particular depth, could have complicated matters seriously had the drive for the Twenty-first Amendment not gone smoothly. The first of these involved the process of repeal itself, which was not as obvious a matter as might appear at first glance. Kyvig's *Repealing National Prohibition*, for example, revealed the extent and sophistication of the organizational and political effort necessary to secure the wet cause at the federal level; significantly, he also noted that repeal advocates in the states worked just as hard. They had to, given the vital role of the states in the constitutional amendment procedure. If they had not, and had drys consequently made a better showing in the state contests, the repeal effort— as well as Roosevelt's plans to skirt the liquor question—could have suffered a serious embarrassment. We need to know, then, as much as possible about the antiprohibitionist campaigns in the states. This presents a major opportunity for the historian.

The fact is that we know relatively little about the repeal movement at the state and local levels. Indeed, we have a much better understanding of dry activities, as the battle to enact the Eighteenth Amendment produced some impressive studies of local politics and reform efforts. While this is not the place to review them all, it is important to stress that monographs such as Norman Clark's *The Dry Years: Prohibition and Social Change in Washington* (1965) and C. C. Pearson and J. Edwin Hendricks's *Liquor and Anti-Liquor in Virginia, 1619– 1919* (1967), to cite only two of many fine examples, have shed considerable light on the regional operations of the prohibitionist crusade.[7] Local political alliances, reform motives, lobbying techniques, personalities, and even conflicts between various temperance groups have all received a good deal of attention, with the result that we know quite a bit about how state and national dry leaders coordinated their efforts. There is still a lot to learn in this regard, and we should welcome additional regional monographs on the temperance movement; but at least at this point, historians of repeal would do well to take the existing works on the dry side of the contest as models for their own.

Studies of repeal on the state level should produce a wealth of insights on the nature of the fight against prohibition. For example, as Kyvig pointed out, the repeal effort provided the only instance in national history of the use of state conventions in the ratification of a constitutional amendment. It behooves us, then, to learn as much about those conventions as possible.[8] How did the states organize them, and how easily did they do so? Were there no legal challenges, and what did the public think? The fact that repeal advocates so easily dominated most of the conventions also deserves further investigation. How did wets and drys prepare for the conventions? Who were the delegates, how did they fight their battles, and did regional issues or circumstances contribute to convention results? Depending upon the findings of such investigations, we could well find that the movement for repeal was as diverse at the grassroots level as the earlier movement for prohibition. Indeed, the few studies we have on the subject, which focus on the repeal efforts in Oklahoma, Ohio, and New York, suggest that this was in fact the case.[9]

Any study of state and local activities must include the roles of the organized repeal groups. At the national level, we know quite a bit about the workings, for example, of the Association Against the Prohibition Amendment. But the picture is not as clear in the states, and future students of the repeal effort would do well to consider how the AAPA consolidated local support for its particular program (for there were other antiprohibitionists on the scene in some areas), as well as how it went about building its state-level political and financial networks. The workings of the Women's Organization for National Prohibition Reform deserve similar attention. Indeed, it merits particular care, given its direct competition with the Women's Christian Temperance Union for the loyalties of American women. A comparative study of the two women's groups, focusing particularly on the backgrounds and values of their respective leaders and memberships, would probably prove enlightening.[10] In fact, in so far as organizational tactics were concerned, a broader comparison between the major wet and dry groups also presents an interesting opportunity: For there is every possibility, that, in an ironic twist of fate, wets simply built upon the organizational techniques pioneered earlier by the drys. Political scientists or practicing politicans, especially those concerned with single-issue causes (of which more later), might benefit considerably from such an inquiry.

Scholarly opportunities also abound in the activities of the archenemies of repeal—those who rallied against it under temperance banners. The story of the temperance movement's fall from grace has already told us much of why the repeal effort succeeded. We know, for example, thanks to the recent work of K. Austin Kerr, that the Anti-Saloon League, previously a political giant, was riven with internal problems and lost some of its most astute leaders as the wet assault gathered momentum. At the same time, the Prohibition party had become little more than a faction, and the WCTU had lost both members and a great deal of the broad reform commitment that had given it earlier vitality.[11] Yet there is considerably more to mine in this vein.

Political history has a good deal of potential here. For instance, it would be useful to simply reverse Kyvig's study of repeal, focusing on the same subject but through the eyes of temperance partisans and organizations. In hindsight, some drys, such as Fletcher Dobyns in *The Amazing Story of Repeal* (1940) or Ernest Gordon in *The Wrecking of the Eighteenth Amendment* (1943), proved remarkably perceptive in their analyses of what had befallen the dry cause in its final days.[12] But they were rather obtuse during the struggle itself, and it is worth asking why. What had happened to the dry constituency that made it blind to its weaknesses; why was it unable to respond to the wet challenge (frankly, even a losing effort could have been conducted with greater competence); and what changes in temperance outlooks and activities did the struggle for repeal engender?

All of these questions involve, at least to some extent, issues of social or political leadership. Yet the fact is that we know relatively little about the lives of those who led the contending prohibitionist and repeal legions. While the antislavery, suffrage, and other reform movements have produced a host of solid biographies, few such studies have emerged from the liquor question. Of those we have, some, such as the lively works on Carry Nation by Herbert Asbury and Robert Lewis Taylor, were written in acid and present obviously stilted views. Even the more careful life of James Cannon, *Dry Messiah*, by Virginius Dabney (1949), played to the hostile stereotypes of temperance leaders.[13] Biography therefore presents an area of major scholarly opportunity.

Indeed, there are signs that historians of the liquor question already are turning in this direction. I have recently completed a *Dictionary of American Temperance Biography* (1984), while Robert S. Bader and Robert Hohner are now at work on new biographies of John P. St. John and Bishop James Cannon respectively.[14] The changing historiography of reform also invites fresh looks at such drys as Neal Dow and Frances Willard; and we have long needed careful studies of the likes of Wayne B. Wheeler, William ("Pussyfoot") Johnson, Lillian M. N. Stevens, and Ernest Cherrington, to name only several candidates. On the wet side of the coin, individuals such as William Stayton and Pauline Sabin also merit full biographies.[15] Probing the contributions, motives, beliefs, and even the foibles of such people—all grist for the biographical mill—should add appreciably to our understanding of the controversies over prohibition and repeal. Indeed, there is every likelihood that even the most stubborn old stereotypes of the struggle and its leaders will soften, and in many cases melt away entirely.

All of the preceding, however, points toward a much greater need in the study of prohibition and repeal. Questions on the *how* of repeal, and of who led the fight for and against it, are in fact parts of the larger problem of *why* repeal occurred at all. Given the recent historiography of prohibition, most of the old explanations of repeal will no longer do. Even Kyvig's political study, revealing as it is, did not fully explore why the public, so ready to accept the Eighteenth Amendment in 1920, so quickly embraced the arguments of the AAPA and repeal only thirteen years later. What had happened in America during those years to radically change popular opinion?

Scholars have not been unaware of the need for further study in this area, and in fact a number of social and intellectual historians have devoted considerable thought to it. Paul Carter, Norman Clark, James Martin, and I, for instance, although with different emphases, have all written of a temperance movement espousing a fairly unified worldview—largely antipluralist, fearful of social disorder, rooted in traditional Protestant values (although not necessarily in a strictly religious sense).[16] Prohibition was imperiled, these writers argue, and repeal became a possibility, with the coming of basic changes in social outlook. The very success of the Eighteenth Amendment in reducing the worst alcohol-related problems made it impossible for dry leaders to maintain the old zeal of the rank and file. Prosperity, at least arguably, altered perceptions of the good life, made rapid industrialization seem less threatening, and along with changing social roles of women and ethnic groups, promoted a cultural and political pluralism previously unknown. All of this was at marked variance with the unitary ideology that had carried so much of the temperance drive. American society, or so these studies suggest, moved beyond the antiliquor crusade; whereas social developments in the nineteenth and early twentieth centuries had worked in favor of the Women's Christian Temperance Union and the Anti-Saloon League, by the late 1920s the times simply were working for the AAPA.[17] Yet as intriguing as these works are, at this point they are only approaches to the subject. They offer theses for others to test, but they need monographic support—or refutation.

There is also the fact, of course, that Americans received plenty of encouragement as their views dimmed on the worth of the temperance crusade. Repeal advocates orchestrated a truly astonishing public relations campaign, hurling invective and sarcasm at drys while barraging the public with supposed evidence of the virtue of the wet cause.[18] We need to know in great detail how proliquor forces used (or is "manipulated" a better word?) the media in shaping popular opinion. Indeed, the repeal experience offers an opportunity for a classic case study of the employment of sophisticated propaganda in behalf of the particular cause. While the matter would be difficult to assess with precision, it still would be worth considering the effect of the wet media blitz *alone* in the downfall of prohibition—that is, the extent to which it operated independently of other forces working for repeal. Drys certainly never learned to cope with it, and historians have failed to appreciate its full impact.

LIVING WITH THE RESULTS: THE CONSEQUENCES OF REPEAL

If the effort to dry out the United States generated any number of significant consequences for the nation, the restoration of legal beverage alcohol did the same. Repeal ultimately touched on federal and state alcohol control policies and politics, public attitudes toward liquor use and related problems, and a complex set of social issues—crime, poverty, and public health, among others—linked closely to drinking behavior over the course of American history. The relationships of repeal to these matters, however, often were less than obvious at first. The depression, hard feelings over national prohibition, and World War II masked a number of immediate effects of repeal, while others, more subtle in their workings, would have become apparent only over time anyway. Readily evident or not, though, the consequences of repeal offer important opportunities to the historian.

Political historians especially have some interesting studies in front of them. As the Roosevelt administration dismantled the apparatus of national prohibition, it became clear that repeal had forced one of those rarest of instances in government, the demobilization of an important bureaucracy. The end of the Volstead laws brought down the Prohibition Bureau, the focus of so much public displeasure as the war against drink went sour. Yet despite the controversy the agency engendered, we know little of its decline and passing.[19] How did the growing repeal movement affect its functions? With the final wet victory, what became of its personnel and leaders, its operations in progress, and the litigation resulting from its actions? How can we reach a final assessment of its role? These are not idle questions, as the Prohibition Bureau, whatever else it became, was first and foremost an institutionalized effort to compel general allegiance to a particular reform effort. Few other social or moral crusades ever developed a police arm, and for that reason alone we might profit from learning what we can about the bureau and its ultimate fate. Repeal, in dooming the agency, created the possibility for an eminently manageable case study (only thirteen years) in the actual enforcement of a reform.

If repeal destroyed a bureaucracy, though, it established another. The Federal Alcohol Control Administration, established under the National Industrial Recovery Act (NIRA) and directed by Joseph Choate, Jr., became one of the more successful agencies of the Roosevelt administration, although it never enjoyed the public or historical prominence of many of the New Deal bureaucracies. It worked well in overseeing the remaining alcohol-related concerns of the federal government (until it passed from the scene when the Supreme Court declared the NIRA unconstitutional), although it avoided the political controversies that placed other Roosevelt-inspired agencies in the headlines. The evident success of Choate's operation, though, raises a variety of questions. As the depression-wracked nation was in desperate need of federal revenues, some of which the new liquor revenues provided (an argument repeal proponents had made with some vigor), it was Choate's job to see that nothing impeded the collection of those funds, although we know little enough about how the Alcohol Control Administration did its work.[20] It might prove interesting to get a better view, as the establishment and operation of the agency offers the best possible example of how the federal government organized itself to cope with repeal.

The Alcohol Control Administration stance toward alcohol problems presents another aspect of the issue. Choate did his best to avoid controversy in this regard; as we have noted already, the last thing Franklin D. Roosevelt wanted was a renewed temperance drive. We should ask, then, how the federal alcohol agency, or for that matter the national government generally, dealt with suggestions that federal authorities assume a more active stance in some new effort against alcohol problems in post-repeal America. For these were such calls: the temperance movement had not completely lost its zeal, and even non-temperance voices were heard on occasion. Among others, the ideas of Professor Yandell Henderson of Yale University, who wanted the alcohol content of beverages strictly limited, come to mind here.[21] Choate and his successors, however, evidently never seriously considered any action to disturb the new status quo; one suspects that a regard for healthy liquor revenues, as much as any fears of reviving the wet-dry wars, lay at the heart of the matter. Yet we only have the broadest view of the federal involvement with alcohol-related issues immediately after repeal, and the entire episode deserves more attention than it has received so far. Such a study would be a welcome successor to others focusing strictly on repeal itself.

For the same reasons, both political and economic historians need to look in greater detail at the relationship between the New Deal (via Choate's office and otherwise) and the liquor industry. Repeal sparked one of the greatest reversals in the history of governmental dealings with a major industry. Having declared ''the traffic'' an outlaw in 1920, national authorities happily became its partner in 1933. This fact alone merits the attention of historians, who in any case have long expressed an interest in governmental-industrial relations in the 1930s.[22] The resurgence of the drink trade offers a compelling chance to study a dynamic example of business growth, marketing techniques, union activities, and, in fact, an economic success story in the midst of the Great Depression. Given business attitudes during the 1930s, what did the liquor industry think of the Roosevelt programs; how did the industry's financial relationship with the government affect its conduct; and how did it so successfully fight off the old charges of its culpability for the nation's alcohol problems? Addressing such questions would lead to welcome additions to the literature of repeal and of the New Deal, while also shedding further light on the change in popular attitudes toward reform generally and temperance specifically.

The shift from dry to wet policies also had a major impact on the states. Indeed, they may well have felt the brunt of repeal, as circumstances forced the individual states to create control systems to regulate liquor sales and distribution. Yet repeal had disclosed the lack of any national consensus on what to do about liquor control (a point to which we will return), and without uniform attitudes or federal guidance, the new state regulatory bodies varied considerably. Some created state monopolies over the trade in distilled spirits and wines, while allowing the private sale of beer; others banned the sale of alcohol beverages by the drink; still others allowed the retail market in alcohol to operate with relatively few restrictions.[23] All gave at least lip service to the desire to avoid the recurrence of the often scandalous abuses of liquor laws and the tolerance of the drinking problems that marked the pre-prohibition years.

The rise of the post-repeal state liquor control efforts pose a number of questions for historians. Aside from a broad view of which states created what kinds of systems, scholars have not looked carefully at how and why the individual legislatures chose their respective regulatory models. Neighboring states could produce remarkably different systems. Pennsylvania, for example, established a monopoly over spirits and wine, while New Jersey chose to regulate a market fully in private hands. Other equally striking variations between adjoining states were fairly common, and it is worth asking what it all meant. Were differences due to local politics, residual temperance strength, opposing reform views, or what? What role did the revived liquor industry play in various areas? Studies such as Clark's on the passing of prohibition in Washington State, and Jimmie Lewis Franklin's *Born Sober: Prohibition in Oklahoma, 1907–1959*, have shown something of how these elements could influence post-repeal liquor policies in the states, although a comprehensive picture of the issue has yet to emerge.[24]

And for that matter, what difference did the control agencies make? No historian has ever assessed the impact of these regulatory efforts on alcohol-related matters, a task which may well prove interesting given recent claims for the partial efficacy of national prohibition. What might a careful comparison between prohibition and the various regulatory approaches show in this regard? These questions are not strictly academic, as the repeal-induced state liquor control systems developed into the agencies in existence today. Conclusions on their origins and performance may well have useful aspects in the present.[25]

The differences in state alcohol control structures serves to emphasize another important aspect of repeal: the Twenty-first Amendment ended America's only experiment with a national alcohol-use policy. For national prohibition, successful or not, was just that: it put the government on record against beverage alcohol and in favor of personal abstinence, implied clearly that the best way to attack drinking problems was to eliminate alcohol (even if this was not actually a part of the Eighteenth Amendment), and just as clearly called for uniform popular attitudes in support of these positions. While it demolished this policy, repeal offered no replacement (unless the government's hands-off position can be considered such). All of this became of particular significance as Americans realized that alcoholism and its attendant difficulties did not disappear with the demise of the Volstead Act. With the old standards gone, how were Americans to react?

This question has only begun to receive adequate historical attention, although several points have become clear. Americans have been unable, for example, to form any consistent views on alcohol use since repeal. Earlier years of prohibitionist indoctrination clearly had their effects. While many people happily went back to their drinking, any number of post-repeal surveys showed that others drank only with mixed emotions. Still other Americans, while allowing alcohol as acceptable for adults, have been anything but sure about allowing it among youth; we have seen decades of sparring over drinking age legislation as a result. Nor are Americans comfortable with how to handle drinking problems generally. Alcoholism is clearly a problem with personal, social, moral, and economic implications, but even as obvious a threat to public safety as drunken driving has defied a uniform or effective response. Who is responsible for the continued existence of alcohol problems? Is it the drinker's fault; is it society's fault for not taking action; or does the issue lie at the feet of the liquor industry for en- couraging drinking? There are proponents of all these positions, al- though few concrete ideas able to win widespread popular support have emerged on what to do about them.[26]

The problem of how to teach school children about alcohol use after repeal has been a prominent case in point. During the heyday of the temperance reform, a campaign of "scientific temperance instruction" sponsored by the Women's Christian Temperance Union brought the dangers of demon rum and the glories of total abstinence vividly be- fore millions of students. While this approach remained stubbornly embedded in some regions after repeal, most of the nation's schools gradually abandoned such tactics. But nothing coherent emerged as a replacement. Gail Gleason Milgram has pointed out that educators, fully aware that alcohol use required some attention, were at a loss as to what to do with the subject. The guidelines were clear on how to han- dle such issues during prohibition, but no one in the post-repeal period could (or can) answer with certainty.[27]

This very ambivalence, however, one of the major legacies of re- peal, holds out rich opportunities for the historian. Not the least of these should be an attempt to explain the roots and persistence of these un- certain attitudes in some comprehensive way. Other disciplines have tried, but have succeeded only in highlighting its various facets (dif- ferences in drinking and attitudes toward it, by sex, ethnic group, age group, and the like) or sketching in only the broadest of fashions the rise of conflicting views.[28] Looking at the question of ambivalence calls for depth and perspective, the sort of things that history can provide admirably if it looks in the right places. What issues, for example, prevented the public from reaching a consensus on alcohol-related issues? Previous studies, as we have noted earlier, have pointed to anger born of the prohibition experience, the depression, then the coming of war. But few authors have actually tried to determine to what extent these elements really made a difference, much less how they intertwined with other questions. Matters of social change potentially cast a major shadow here. Did Americans, with their rampant pluralism, simply outgrow the ability to reach agreement on such an issue? Had society changed to an extent that even the resurgence of such old problems as alcoholism and alcohol-related violence and waste could no longer evoke a politically powerful response? A number of authors have suggested as much, and if future studies confirm their tentative conclusion, then the roots of modern ambivalence may be far more significant than the frustrations born of prohibition, depression, and war.[29] Shed light on all of this, and such matters as the confusion in alcohol education and the differences between state liquor control systems become much more explicable.

At the same time, and somewhat ironically, this confused state of affairs allowed the evolution of some significant new thinking on alcohol problems. And if the resulting ideas never produced a crusade of the magnitude of the temperance movement, they have had an important modern impact and must stand as a major additional legacy of repeal. Perhaps the most salient of these has been the emergence of the modern alcoholism research and treatment effort, loosely termed the alcoholism movement. The Twenty-first Amendment, in striking down enforced abstinence as a national policy, had cleared the way for nontemperance solutions to problem drinking. The decades following 1933 saw the rise of Yale (later Rutgers) Center of Alcohol Studies, the birth of Alcoholics Anonymous, the work of E. M. Jellinek and other alcohol researchers, the founding of the National Council on Alcoholism, and the popularization of the old disease conception of alcoholism. All of this happened, we should note, largely as the result of private initiative; government—local, state and federal—came back into the picture only later. What happened was a cautious rebirth of public concern over alcohol problems, although it overtly avoided prohibitionist rhetoric and goals and did not immediately resort to legal means.

We already have a fairly broad view of how the transition from the temperance movement to the alcoholism movement took place. There are some excellent studies on specific aspects of the change.[30] But the subject had so many facets—touching as it does on popular attitudes, the nature of post-repeal drinking problems, public health concerns, medical and psychological developments, and the roles of central individuals—that its full dimensions and import will not emerge before a great deal of further study. We need to know more, for instance, about how the remnants of the dry crusade interacted with those who orchestrated the new research and treatment effort. Jay Rubin has demonstrated that they did not start out as enemies, and their eventual divergence over the 1940s needs to be traced with care.[31] It can shed considerable new light on the dry crusade's inability to adapt to the post-repeal world, as well as how modern alcohol studies gained a respectable place in the academic and medical communities. Studies focused specifically on the growth of the Yale Center of Alcohol Studies, on the National Council on Alcoholism, and on early corporate-based alcoholism programs and treatment facilities will be helpful in this regard as well. Indeed, they present excellent opportunities for institutional histories.

A word of caution is in order here, however. Such studies, while they promise to be revealing, will be complex affairs. Sources are scattered and buried in institutional archives, often with limited accessibility and without having been cataloged or otherwise organized to aid a research effort (a problem to which we will return). Moreover, authors will have to deal with questions as diverse as public health policy, the growth of medical and psychological understanding of alcohol use, the nature of institutional research, and the politics and public relations programs inherent in trying to rebuild national interest in drinking problems. Ernest Kurtz's superb history of Alcoholics Anonymous has shown how good studies of this kind can be, and how a wealth of evidence drawn from social and intellectual history, medicine, the social sciences, and even philosophy can blend into a penetrating work.[32] Future inquiries in this vein thus are likely to show the social effects of repeal at their most complex, and perhaps at their most surprising given the limited original goals of those who proposed the Twenty-first Amendment.

We should also consider the matter of the individual drinker in this context. It was, after all, the behavior of drinkers, both alcoholics and not, that sparked the liquor question in the first place. The prohibition movement had defined (or at least had attempted to define) drinking as deviant behavior and had established social norms such that drinkers lay beyond public respectability.[33] Repeal restored the drinker to a measure of social acceptance, or at least officially confirmed a change in popular attitudes that already had taken place anyway. It was quite a shift in values, although it has escaped most historians. Indeed, only a few studies have looked at how drinkers figured in the debates over American liquor. W. J. Rorabough has offered some sugggestive ideas on the meaning of drinking and its value to drinkers in the early republic, and a few studies have explored popular views of the alcoholic.[34] But no one has undertaken a serious examination of the specific values Americans have attached to their personal alcohol use in the past, or of how these same drinkers viewed the appeals of wets and drys. In other words, in considering the debate over legal liquor, historians have overlooked possible relationships between reformers and "reformees." In 1976 Norman Clark observed that we needed a history of "Drinking American," and we still do.[35]

While there is little way to predict what form such a history (or histories) might take, there are some useful precedents for this kind of study. The literature already has fine examples of research on the bonds between reformers and the intended subjects of their reforms: one thinks here of the studies of the abolitionists and the slaves, suffrage crusaders and American women, and the Progressive reformers and the groups they sought to influence.[36] Investigations along similar lines, focusing on drinkers, would prove equally revealing, and again would provide opportunities for historians to draw on the rich alcohol-related literature in the social sciences, medicine, and psychology (indeed, a psychohistorical study could well emerge here), as well as more traditional sources. How drinkers perceived themselves should give us a much better view of what drinking has meant in American culture. And, given social vacillation on the status of the problem drinker—is he a victim and a candidate for the health care system, or an irresponsible profligate suited to the criminal justice system, or what?—we need a careful study of how Americans have felt about (and dealt with) the alcoholic. Such studies will deal with the social meaning of drink at its most basic level and probably offer one of the best views to be had of what was won and lost in the fight for repeal.

In some cases it might even be possible to measure what was won and lost, a circumstance which suggests a series of studies on the actual effectiveness of repeal. The word "effectiveness" in this context, however, requires some justification, for in serving some of its intended purposes—getting rid of Volsteadism, removing the liquor question from the federal agenda—repeal certainly succeeded. But in arguing for repeal, its proponents promised the public a series of positive social, political, and economic results to follow the wet victory (just as prohibitionists, in an earlier day, had made promises of a golden age to flow from the Eighteenth Amendment); and in asking for an assessment of the effectiveness of the Twenty-first Amendment, I am really asking for a comparison of pre-repeal rhetoric with post-repeal reality in these areas.[37] This is not an easy assignment, for any such measures will be subjective to at least some extent. Indeed, if we concede that neither drys nor wets could actually deliver all of their promises, to what extent did even partial results constitute success? A determination of how to measure the impact of pro- and anti-liquor laws would by itself be an important contribution to the literature.

If we proceed with this caveat in mind, however, the subject still holds a number of interesting possibilities. Assessments of repeal will necessarily build directly on the continuing study of prohibition. It can hardly be otherwise, because any judgment on the impact of repeal will, in great measure, depend on our conclusions on the effectiveness of the dry laws in accomplishing their purposes. But if we use such a comparative approach, we can ask a number of important questions about both repeal and prohibition and probably shed new light on old assumptions. We need a careful study of the effects of both wet and dry legislation on an entire range of alcohol-related problems, beginning with the issue of consumption levels. Indeed, as long ago as 1932, wet economist Clark Warburton suggested that the key question was whether or not prohibition actually prohibited, as so many other social and health complications were tied to actual drinking rates. The historical literature on this question has grown steadily since the late 1960s, but a comprehensive investigation of the matter has yet to emerge.[38]

Public drinking is a related subject and was also a major public concern during the battle over prohibition. In his recent study *The Saloon: Public Drinking in Chicago and Boston, 1880–1920*, Perry Duis has presented astonishing detail on the socioeconomic milieux of the drinking establishments and their patrons, explaining why the bars were popular in some quarters while provoking fury in others.[39] The critics of the barrooms, of course, carried the day by 1920, and even with repeal President Roosevelt warned against the return of the saloon in its previous guise. But did it return? The answer is hazy, for we have no adequate comparative studies of drinking places before and after prohibition. Nor, for that matter, do we know enough about the illegal establishments that operated in violation of the Volstead Act. There is plenty of room, then, for studies focusing directly on the speakeasies and the bars that opened after repeal. If such efforts prove as fruitful as Duis's research, we should be better able to gauge the success of prohibition against the alleged vices of the saloon and to assess the claims of wets that repeal would lead to an improvement over the state of public drinking as it existed under the Eighteenth Amendment.

The list of possible topics grows quickly after this: What impetus did prohibition really give to the growth of criminal activity, and did repeal subsequently improve the situation? Were there major economic benefits of prohibition, as drys claimed, and how did they compare to economic growth attributed to repeal? The Eighteenth Amendment allegedly alleviated problems of the urban poor, as less family money supposedly went to alcohol and more to savings and necessities.[40] But was this in fact true? And did spending patterns change again as a result of repeal? The personal and public health aspects of prohibition and repeal also invite comparison. Some historians have argued persuasively that national prohibition had a clearly positive impact on the health of the country. But they have argued from limited (albeit very suggestive) data, some of it open to other interpretation. A careful look at this issue, including an equally close look at how conditions changed (if at all) after the demise of the "noble experiment," would be welcome.[41] It has been fifty years—time enough for changes to have become apparent, and time for historians to deal with them.

REPEAL AND THE PRESENT: WERE THERE ANY LESSONS?

Drawing lessons from history is always a tricky business. With all due regard for Lord Acton's sentiments on the matter, history does not repeat itself, and considerable prudence ought to inform all comparisons between past and present—much less between past and future. Yet part of the appeal of history is the possibility that it can shed some light on the nature of human conduct, and as long as that appeal is there, we will continue, for better or worse, to use the past as at least a rough guide to what lies ahead. Certainly the history of national prohibition has served (and still serves) in this capacity. Partisans involved in the controversies over modern alcohol and drug issues have drawn freely on supposed parallels to the battles of the 1920s and 1930s, and there are no signs that such appeals to history will stop. Historians, then, should indeed look at the repeal experience with an eye toward assessing its utility for dealing with the present—if only to point out the limitations and problems inherent in such historical comparisons.

The modern debate over the legalization of marijuana (and to a lesser extent other drugs) has given rise to the most frequent—and most heated—arguments from history. Indeed, the subject now has a considerable literature, and while some of it is argued in detail and at length, most of it boils down to a few critical assumptions and comparisons: First, and centrally, this wisdom holds that legal prohibitions of anything that people really want will fail. That national prohibition failed is an article of faith here, and thus it follows that the prohibition of marijuana must also fail. Second, there is the insistence that the consequences of failed prohibitions will be similar. If the Volstead years supposedly led to increased alcohol use, more crime, disrespect for law, and a multitude of other alleged calamities, the illegal status of cannabis has been productive of the same results—or so goes the argument.[42]

All of this, of course, is a doubtful exercise. It shows either a ghastly ignorance of the recent historiography of prohibition, or makes assumptions about the "noble experiment" that go far beyond available evidence. And if the purpose of such reasoning is to make a case for the legalization (or the decriminalization) of marijuana, perhaps national prohibition is not even the right starting point for analysis of this kind. In fact, repeal is arguably more instructive: it would be equally plausible to insist that if we want to predict the possible results of a repeal of marijuana control laws, we should look at what happened when we got rid of the statutes banning alcohol. I have already suggested a similar study in another context, but it would be particularly helpful here. It could start with the promises of repeal advocates: more liquor revenues, fewer alcohol problems, less crime, more faith in the law, and so forth. How did these pre-repeal promises compare with later performance? The answers will no doubt invite considerable controversy (alcohol problems, for example, hardly went away; and did a revival of the liquor industry really reduce alcohol-related crime?), a fact which is in itself instructive. It may well be that repeal was a mixed blessing—and how would proponents of a modern repeal feel about such a conclusion? Do you build a cause based on such a dubious foundation? At the very least, then, it might well be that the lessons of history are hardly as clear as some promarijuana partisans would have us believe. If they favor change in the current laws, they might do better to fight their battles on the merits of their case as it is today, for any "justification" from the historical record will certainly be open to challenge, and in part, probably to repudiation. Even so, given the frequency of appeals to history in the marijuana debate, a full demonstration of this point in a careful comparative study would be a genuine public service.

The prohibition of marijuana, however, is by no means the only area with intriguing possibilities for comparative study. There are others with equal or even greater potential. For example: Whatever else the temperance movement was during its ascendency, by its fall it had become a largely single-issue crusade. Opposing it were repeal advocates who had organized a single-issue campaign of their own. How both wets and drys conducted themselves might therefore prove instructive in assessing the impact of modern groups organized along similar lines. One thinks here of anti-abortion groups, the nuclear freeze movement, and lately, even certain animal rights organizations. Yet before any meaningful comparisons are possible, we need considerable spadework on why the temperance movement, so closely allied to other reforms in its early years, ultimately tied its fortunes so securely to the prohibition issue alone. What happened to its broad-based reform vision? Jack S. Blocker, Jr., has explored this question in regard to the Prohibition party; but such groups as the Women's Christian Temperance Union and the Anti-Saloon League, as well as temperance ideology generally, need similar treatment. What happened, for example, to the "do everything" policy of the Women's Christian Temperance Union after the death of Frances Willard? Why did the Anti-Saloon League, whose leaders often had far-ranging interests and splendid records in other reform endeavors, finally pin all of its hopes on the Eighteenth Amendment?[43] These questions need asking, for there may have been a middle ground for drys in the fight to save prohibition, one short of total victory (some modification of the Volstead Act to allow light wines or beers, perhaps?), but well beyond the eventual total defeat inflicted by the forces of repeal.[44]

Whatever the answers, they are likely to have both reassuring and disturbing aspects. Drys and, as Kyvig's study has shown, wets as well, proved able to enact their pet reforms into law, and on the highest levels. Thus single-issue politics today builds on a potent legacy of success. But can such success endure? The temperance example suggests that if reformers lose touch with the popular pulse and allow their own zeal to lapse, even a measure as seemingly secure as a constitutional amendment is open to counterattack. On the other hand, the AAPA suffered a major check when, reconstituted in part as the American Liberty League, it tried to use its techniques and arguments in an arena beyond the repeal struggle.[45] How far, then, can a single-issue group venture beyond its original turf? If the wet-dry controversy itself seems dated today, the efforts of the combatants—especially their organizational and political techniques—may still hold lessons worth learning.

The modern alcoholism movement might also benefit from a similar consideration of the wet-dry controversy. When repeal took the federal government out of the business of making alcohol policy, it also set the stage, as we have seen earlier, for the rise of such groups as the Center of Alcohol Studies and the National Council on Alcoholism. In a somewhat ironic turn, the activities of these new organizations set events in motion that ultimately, during the 1960s and early 1970s especially, brought national authorities back into the picture. We need not only a thorough study of how this came about (which alone will be a major project) but also an examination of the new movement as it has taken on concrete and permanent form. Its various constituents—research laboratories, professional organizations, treatment units, the National Council on Alcoholism, the National Institute on Alcohol Abuse and Alcoholism, and other groups—have, at least arguably, begun the normal process of developing internal concerns which color their views of their work. Impulses to help the alcoholic, learn what we can about alcohol use, and ameliorate drinking problems have merged with the requirements of the political process, fund-raising and administration, and even bureaucratic conservatism. For instance, in *The Politics of Alcoholism*, Carolyn L. Wiener has shown how this process transformed or even muted some of the original reform enthusiasm of the alcoholism movement. Her monograph focused on California, but it clearly demonstrated the promise of this line of investigation. Similar studies, however, might be even more revealing if informed by the experience of national prohibition. The "noble experiment" was never able to make the transformation from crusade to institution, at least not to the satisfaction of most citizens. Enmeshed in day-to-day affairs, its ardor cooled as it failed to make good on all it promised; and as controversy engulfed its operations, it became ripe for repeal. The modern movement, which has labored under internal conflicts of its own (the "controlled drinking" controversy and its reluctance to seriously consider strict controls on alcohol consumption as a national prevention policy both come to mind here) would do well to keep the fate of the prohibitionist cause in view as it charts its own future.[46]

A FINAL NOTE: REPEAL AND THE SOURCES

There is a final topic to consider in suggesting any further work on repeal. The subject lacks adequate documentation of critical source collections, contributions to which would be of major benefit to historians. Over the past several years, the situation has begun to improve. Recent work on the Anti-Saloon League, for example, has uncovered more primary source material than most researchers knew existed.[47] Microfilm editions, properly arranged, of the papers of the AAPA and the Women's Organization for Prohibition Reform have also become available.[48] At the Rutgers Center of Alcohol Studies, Penny Booth Page has published a model collection inventory, for the first time allowing adequate access to the thousands of documents (manuscript and print) of historical significance in the center's library.[49] These are all steps in the right direction, but in general, bibliographical aides, manuscript catalogs, collection inventories, and even attempts to preserve pertinent sources from loss or deterioration are not on a par with those of other fields. The papers of the Washingtonian Hospital, for instance, the first alcoholism-treatment facility in the nation, now lie uncataloged and inadequately protected in a private garage. While this is an extreme example, it is hardly unique, and even collections not in immediate physical danger are frequently inaccessible.[50] The field therefore needs to bring its sources to light and to make them available to the research community. The fate of a good deal of the work suggested in this essay probably depends, at least in some measure, on such a continuing bibliographic effort.

The issues addressed in this essay are only the tip of a scholarly iceberg. I have asked only the most obvious questions, pointed only to the clearest needs. Future studies will go far beyond the areas touched on here, especially as interesting results provoke further inquiry. But even this brief look at the matter has suggested something of the range of opportunities open in the study of repeal. At least I hope it has, for the significance of the Twenty-first Amendment—and the national prohibition it brought down—reaches quite beyond the mere politics of alcohol. It involves nothing less than our ability to mold national values and to solve social problems in a complex, pluralistic, and democratic society.

NOTES

1. *New York Times*, December 6, 1933 p. 22; Pauline Sabin quoted in Mark Edward Lender and James Kirby Martin, *Drinking in America: A History* (New York: Free Press, 1982), p. 135.

2. *See*, for examples, Andrew Sinclair, *Prohibition: The Era of Excess* (Boston: Little, Brown, 1962); Herbert Asbury, *The Great Illusion: An Informal History of Prohibition* (Garden City, N.Y.: Doubleday, 1950); John Kobler, *Ardent Spirits: The Rise and Fall of Prohibition* (New York: Putnam, 1973).

3. For the paucity of studies on the Twenty-first Amendment, especially in comparison with other studies on the Constitution, see Earlean M. McCarrick, *U.S. Constitution: A Guide to Information Sources*. American Government and History Information Guide Series, vol. 4 (Detroit: Gale Research, 1980), especially chap. 12; Alpheus T. Mason and D. Grier Stephenson, Jr., comps., *American Constitutional Development* (Arlington Heights, Ill.: Harlan Davidson, 1977); Stephen M. Millett, *A Selected Bibliography of American Constitutional History* (Santa Barbara, Calif.: Clio Books, 1975); and Lester B. Orfield, *The Amending of the Federal Constitution* (Ann Arbor: University of Michigan Press, 1942).

4. David E. Kyvig, *Repealing National Prohibition* (Chicago: University of Chicago Press, 1979).

5. For an insightful and influential essay in this vein, *see* John C. Burnham, "New Perspectives on the Prohibition 'Experiment' of the 1920s," *Journal of Social History* 2 (1968): 51–68. The most recent statement of this view is in Lender and Martin, *Drinking in America*, pp. 136–39.

6. Quoted in Lender and Martin, *Drinking in America*, p. 170.

7. Norman Clark, *The Dry Years: Prohibition and Social Change in Washington* (Seattle: University of Washington Press, 1965); C. C. Pearson and J. Edwin Hendricks, *Liquor and Anti-Liquor in Virginia, 1619–1919* (Durham: Duke University Press, 1967). For examples of other fine state studies, see Earl C. Kaylor, Jr., "The Prohibition Movement in Pennsylvania, 1865–1920," Ph.D. thesis, Pennsylvania State University, 1963; Gilman Ostrander, *The Prohibition Movement in California, 1848–1933* (Berkeley: University of

California Press, 1957); Paul E. Issac, *Prohibition and Politics: Turbulant Decades in Tennessee, 1885–1920* (Knoxville, Tenn.: University of Tennessee Press, 1965); Jimmie Lewis Franklin, *Born Sober: Prohibition in Oklahoma, 1907–1959* (Norman, Okla.: University of Oklahoma Press, 1971); and Larry Engelman, *Intemperance: The Lost War Against Liquor* (New York: Free Press, 1979) on Michigan.

8. Kyvig, *Repealing National Prohibition*, pp. 172–82. For a revealing analysis of the conventions soon after their work, *see* Everett S. Brown, "The Ratification of the Twenty-first Amendment," *American Political Science Review* 29 (1935): 1005. *See also* Noel T. Dowling, "A New Experiment in Ratification," *American Bar Association Journal* 19 (1933): 383–87, Elmer Davis, "How the Wets Won," *Current History* 34 (1933): 276–84; and Everett Somerville Brown, comp., *Ratification of the Twenty-first Amendment to the Constitution of the United States: State Convention Records and Laws* (Ann Arbor: University of Michigan Press, 1938).

9. Robert S. Walker and Samuel C. Patterson, *Oklahoma Goes Wet: The Repeal of Prohibition* (New York: McGraw-Hill, 1960); Leslie Joseph Stegh, "Wet and Dry Battles in the Cradle State of Prohibition: Robert J. Bulkley and the Repeal of Prohibition in Ohio," Ph.D. thesis, Kent State University, 1975; William John Jackson, "Prohibition as an Issue in New York State Politics, 1836–1933," Ph.D. thesis, Columbia University, 1974.

10. Such studies will benefit from the recent microfilm editions of the Papers of the Association Against the Prohibtion Amendment and of the Women's Organization for National Prohibition Reform (Wilmington, Del.: Scholarly Resources, 1982) edited by David E. Kyvig.

11. Indeed, the Prohibition party never really was more than a faction, but its retreat from political significance is traced in Jack S. Blocker, Jr., *Retreat from Reform: The Prohibition Movement in the United States, 1890–1913* (Westport, Conn.: Greenwood, 1976). The problems of the Anti-Saloon League during these critical years are examined in Norman H. Dohn, "The History of the Anti-Saloon League," Ph.D. thesis, Ohio State University, 1959; and in K. Austin Kerr, "Organizing for Reform: The Anti-Saloon League and Innovation in Politics," *American Quarterly* 32 (1980): 37–53. Kerr will treat the subject in greater depth in his forthcoming *Organized for Reform: A New History of the Anti-Saloon League* (New Haven: Yale University Press, 1985). *See also* Kyvig, *Repealing National Prohibition*, pp. 135–36. On the narrowing reform commitments of the Women's Christian Temperance Union, *see* Lender and Martin, *Drinking in America*, pp. 160–61; Norton H. Mezvinsky, "The White Ribbon Movement, 1874–1920," Ph.D. thesis, University of Wisconsin, 1959; and Samuel Ungar, "A History of the National Women's Christian Temperance Union," Ph.D. thesis, Ohio State University, 1933.

12. Fletcher Dobyns, *The Amazing Story of Repeal: An Expose of the Power*

of Propaganda (Evanston, Ill.: Clark, 1940); Ernest Gordon, *The Wrecking of the Eighteenth Amendment* (Francestown, N.H.: Alcohol Information Press, 1943).

13. Herbert Asbury, *Carry Nation: The Woman with the Hatchet* (New York: Knopf, 1929); Robert Lewis Taylor, *Vessel of Wrath: The Life and Times of Carry Nation* (New York: New American Library, 1966); Virginius Dabney, *Dry Messiah: The Life of Bishop Cannon* (New York: Knopf, 1949).

14. Mark Edward Lender, *Dictionary of American Temperance Biography: From Temperance Reform to Alcohol Research, the 1600s to the 1980s* (Westport, Conn.: Greenwood, 1984). For an older work on St. John, *see* Edna Tutt Frederickson, "John P. St. John: The Father of Constitutional Prohibition," Ph.D. thesis, University of Kansas, 1930.

15. Biographical sketches of all of these individuals except Stayton and Sabin are in Lender, *Dictionary of Temperance Biography*, *passim*. For older titles, all in need of revising, *see* Frederick A. McKenzie, *"Pussyfoot" Johnson, Crusader—Reformer—A Man Among Men* (New York: Revell, 1920); Justin Steuart, *Wayne Wheeler, Dry Boss: An Uncensored Biography of Wayne B. Wheeler* (New York: Revell, 1928). The best biographical sketch of Stayton is in Kyvig, *Repealing National Prohibition*, pp. 39–42; but *see also* "William H. Stayton," *Repeal Review* 7 (1942): 3. For Sabin, *see* scattered sources cited in Kyvig, *Repealing National Prohibition*, p. 226, note 11; and *Notable American Women: The Modern Period* (Cambridge: Harvard University Press, 1980), pp. 618–19.

16. *See*, for examples, Paul A. Carter, "Prohibition and Democracy: The Noble Experiment Reassessed," *Wisconsin Magazine of History* 56 (1972): 189–201; Paul A. Carter, *The Twenties in America* (rev. ed., New York: Crowell, 1975); Norman A. Clark, *Deliver Us from Evil: An Interpretation of American Prohibition* (New York: Norton, 1976); Lender and Martin, *Drinking in America*.

17. Lender and Martin, *Drinking in America*, pp. 150–53, 159–67.

18. Kyvig, *Repealing National Prohibition*, *passim*, covers the political agitation of the AAPA in this regard. *See also* Dayton E. Heckman, "Prohibition Passes: The Story of the Association Against the Prohibition Amendment," Ph.D. thesis, Ohio State University, 1939; and Andrew C. McLaughlin, "Satire as a Weapon against Prohibition, 1920–1928: Expression of a Cultural Conflict," Ph.D. diss., Stanford University, 1969. For a dry view of the subject, *see* Dobyns, *The Amazing Story of Repeal*.

19. For an enforcement view of the bureau, *see* Mabel Walker Willebrandt, *The Inside of Prohibition* (Indianapolis: Bobbs-Merrill, 1929); for views of the bureau in its later years, *see* Kyvig, *Repealing National Prohibition*, pp. 106–7, 111–12.

20. Kyvig, *Repealing National Prohibition*, pp. 189–90.

21. Yandell Henderson, *A New Deal in Liquor: A Plea for Dilution* (Garden City, N.Y.: Doubleday, Doran, 1934).

22. Part of this question involves the Federal Alcohol Control Administration under the National Recovery Administration (*see* note 20, above); but the liquor business did well, and avoided confrontation with the federal government, even after the fall of the National Recovery Administration. *See also* Carl W. Badenhausen, "Self-Regulation in the Brewing Industry," *Law and Contemporary Problems* 7 (1940): 689–95.

23. For contemporary views of this issue, *see* Grace C. Root, ed., *Thirty-seven Liquor Control Systems of Today* (n.p., 1932); and *More Liquor Control Systems of Today* (n.p., 1933); Leonard V. Harrison and Elizabeth Laine, *After Repeal: A Study of Liquor Control Administration* (New York: Harper, 1936); and George A. Shipman, "State Administrative Machinery for Liquor Control," *Law and Contemporary Problems* 7 (1940): 600–20. For a legal analysis in historical perspective, *see* David S. Kersfelt, "The Effect of the Twenty-first Amendment on State Authority to Control Intoxicating Liquors," *Columbia Law Review* 75 (1975): 1578–1610.

24. *See* the sources cited above (note 23), as well as Franklin, *Born Sober*, and Clark, *The Dry Years*.

25. Lender and Martin, *Drinking in America*, pp. 180–81. This may be true particularly when local control systems reflect something of regional views toward alcoholism treatment, alcohol education, minimum drinking-age laws, and other alcohol-related issues.

26. Ibid., pp. 177–95. *See also*, for differing views of modern drinking and on its implications, Cooperative Commission on the Study of Alcoholism, *Alcohol Problems: A Report to the Nation*, ed. Thomas F. A. Plaut (New York: Oxford University Press, 1967); Carolyn L. Wiener, *The Politics of Alcoholism: Building an Arena Around a Social Problem* (New Brunswick, N.J.: Transaction, 1981); and Dan Edward Beauchamp, "Precarious Politics: Alcoholism and Public Policy," Ph.D. diss., Johns Hopkins University, 1973.

27. Gail Gleason Milgram, "A Historical Review of Alcohol Education: Research and Comments," *Journal of Alcohol and Drug Education* 21 (1976): 1–16.

28. *See*, for an example in this regard, Selden D. Bacon, "The Classic Temperance Movement of the U.S.A.: Impact on Attitudes, Action, and Research," *British Journal of Addiction* 62 (1967): 5–18. Bacon, a sociologist, focuses on a narrow portion of temperance opinion in tracing the roots of modern views toward drinking. For a wider study, reflecting the diversity of sociocultural data involved in shaping patterns of alcohol use, *see* Don Cahalan, Ira Cisin, and Helen Crossley, *American Drinking Practices: A National Study of Drinking Behavior and Attitudes* (New Brunswick, N.J.: Center of Alcohol Studies, 1969).

29. *See*, for example, Lender and Martin, *Drinking in America*, p. 192.

30. For an overview of the issue, *see* ibid., pp. 181–93. For specific studies, *see* Wiener, *The Politics of Alcoholism*; Jay L. Rubin, "Shifting Perspectives on the Alcoholism Treatment Movement, 1940–1955," *Journal of Studies on Alcohol* 40 (1979): 376–86; Mark Edward Lender, "Jellinek's Typology of Alcoholism: Some Historical Antecedents," *Journal of Studies on Alcohol* 40 (1979): 361–75; Mark Keller, "Mark Keller's History of the Alcohol Problems Field," *Drinking and Drug Practices Surveyor* 14 (1979): 1–28; and an important paper by Penny Booth Page, "The Origins of Alcohol Studies: E. M. Jellinek and the Documentation of the Alcohol Research Literature," History of Science and Technology Seminar, Rutgers University, 1984.

31. Rubin, "Shifting Perspectives on the Alcoholism Treatment Movement," pp. 376–86.

32. Ernest Kurtz, *Not-God: A History of Alcoholics Anonymous* (Center City, Minn.: Hazelden Educational Services, 1979).

33. For this argument, *see* Joseph R. Gusfield, *Symbolic Crusade: Status Politics and the American Temperance Movement* (Urbana: University of Illinois Press, 1963). "Status politics" has not fared well in recent historiography, but Gusfield's contention that organized temperance tried to place drinking beyond the pale of social acceptability has considerable force.

34. W. J. Rorabaugh, *The Alcoholic Republic: An American Tradition* (New York: Oxford University Press, 1979); Mark Edward Lender and Karen R. Karnchanapee, " 'Temperance Tales': Antiliquor Fiction and American Attitudes toward Alcoholics in the Late 19th and Early 20th Centuries," *Journal of Studies on Alcohol* 38 (1977): 1347–70.

35. Clark, *Deliver Us from Evil*, p. 225.

36. Reviews of the historiography of other reforms are conveniently provided in C. S. Griffin, *The Ferment of Reform, 1830–1860* (New York: Crowell, 1967), pp. 92–97; and Arthur S. Link and Richard L. McCormick, *Progressivism* (Arlington Heights, Ill.: Harlan Davidson, 1983), pp. 119–40. *But see*, for a specific example of this kind of approach, Roy Lubove, "The Progressive and the Prostitute," *Historian* 24 (1962): 308–30.

37. For the promises of repeal advocates, *see* Kyvig, *Repealing National Prohibition, passim.*

38. For consumption estimates from the prohibition years, *see* Clark Warburton, *The Economic Results of Prohibition* (New York: Columbia University Press, 1932); and Irving Fisher, *Prohibition at Its Worst* (rev. ed., New York: Alcohol Information Committee, 1927). For AAPA figures, *see* John C. Gebhart, "Prohibition: Statistical Studies of Enforcement and Social Effects," in *Statistics in Social Studies*, Stuart A. Rice, ed. (Philadelphia: University of Pennsylvania Press, 1930) pp. 111–49. Modern estimates are in Burnham, "New Perspectives on the Prohibition 'Experiment' "; Rorabaugh, *The Alcoholic*

Republic; and Merton M. Hyman, Marilyn A. Zimmermann, Carol Gurioli, and Alice Helrich, *Drinkers, Drinking and Alcohol-Related Mortality and Hospitalizations: A Statistical Compendium* (New Brunswick, N.J.: Center of Alcohol Studies, 1980).

39. Perry R. Duis, *The Saloon: Public Drinking in Chicago and Boston, 1880–1920* (Urbana, Ill.: University of Illinois Press, 1983).

40. Drys argued forcefully that such benefits were quite pronounced. *See*, for specific cases, Evangeline Booth, *Some Have Stopped Drinking* (Westerville, Ohio: American Issue Press, 1928); Martha Bensley Bruere, *Does Prohibition Work?* (New York: Harper, 1927); Fisher, *Prohibition at Its Worst.*

41. *See*, for example, Burnham, "New Perspectives on the Prohibition 'Experiment;' " Clark, *Deliver Us from Evil*, pp. 145–51; Lender and Martin, *Drinking in America*, pp. 136–47.

42. For a popular statement of this position, *see* the National Task Force on Cannabis Regulation, *The Regulation and Taxation of Cannabis Commerce* (n.p., 1982); John Kaplan, *Marijuana: The New Prohibition* (New York: World Publishing, 1970). For a useful collection of essays in this vein, *see* K. Austin Kerr, ed., *The Politics of Moral Behavior: Prohibition and Drug Abuse* (Reading, Mass.: Addison-Wesley, 1973).

43. For the prohibitionists, *see* Jack S. Blocker, Jr., *Retreat from Reform.* On this trend generally, *see* Lender and Martin, *Drinking in America*, pp. 159–61.

44. Some wets, for example, simply did not believe complete repeal of the Eighteenth Amendment was possible at first. Even such implacable foes of Volsteadism as Clarence Darrow initially were ready to settle for a more liberal definition of a legally intoxicating beverage. On Darrow, and the general hardening of wet and dry positions, *see* Lender and Martin, *Drinking in America*, pp. 156–57.

45. Kyvig, *Repealing National Prohibition*, pp. 191–96; *see also* Kyvig's essay "Objection Sustained: Prohibition Repeal and the New Deal," in *Alcohol, Reform and Society: The Liquor Issue in Social Context*, ed. Jack S. Blocker, Jr. (Westport, Conn.: Greenwood, 1979), pp. 211–34.

46. Wiener, *The Politics of Alcoholism*, pp. 207–15; *see also* Don Cahalan, "Why Does the Alcoholism Field Act Like a Ship of Fools?" *British Journal of Addiction* 74 (1974): 235–38; for the controlled drinking flap, much of which centered on the reaction of such groups as the National Council on Alcoholism and Alcoholics Anonymous to the publication of the Rand Report, suggesting in the mid-1970s that some alcoholics could return to a limited use of alcohol, *see* Lender and Martin, *Drinking in America*, pp. 192–93.

47. Kerr, "Organizing for Reform," and *Organized for Reform.*

48. See above, note 10.

49. Penny Booth Page, *The Center of Alcohol Studies—Rutgers University:*

Archives and Manuscripts: An Inventory (1789–1981) (New Brunswick, N.J.: Center of Alcohol Studies, 1982).

50. The Washingtonian Hospital papers are now in the possession of Professor Leonard U. Blumberg of Temple University, Philadelphia. The Rutgers Center of Alcohol Studies, in another example, has a major collection (perhaps the largest in existence) of foreign language publications of the Anti-Saloon League. While they are protected from deterioration, these materials remain uncataloged, and thus unavailable to scholars, because of financial and space problems.

Index

Contributors

NUALA MCGANN DRESCHER, Professor of History, State University of New York, Buffalo, and President, United University Professions, American Federation of Teachers, A.F.L.-C.I.O., author of *The Opposition to Prohibition, 1900–1919* (Ann Arbor, Mich.: University Microfilms, 1978).

STEVEN GOLDBERG, Associate Professor of Law, Georgetown University, author of "The Constitutional Status of American Science," *University of Illinois Law Forum* (1979).

MARK H. HALLER, Professor of History, Temple University, author of "Bootleggers and American Gambling, 1920–1950" in Commission on the Review of National Policy toward Gambling, *Gambling in America*, Appendix I (Washington, D.C.: GPO, 1976).

MARK KELLER, Professor of Documentation, Emeritus, Rutgers University, former editor of the *Journal of Studies on Alcohol*.

DAVID E. KYVIG, Professor of History, University of Akron, author of *Repealing National Prohibition* (Chicago: University of Chicago Press, 1979), and editor of *Papers of the Association Against the Prohibition Amendment and the Women's Organization for National Prohibition Reform* (Wilmington, Del.: Scholarly Resources, 1982).

MARK EDWARD LENDER, Director of Grants, Kean College of New Jersey, co-author with James Kirby Martin of *Drinking in America: A History* (New York: Free Press, 1982), and author of *Dictionary of American Temperance Biography: From Temperance Reform to Alcohol Research, the 1600s to the 1980s* (Westport, Conn.: Greenwood, 1984).

PAUL L. MURPHY, Professor of History and American Studies, University of Minnesota, author of *The Constitution in Crisis Times, 1918–69* (New York: Harper and Row, 1972) and *World War I and the Origins of Civil Liberties in the United States* (New York: W. W. Norton, 1980).

HUMBERT S. NELLI, Professor of History, University of Kentucky, author of *The Business of Crime: Italians and Syndicate Crime in the United States* (New York: Oxford University Press, 1976).

RAYMAN L. SOLOMON, Research Attorney, American Bar Foundation, author of *History of the Seventh Circuit: 1891–1941* (Chicago: Seventh Circuit, 1981).

WILLIAM F. SWINDLER, before his death in 1983 John Marshall Professor of Law Emeritus, College of William and Mary, author of *Court and Constitution in the Twentieth Century*, 2 vols. (Indianapolis: Bobbs-Merrill, 1969–70).

CLEMENT E. VOSE, Professor of Government, Wesleyan University (until his death in 1985), author of *Constitutional Change: Amendment Politics and Supreme Court Litigation since 1900* (Lexington, Mass.: Lexington Books, 1972).

Recent Titles in
Contributions in American History
Series Editor: Jon L. Wakelyn

MASTERS OF
GREATNESS

Book Two of the God-Mind Plan
for Saving Both Planet and Man

As revealed by the Brotherhood of God

To Jean K. Foster

Note to readers:
Words in italics are those of the writer, Jean K. Foster, including conversations with her spirit teacher. Words of the Brotherhood of God are printed in regular type.

This book is manufactured in the United States of America. Distribution by TeamUp. Cover design by Phil Reynolds. Jean Foster portrait by Jim Wiltse. Printing by Walsworth Publishing Company.

ISBN #0-9626366-0-6
Library of Congress Catalog Card Number: 90-90149